CONSTRUCTING PREDICTABLE REAL TIME SYSTEMS

THE KLUWER INTERNATIONAL SERIES IN ENGINEERING AND COMPUTER SCIENCE

REAL-TIME SYSTEMS

Consulting Editor

John A. Stankovic

CONSTRUCTING PREDICTABLE REAL TIME SYSTEMS

by

Wolfgang A. Halang
University of Groningen

Alexander D. Stoyenko
New Jersey Institute of Technology

KLUWER ACADEMIC PUBLISHERS
Boston/Dordrecht/London

Distributors for North America:
Kluwer Academic Publishers
101 Philip Drive
Assinippi Park
Norwell, Massachusetts 02061 USA

Distributors for all other countries:
Kluwer Academic Publishers Group
Distribution Centre
Post Office Box 322
3300 AH Dordrecht, THE NETHERLANDS

Library of Congress Cataloging-in-Publication Data

Halang, Wolfgang A., 1951 -
      Constructing predictable real time systems / by Wolfgang A.
Halang, Alexander D. Stoyenko.
      p.   cm. -- (The Kluwer international series in engineering and
computer science ; 146. Real-time systems)
      Includes index.
      ISBN: 0-7923-9202-7 (acid- free paper)
      1. Real-time data processing. 2. System design. I. Stoyenko,
Alexander D., 1962 -   . II. Title. III. Series: Kluwer
international series in engineering and computer science ; SECS
146. IV. Series: Kluwer international series in engineering and
computer science. Real-time systems.
QA76.54.H35   1991
004'.33--dc20   91-19988
                                  CIP

To our wives Bertha and Lana

Contents

List of Figures

List of Tables

Authors

Wolfgang A. Halang studied mathematics and theoretical physics at Ruhr-Universität Bochum, Germany. He received a doctorate with a thesis on numerical analysis in 1976. Subsequently, he studied computer science at Universität Dortmund concluding with a dissertation on function oriented structures for process control computers. Simultaneously with the latter, he worked with Coca-Cola GmbH in Essen where he was in charge of real time applications in the chemical Research and Development Department. From 1985 to 1987, he was an assistant professor for Systems Engineering at the King Fahd University of Petroleum & Minerals in Dhahran, Saudi Arabia, teaching courses mainly on real time and computer control systems. During the academic year 1987/88 he was a visiting assistant (research) professor with the Department of Electrical and Computer Engineering and with the Computer Systems Group at the Coordinated Science Laboratory at the University of Illinois at Urbana-Champaign. From June 1988 to May 1989 he was back in Germany working in the process control division of the Bayer AG. Since June 1989 he is a full professor at the University of Groningen in the Netherlands holding the chair for applications-oriented computing science, and since 1990 he is head of the Department of Computing Science as well. His research interests comprise all major areas of hard real time systems with special emphasis on innovative and function oriented architectures and on application specific peripheral components for process control computers. Presently, he concentrates his interest on predictable system behaviour and on rigorous software verification and safety licensing. He is the founder and European editor-in-chief of "Real-Time Systems", the international journal of time critical computing systems, has authored numerous publications and given many guest lectures on topics in this area, and is active in various professional organisations and technical committees as well as involved in the program committees of many conferences.

Alexander D. Stoyenko received a doctorate in computer science from the University of Toronto in 1987. Subsequently, he joined IBM T. J. Watson Research Center as a Research Staff Member. Since autumn 1990, he has been employed as an assistant professor with the Department of Computer and Information Science at New Jersey Insti-

tute of Technology. Dr. Stoyenko has also held temporary and visiting
appointments at the University of Toronto, Wang Institute of Graduate
Studies, Stanford University, IBM Zürich Research Laboratory and the
Bank of Montreal. His research interests are in the areas of real time systems, system integration, distributed systems, programming languages
and network management. Dr. Stoyenko is the inventor of Real-Time
Euclid, the first designed and implemented high level language with the
property that every program formulated in the language can be statically
analysed for adherence to critical timing constraints. To refer to this
form of program analysis he coined the term "schedulability analysis".
Dr. Stoyenko has published in various journals and conferences, and
has served on North American and international programme committees and professional society boards. He has given a number of invited
lectures and was the keynote speaker at the PEARL '90 conference. Dr.
Stoyenko is a member of the IFAC TC on Computers Working Group
on Real Time Programming, the Computer Society of the IEEE, and
the ACM.

Vorwort

In der Natur entwickelten sich die Echtzeitsysteme seit einigen 100 Millionen Jahren. Tierische Nervensysteme haben zur Aufgabe, auf die Nachrichten aus der Umwelt die Steuerungsbefehle an die aktiven Organe zu geben. Dabei spielen zum Beispiel bedingte Reflexe eine wichtige Rolle. Vielleicht kann man die Entstehung des Menschen etwa zu der Zeit ansetzen, als sein sich allmählich entwickelndes Gehirn Gedanken entwickelte, deren Bedeutung in vorausplanender Weise über die gerade vorliegende Situation hinausging. Das führte schliesslich unter anderem zum heutigen Wissenschaftler, der seine Theorien und Systeme aufgrund langwieriger Überlegungen aufbaut.

Die Entwicklung der Computer ging im wesentlichen den umgekehrten Weg. Zunächst diente sie nur der Durchführung "starrer" Programme, wie z.B. das erste programmgesteuerte Rechengerät Z3, das der Unterzeichner im Jahre 1941 vorführen konnte. Es folgte unter anderem ein Spezialgerät zur Flügelvermessung, das man als den ersten Prozessrechner bezeichnen kann. Es wurden etwa vierzig als Analog-Digital-Wandler arbeitende Messuhren vom Rechnerautomaten abgelesen und im Rahmen eines Programms als Variable verarbeitet. Aber auch das erfolgte noch in starrer Reihenfolge.

Die echte Prozesssteuerung — heute auch Echtzeitsysteme genannt — erfordert aber ein Reagieren auf beständig wechselnde Situationen. Eine "Bedingungskombinatorik", welche mit den formalen Werkzeugen der mathematischen Logik arbeitet, so wie sie vom Unterzeichner 1936 in den mechanischen Computer Z1 eingebaut und später (1945) im Plankalkül in ihren verschiedenen Möglichkeiten ausgearbeitet wurde, machte sehr flexible und lebendige Systeme möglich. Das gilt auch für die Computer, die immer beweglicher wurden. Diese schon früh erkannte Möglichkeit, z.B. auch Programme zu speichern, führt oft zu unübersehbaren Verschachtelungen der Programmabläufe, was gerade bei den Echtzeitsystemen sehr unangenehme Folgen haben kann. Das führt wiederum zu dem Wunsch, solche Systeme "vorhersehbar" zu machen, was sich aber im wesentlichen auf die Überschaubarkeit der Abläufe in zeitlicher und logischer Hinsicht auswirkt und nicht, wie man zunächst meinen möchte, auf die Vorhersehbarkeit und Ergebnisse der

Rechnungen. Je weiter die Computer in unser Leben, insbesondere in technischer und wissenschaftlicher Hinsicht, eindringen, desto komplexer und eigenmächtiger werden die von ihnen gesteuerten Systeme. Für uns Menschen wird es immer wichtiger, die Dinge im Griff zu behalten. Ein Versagen eines Steuerungssystems, und sei es auch nur durch Überlastung, kann zu katastrophalen Folgen führen. Die Verantwortung des Programmierers steigt dadurch immer mehr.

Das vorliegende Buch zeigt nun Wege, wie man auch bei Ausnutzung der verschiedenen gut ausgeklügelten Programmierungsmöglichkeiten die Übersicht über die Folgen und Reaktionen eines Systems behalten kann. Damit leistet dieses Buch eine wichtige Hilfestellung in unserer Zeit der ständig wachsenden Bedeutung des Computers, und ich glaube, dass seine positive Auswirkung vorhersehbar ist.

Konrad Zuse

Foreword

The following is an English translation of the original German Foreword as presented above.

In nature, real time systems have existed for some 100 million years. Nerve systems of animals have the task of sending control signals to the active organs, in response to messages from the environment. Conditional reflexes, for instance, play an important rôle in this context. Perhaps, the origin of man can be associated with approximately the time, when his gradually developing brain commenced to have thoughts, whose meaning went beyond the present situation in a planned way. Eventually, among other humans, the modern scientist type has emerged, who establishes his theories and systems based on tedious, planning considerations.

The development of computers essentially has gone in the opposite way. First, computers were used to carry out "fixed" programs, such as, for instance, the first program controlled calculation device Z3, which was developed and could be presented by the undersigned in the year 1941. Among the early computers that followed, was a special device for the survey of aircraft wings, that could be called the first real time computer. This automatic computer read values from some forty sensors working as analogue-to-digital converters, and processed these values as variables within a program. Still, this process proceeded in a fixed sequence.

The true control of (technical) processes — today also referred to as real time systems — however, requires computers to react to constantly changing situations. A "combinatorics of conditions", which works with the formal tools of mathematical logic, such as the one implemented by the undersigned in 1936 in the mechanical computer Z1, and and later (1945) elaborated in its various potentials in The Plankalkül, enables very flexible and lively systems. The same holds true for the modern computers as well. Thus, both the computers and the programming languages have become increasingly more flexible. The side-effects of this early recognised flexibility phenomenon, e.g. the possibility to store program code in computer memories, has often led to incalculable nesting of program sequences, which in turn can have very unpleasant consequences, especially in real time systems. That, again, leads to the wish to make such systems "predictable", in turn essentially affecting the manageability of processes with respect to their temporal and logical behaviour, but not, as one first might think, the predictability and results of the calculations. The more computers penetrate our lives, especially with regard to science and technology, the more complex and arbitrary become the systems controlled by the computers. For us human beings, it thus becomes increasingly more important to keep things under control. A failure of a control system, even if it is only caused by an overload, may have catastrophic consequences. The programmer's responsibility is therefore constantly increasing.

The present book shows how real time control of the effects, operation and reactions of a system can be maintained, even when using various highly sophisticated programming techniques. Thus, this book provides important assistance in these times of the constantly growing significance of the computer, and I believe, that the book's positive contribution is predictable and certain.

Konrad Zuse

Preface and Abstract

The use of embedded real time computing systems to control industrial, medical, scientific, consumer, environmental and other processes is
rapidly growing. A failure of an embedded computing system to properly
control its real time process may lead to major losses, possibly including the loss of human life. A real time application thus demands from
its embedded computing system not only significant computation and
control processing, but also, and even more importantly, a guarantee of
predictable, reliable and timely operation.

Owing to the hazards its failure may cause, a real time system must
not be put to use without a thorough a priori assessment of its adherence
to inherent, time-constrained, functional requirements of the process the
system is intended to control. The focus of the assessment must be on
predictability of system behaviour. This assessment, once completed,
will serve as a basis for design and implementation evaluation, feedback,
requirements correlation and, ultimately, official safety licensing of the
system.

It is the thesis of this book that real time computing systems with
predictable behaviour can indeed be realised. This thesis is established
constructively, i.e. from an engineering point of view. It is demonstrated how the requirement of predictable system behaviour, given
time-constrained, functional specifications of the environment, can be
embodied into programming language, operating system, hardware and
other aspects of real time systems. It is further demonstrated how
the resulting real time computing system is made subject to an a priori assessment of predictable behaviour. We refer to this assessment
as *schedulability analysis* — a term introduced by one of the authors
[170, 169, 168, 101]. The ideas are validated through a qualitative and
empirical evaluation, drawing from the existing body of knowledge in
real time systems engineering and the experience of the authors.

The book commences with an introduction to real time computing.
The need for predictable embedded real time computing systems is mo-
tivated by drawing the reader's attention to typical control applications
selected from different fields. Based on the application needs identified, specific requirements are established for real time programming

languages, operating systems, and hardware architectures.

A two-part comparative survey of high level real time programming languages, both actually used, proposed and experimental, reveals the degrees of inadequacy of these languages to meet their real time requirements. Two languages are identified for further consideration: Real-Time Euclid and PEARL. Real-Time Euclid has been specifically designed to yield predictable and schedulability analysable software. However, Real-Time Euclid has only so far been implemented and used in a research environment. PEARL, on the other hand, is standardised and in wide industrial use. Among industrially used languages, PEARL represents the closest match with respect to the identified real time requirements. On the basis of the ideas introduced by Real-Time Euclid and the real time needs not already addressed, PEARL extensions are proposed.

Currently, real time systems programmers perform schedulability analysis in a manual, non-systematic, error-prone way. Attempts to systematise schedulability analysis have so far resulted in techniques which can adequately model and analyse only simple real time systems. When applied to realistic real time systems, these techniques yield overly pessimistic worst-case time bounds. The failure to produce tight bounds can largely be attributed to the lack of detail exploited. This means, practically all information about the language, its implementation, program organisation, and hardware configuration is not used or is reduced to a small number of parameters. Schedulability analysis is presented, based on a new technique referred to as *frame superimposition*, that utilises knowledge of implementation- and hardware-dependent information, and provides tight worst-case time bounds and other schedulability information. The analysis is applied first to Real-Time Euclid, and then, to extended PEARL.

Conventional architectures embody many features, such as hierarchical memories and DMA cycle stealing, that introduce formidable, sometimes insurmountable obstacles in the way of an a priori assessment of predictable real time performance. Furthermore, architectural support is needed both to enable the implementation of various real time language constructs and, generally, to facilitate the building of predictable real time systems. Whereas numerous high level language machines have already been defined or realised, there has been no machine architecture defined yet to support a real time language. An architecture is presented here, which integrates the hardware with the operating system kernel software. The kernel directly supports the real time features of extended PEARL. The hardware consists of a master-slave dual processor and special-purpose peripherals. Application code is run on one processor, and the kernel code on the other. Both the hardware and the kernel operate predictably under all circumstances.

A study evaluating Real-Time Euclid is reported. Real-Time Euclid has been implemented and beta-tested in an experimental research environment. The study demonstrates the suitability of Real-Time Euclid for constructing predictable real time applications. While no implementation of extended PEARL and its architecture exists yet, a qualitative study is carried out, that establishes how a suitable implementation may be realised.

The book presents concepts and techniques, that the authors sincerely hope will soon become the state-of-the-art in the engineering of real time systems. To facilitate the construction of predictable real time systems, schedulability analysable languages, such as Real-Time Euclid or extended PEARL, need to be used. The systems should be supported by suitable architectures, such as the one described in this book. A priori assessments of the systems' adherence to their real time requirements, such as the frame-superimposition-based schedulability analysis, will become an indispensable part of the quality assurance process of real time systems.

This book is neither a detailed design specification for a real time system nor a comprehensive textbook, complete with definitions, examples and problem sets. Yet, the authors have felt that it was important to collect their thoughts on predictable real time computing, and to include them in a single manuscript. The authors hope that this book will serve as a useful set of suggestions to the practitioners in the field, as well as contribute to lecture notes on real time systems.

Disclaimers and Acknowledgements

This book is based on some of the research undertaken previously by the authors. Some of the work has already been presented in scientific articles and at conferences, other has been submitted to such articles or conferences and is currently under review, and yet other may be submitted in the future. The relevant research by the second author has been supported in part by NSERC (Canada) Grants A-5192 and A-8647, and an NSERC Postgraduate Scholarship.

The authors are deeply indebted to Prof. Dr. mult. h.c. Konrad Zuse for writing a foreword for the book. Ronald Tol has carefully and diligently validated the algorithms of Chapters 4, 5, and 6. A number of figures in Chapters 4 and 5 were prepared by Winfried Stockmann. Special thanks go to Carl Hamacher and Ric C. Holt who co-supervised the second author during his study at the University of Toronto. The Real-Time Euclid project which the second author ran and which produced some of the results reported here simply would not have happened nor succeeded without the project team members: Gene Kligerman, Chris Ngan, Scott Thurlow, Gerry Parnis, Greg Nymich and Victor Anderson. The second author's wife Lana and parents David and Irene endured through much and always provided the author with their love and support.

CONSTRUCTING PREDICTABLE REAL TIME SYSTEMS

Chapter 1

Introduction

1.1 Motivation

How is running a dedicated chemical process control program different from running a compiler on a time-sharing system? Apart from the obvious difference in function, the two programs also differ in another fundamental way.

The time it takes the compiler to execute depends on such factors as the system load and program mix. Sometimes, the user must wait for a relatively long time for the compilation to complete, and at other times the compilation runs quickly. The user does not like waiting, but probably tolerates occasional long compilations as long as most compilations take relatively little time. Even if most of the compilations take a long time, because the system is very busy, probably the only harmful effects of this are making the user frustrated. The reason the user often tolerates long compilations is that there are no real timing constraints associated with them.

Once the chemical process control program is started, however, it must not take arbitrarily long to execute. Moreover, the program must keep pace with the external process it controls, i.e., the program processing must be temporally synchronised with the events occurring in the process. If it does not, the result may be plant damage or even loss of human life. The reason the control program needs to operate in a

1

timely manner is that the chemical process itself imposes critical timing constraints on the program.

We say that the process control program (or system) is *real time*, while the compiler program is not. Real time systems are embedded in external, larger environments and, thus, are often also called "embedded systems". More generally, an embedded real time computer system may be defined as

> ... one which controls an environment by receiving data, processing them, and taking action or returning results sufficiently quickly to affect the functioning of the environment at that time.[126].

The definition of real time is further refined in [52]:

> **Real time operation is the operating mode of a computing system, in which the programs for the processing of data arriving from the outside are permanently ready in such a way, that the processing results become available within a priori given time frames.**

Still in [52], the definition specifies the arrival of external data in more detail:

> **According to the application, the data may become available for processing either at randomly distributed instants or at predetermined points in time.**

Observe that the emphasis in the above definitions is on the system performing required functions *sufficiently* quickly, and not on the absolute speed of the system.

Today there is a large, fast growing number of real time applications. Further in this Section we consider three applications drawn from different areas, and see how computer systems are used as control elements.

The main objective for the employment of process control computers in industrial environments is to increase productivity. To this end the operation costs are to be lowered, especially by automating routine work, and participating resources are to be utilised most efficiently. The latter are not confined to computer or operating system resources — men, machines, material, and energy are also included. In pursuing these goals, certain boundary conditions are to be observed. First, the security of the working people and of the capital invested into the process needs to be guaranteed. Then, the processing is subject to timing constraints with only small tolerances; and last but by no means least, reliable system operation characterised by high availability and low maintenance expense is expected.

In scientific applications slightly different requirements come to the fore. Here process control computers are mainly utilised for the acquisition and evaluation of measuring data originating in directly connected experimental set-ups. Hence, efficiency aspects become less important whereas tighter timing constraints are to be observed. The reasons for this are that the exact instants of monitoring operations are prescribed by the evaluation algorithms and that data may be received with very high frequencies.

Finally, for military use of real time systems, emphasis is shifted towards security and reliability aspects, since great many human lives depend on these systems' faultless functioning. The design of such systems has to provide enough capacity reserves and redundancy in order to be able to cope with extraordinary requisitions.

1.1.1 A Chemical Process Application

Life in a modern society is inconceivable without synthetic materials. They are used to make products like petrol, paints, video tapes, and polyester shirts. Synthetic materials are manufactured at chemical plants by means of chemical processes.

Three typical chemical process configurations are studied experimentally by researchers in the System Control Group of the Department of Electrical Engineering at the University of Toronto [49]. The basic configuration consists of a reservoir, a drain pipe, a pump connected to the pipe, and a "noise-source" pipe going from the pump back to the reservoir. Both pipes have computer controlled valves attached to them. The water level in the reservoir is measured by a computer accessed pressure transducer. The pump operates at a constant rate. The control problem studied on this single-input-single-output configuration is the one of water level control.

The second configuration is obtained by connecting the reservoirs of two basic configurations via a valve controlled pipe. This configuration is also used to study level control, this time in the two interacting reservoirs.

The third and most complex configuration is constructed from making the two feeding pipes of the second configuration go to a mixing chamber, and taking two new feeding pipes from the chamber to the reservoirs through heat exchangers. Each reservoir's heat exchanger restores the incoming water's temperature to the one in the reservoir. One reservoir contains cold water, and the other contains hot water. The output of the mixing chamber is monitored with a flow rate transducer and a temperature transducer. The control problem studied under the third configuration is the one of mixing chamber output flow rate and temperature control, also referred to as the "shower problem".

To solve the required control problems, programs written in assembly language, BASIC and Pascal are run under the P-DOS operating system on a TI-990 single board computer attached to the controlled configuration. The software periodically polls various transducers for water pressure, flow rate and temperature, checks data for consistency, computes the adjustments necessary to achieve the level and temperature objectives, and commands the valves to adjust accordingly. Up to five tasks are run concurrently: one to control the water level, one to control the temperature, one to generate the noise, one to vary parameters (i.e. the objectives), and one to record and print the log of the experiment. The tasks are executed periodically, typically once every couple of seconds.

Should the water level or temperature leave their acceptable ranges and stay there longer than their acceptable stabilising times, or should the level or temperature go way out of range, the experiment fails. Consequently, computer tasks operate in a time-constrained way, so that output parameter deviations are spotted and compensated for on time.

1.1.2 A Power Plant Application

Today's ever growing need for electrical power has led to construction of very large power plants. As the complexity of running these plants increased, plant engineers found it effective and cost-efficient to control the plants with computers.

A typical real time system was installed at a power plant in Mobil Oil's Refinery at Paulsboro, New Jersey [112]. The plant is a cogeneration environment (producing both steam and electricity). Its nonstop operation is important, because the plant is a major power source, and even a short service interruption would lead to significant losses.

Each of nine individual boilers is controlled by microprocessor based controllers, three controllers per boiler, with eight control loops per controller. The real time boiler control functions are fuel, air and steam flow management. Individual boiler and other data obtained by controllers are collected and brought to a mainframe computer, which performs boiler optimisation (economic boiler load allocation), printing of logs and reports, historical data gathering, colour graphics, multipoint trends, efficiency, mass balance, and electrical power computation. Most control functions are periodic. The periods vary from several seconds to 24 hours. Boiler load reallocation and other functions can be invoked by human operators. The control system is, nevertheless, able to operate 24 hours a day, 365 days a year with a minimum of human interference.

1.1.3 A Fighter Aircraft Application

Using computers to assist in flying military aircraft is not a new idea. In fact, all modern military aircraft have on-board computer control systems. The rule has been, however, that the computer system can be bypassed in cases of malfunction, and the aircraft will then be flown manually.

There are exceptions, however. The revolutionary forward-swept-wing X-29 aircraft, built for the U.S. Defense Advanced Research Projects Agency by Grumman Aerospace Corp. at Bethpage, New York, cannot be flown at all without its computer system [94]. The X-29 is highly maneuverable, fast, aerodynamically efficient, but also statically unstable. Even the most experienced and quickest pilots would be too slow to maintain the aircraft's attitude and prevent excessive up or down movement that could drive it out of control. The way the plane is flown is as follows: the pilot sets directions, and the X-29 computers monitor and adjust the position of the airplane's control surfaces every 25 milliseconds to follow these directions.

The on-board computer system consists of three redundant primary digital computers backed up by three redundant analogue computers. Each of the six computers is capable of controlling the aircraft fully, and has its own set of sensors such as pressure and temperature sensors for speed measurement, synchros to measure angular position, accelerometers, and angular velocity gyros.

Each computer receives the pilot's commands given through a stick and pedals, accepts data from its sensors, and computes commands to be sent to command actuators that move control surfaces such as the canards, flaperons, strake flaps, and the rudder. The three sets of sensor data are compared and a midvalue set[1] is computed to be used in command derivation. The three sets of commands are compared bit by bit, and again a midvalue set is taken.

Should the command set of one of the computers deviate significantly from the other two, it is discarded and the two remaining sets are used in the midvalue set computation. Should one digital computer fail, the system continues to operate directed by the other two digital computers. Should two digital computers fail, the system turns to the analogue computers.

The aircraft was thus designed to be two-fault tolerant, and to have fewer than three failures every six million hours of flight — typical of today's high performance military aircraft. A reliability analysis actually indicates that the X-29 is ten times more reliable than that [94].

In this Section we looked at three real time applications. They were drawn from very different areas, yet they all have one property in common: to insure predictable, safe and proper operation, they have to be continuously computer controlled in real time. Real time computer con-

---

[1] Each data value in the midvalue set is the average of its three peer values: one from each of the three data sets.

trol is used in many other applications. Some of these are wind-tunnel control [185], astronomical data acquisition [97], space shuttle control [33], overcurrent and high impedance fault relaying [12], radar applications [62], amusement park ride control [135], and positron emission tomography [184]. Due to space considerations we choose not to describe them in detail here, but it will suffice to say that they all greatly benefit from or even require continuous real time computer control. Abstracting from the motivating examples we have considered, in the next Section we want to set up the general requirements, which real time systems are to fulfill.

1.1.4   Real Time System Requirements

As we have seen above, real time operation distinguishes itself from other forms of data processing by the explicit involvement of the dimension *time*. This is expressed by the following two fundamental user requirements, which real time systems must fulfill under all, including extreme, load conditions:

- **timeliness** and

- **simultaneity**.

These requirements are supplemented by two further ones of equal importance:

- **predictability** and

- **dependability**.

Upon request from the external process, data acquisition, evaluation, and appropriate reactions must be performed on time. Observe that the speed with which these requests are processed plays but an indirect rôle, while the timeliness, within predefined and *predictable* time-bounds, of the reactions is decisive. Hence, it is characteristical for real time systems that their functional correctness depends on not only the processing results themselves, but also upon the instants, when these results become available. Correct instants are determined by the external environment, which cannot be forced to yield to the computer's processing speed, as is the case with batch and time-sharing systems. Depending on the nature of the critical timing constraints imposed by their external environments, embedded real time systems may be classified as *hard* or *soft*. The distinction lies in the consequences of violating the timeliness requirement: whereas soft real time environments are characterised by costs rising with increasing lateness of results, no lateness can be tolerated in hard real time environments, where late computer reactions are either useless or dangerous. In other words, the costs for missing deadlines in hard real time environments are infinitely high. Hard time constraints can be determined precisely and typically result from the physical laws governing the technical processes being controlled [81].

The second requirement for simultaneous processing of external process requests implies, that real time systems must be essentially distributed and must also provide parallel processing capabilities.

The definition of the real time operating mode has important consequences for the *dependability* of real time systems, since the demanded permanent readiness of computers working in this mode can only be provided by fault tolerant and — especially with respect to inadequate error handling — robust systems. The dependability requirement holds for both hardware and software. It is particularly important for those applications where computer malfunctions not only cause loss of data, but also endanger people and major investments. Naturally, the demand for high dependability does not imply an unrealistic expectation that a system will never fail. Indeed, no technical system is absolutely reliable. However, using appropriate measures, one must strive to make the violation of deadlines and corresponding damages quantifiable and as unlikely as possible. In doing so, the individual limitations of a real time system must be recognised and the risk of its utilisation in process control must be carefully pondered [81].

Data to be processed may arrive randomly distributed in time, according to the definition of the real time operating mode. This fact gave rise to the widespread conclusion, that the behaviour of real time systems cannot be and may not be made deterministic. This conclusion, which has led to a number of corresponding technical decisions, including the non-determinism in the selection of a rendezvous partner in the Ada language, *is based on a thinking error!* Indeed, the external technical process may be so complex, that its behaviour appears to be at random. However, each external event must be handled predictably within its associated timing constraints. The reactions to be carried out by the computer must thus be precisely planned and fully predictable. Predictable real time response must be ensured even in such difficult cases as when several events, competing for the same service and resources, occur simultaneously, and when transient overload and other problems are present in the system. Any performance degradation must occur gracefully, predictably and in as localised fashion as possible.

Only those programmable devices and system components that exhibit deterministic, predictable behaviour should ultimately be licenced as appropriate for safety critical real time applications. The notion of predictability and determinism appropriate in this context is illustrated in the following example: while the residents of a city do not know when the next fire will happen, they expect the city's fire brigade to respond within a sufficiently short time duration when the fire does occur.

Predictability of system behaviour is, as we have seen, of central importance for the real time operating mode. It supplements the timeliness demand. for The latter can only be guaranteed, if the system behaviour is precisely predictable, both in time and with respect to external event reactions.

1.2   Predictability and Simplicity

The current state of affairs in real time systems is at best inadequate.

> Military missions and commercial applications involving real time systems at their base are becoming rapidly prevalent while the science and technology to support the credible design, construction, and enhancement of such systems is woefully deficient. [182]

If future real time systems are not to fail as the very early, fully centralised ones, the VLSI-technology driven hardware development needs

to be influenced by the requirements discussed earlier. The development
further needs to be made part of a consolidating effort with respect to
architectural and software issues, aimed at producing timely, predictable
and dependable systems. To achieve these objectives, we should follow
Dijkstra's advice and choose *simplicity* as the fundamental design principle:

> **Computing's core challenge is how not to make a
> mess of it.**
>
> **... so we better learn how not to introduce complex-
> ity in the first place.**
>
> **It is only too easy to design resource sharing sys-
> tems with such intertwined allocation strategies that
> no amount of applied queueing theory will prevent
> most unpleasant performance surprises from emerg-
> ing. The designer that counts performance predicta-
> bility among his responsibilities tends to come up
> with designs that need no queueing theory at all.**
>
> **The moral is clear: prevention is better than cure,
> in particular if the illness is unmastered complexity,
> for which no cure exists.**
>
> **... both the final product and the design process
> (must) reflect a theory that suffices to prevent a com-
> binatorial explosion of complexity from creeping in.**
>
> **It is time to unmask the computing community as a
> Secret Society for the Creation and Preservation of
> Artificial Complexity.** [51]

Since most if not every real time system must make provisions for
safety, the non-temporal requirement of dependability and high integrity
is of paramount importance. We must come to a stage when real time
systems can be engineered with a sufficient degree of confidence in their
dependability to allow the licensing authorities to approve formally their
utilisation for safety critical control purposes. Given the present state
of affairs, simplicity is a precondition for dependable engineering. The
fundamental importance of simplicity is established by its position in

the following causal chain:

$$Simplicity \Rightarrow (easy) \; Predictability \Rightarrow Dependability$$

At first, it is surprising to have to stress the notion of predictability in the context of computing since, in principle, all digital computers work fully deterministically and are, therefore, predictable in their behaviour. To express the special meaning of predictability precisely, and as a fundamental concept of real time computing, the adjective "easy" was used in the above implication. It qualifies the notion of predictability, defined in [165] as

> Predictability means that it should be possible to show, demonstrate, or prove that requirements are met subject to any assumptions made, for example, concerning failures and workloads.

by paying tribute to the economic and intellectual effort which needs to be invested in order to establish the property for a given real time system. A simple system is easier to understand. In turn, understanding is the main step towards the verification of the system's correct behaviour in the sense of Descartes: "verum est quod valde clare et distincte percipio".

1.3 New Thinking Categories and Optimality Criteria

The definition cited in Section 1.1 implies that some prevailing misconceptions (additional to the ones mentioned in [164]) about real time systems need to be overcome: neither time-sharing nor fast systems are necessarily real time. Commencing the processing of tasks in a timely fashion is much more significant than speed. The thinking in probabilistic or statistical terms, which is common in computer science with respect to questions of performance evaluation, is as inappropriate in the real time domain as is the notion of fairness for the handling of competing requests or the minimisation of average reaction times as an optimality criterion of system design. Instead, worst cases, deadlines, maximum run-times, and maximum delays need to be considered. For the realisation of predictable and dependable real time systems, reasoning in static terms and the acceptance of physical constraints is a must — all dynamic and "virtual" features are *considered harmful.*

Despite the best planning of a system, there is always the possibility of a transient overload in a node resulting from an emergency situation. To handle such cases, load-sharing schemes have been devised, which migrate tasks between the nodes of distributed systems. In industrial embedded real time systems, however, such ideas are generally not applicable, because they only hold for computing tasks. In contrast to this, control tasks are highly I/O bound and the permanent wiring of the peripherals to certain nodes makes load-sharing impossible.

Maximum processor utilisation is a major issue by the thinking criteria of classical computer science, and still the subject of many research articles. For embedded real time systems, however, whether processor utilisation is optimal or not is totally irrelevant. Instead, costs have to be seen in a larger context, i.e., in the framework of the controlled external process and with regard to the latter's safety requirements. When the total cost of a failed external process is considered (including the damage caused by the failure), the cost of any processor involved is usually negligible. This is true even for relatively inexpensive environments. For instance, one hour production stoppage of a medium-size chemical facility due to a computer malfunction and the required clean-up cost some $ 50,000. This is about the price of the entire computer controlling the process itself. A processor board costs only a minor fraction of that amount. Moreover, given the fact that hardware costs are declining, while general industrial costs are rising, the relative cost of computer components is of fast decreasing significance. Hence, processor utilisation is not an appropriate design criterion for embedded real time systems. Lower processor utilisation is a — cheap — price to be paid for system and software (an experienced system engineer costs some $ 1,600 per day) simplicity as prerequisite to achieve dependability and predictability.

1.4 Guiding Principles for Predictable, Verifiable Real Time Software and Hardware

To ensure that a real time application acts in a predictable, timely manner, the environment of the application must meet a number of requirements.

A real time application imposes critical timing constraints on the software and hardware that control it. The very nature of the application thus requires that the software and hardware adhere predictably to these constraints. The fundamental assumption we make is that only software and hardware that can be checked (i.e., analysed for schedulability) for adherence to the constraints *before the application is run* fit the requirements of predictable real time applications.

1.4.1 Language Assumptions

We assume that a real time language makes sufficient provisions for schedulability analysis. Thus, every program can be analysed at compile time to determine whether or not it will guarantee to meet all time deadlines during execution.

The language is to allow concurrent, real time processes (tasks). Each process is associated with a *frame* (a minimum period). The frame is usually dictated by the external environment, and corresponds to the minimum frequency of the occurrence of the physical task controlled by the process. The process can be activated periodically, by a signal (from another process or an external activity, this is denoted as an **atEvent** activation), or at a specific compile-time-specified time (this is denoted as an **atTime** activation). Once activated, a process must complete its task before the end of the current frame. Furthermore, once activated, a process cannot be reactivated before the end of the current frame. To enable **atEvent** activations, in between activations a process is assumed to be blocked attempting to open a special, busy activation bracket (see below). As expected, the activation signal closes that bracket.

A real time language must have primitives for inter-process synchronisation. At the implementation level, most if not all primitives of synchronisation used in higher level languages are supported essentially the same way. A kernel call blocks until a desired, shared resource is free, then claims the resource and returns. All subsequent attempts to claim the same resource will block until the process that has the resource executes another kernel call that releases the resource. Some primitives of synchronisation (critical sections, MUTEX BEGIN/END, LOCK/UNLOCK, semaphores and so on) map directly to this model. Others, such as the rendezvous or monitors-waits-signals in the sense of [82] break down into groups of these claim-resource/release-resource brackets. We assume that the primitives used in the language are implemented using such possibly nested claim-resource/release-resource brackets, which we refer to simply as *brackets*. To the kernel calls that claim and release resources we refer to as *opening* and *closing* brackets.

Finally, we assume that the language has no constructs that can take arbitrarily long to execute. Thus, a number of familiar conventional constructs, such as, for instance, a general while-loop, are banned from the language. Indeed, an iterative computation that has a deadline must be expressible in. terms of a constant-count loop. Otherwise, the computation may miss its deadline and thus fail. If, on the other hand, unbounded iteration is called for in an real time application, then it must be the case that the iterative computation has no inherent deadline associated with it. Then, a proper way to implement the computation is to make every single iteration (or a bounded number of iterations) a process activation.

The only loops allowed are constant-count loops. We prefer constant-count loops over time-bounded loops, since it makes little semantic sense to time out somewhere in the middle of a loop. Recursion and dynamic variables are either disallowed or their use is restricted to allow compile-time-known bounds on their use (both time- and storage-wise). Wait- and device-condition variables time out if no signal is received during a specified time **noLongerThan** delay. Furthermore, all waits and signals, and device-access statements go through the kernel, where they can be modelled as open- and close-bracket operations.

1.4.2   System Software and Hardware Assumptions

The very nature of schedulability analysis requires predictable system software and hardware behaviour. It must be known how much time each machine instruction takes to execute. The hardware must not introduce unpredictable delays into program execution. Hardware faults and recovery from such faults are not accounted for in this book. Hierarchical memories can lead to unpredictable variations in process execution timing. Thus, caching, paging and swapping must either be disallowed or restricted. Cycle stealing slows down the processors in an unpredictable way. Consequently, DMA operations in a real time computer system are a source of difficulty when determining process execution timing. Knowing the maximum flow rates from DMA device controllers allows calculation of a worst-case bound on process slow-down. However, it is difficult to use this bound in other than a very pessimistic way, unless the relative amount and relative positioning of DMA activity is known. Modeling such activity has not been incorporated into the schedulability analysis techniques described in Chapter 3. A prototype multiprocessor used to experimentally evaluate the schedulability analyser is described in Chapter 6. Neither paging nor swapping of processes is present and there are no memory caches and no DMA cycle stealing activities in this system. In this book we do not explicitly consider network communications. If a system is distributed, we assume that the network protocol organises communications in such a way that a priori known time bounds can be guaranteed for each kind of transfer.

Much like their language counterparts, the system software and hardware assumptions certainly differ significantly from the traditional assumptions made in non-real-time areas of computing. However, these assumptions are not as unrealistic as they may seem. Not only can realistic systems closely fitting these assumptions be assembled from existing components, a number of sources indicate that entire such system software and hardware systems used in time critical real time applications can, should be and are being designed this way [74, 73, 38, 107, 139, 153, 174, 178].

1.5   Book Outline

In distinct contrast to the customary procedure of basing process control systems on hardware with (almost) minimum capabilities, we want to proceed from the special requirements of hard real time environments and to make use of a holistic view when developing apt computer systems. One objective of such a top-down approach is the definition of a hardware architecture as closely adapted to these applications and supporting specific operating system features as the state-of-the-art in hardware technology allows. As a prerequisite for carrying through this task, a synopsis is required of the elements which need to be implemented in order to meet our goals. Therefore, we shall commence our considerations in the next Chapter by discussing the conditions imposed by industrial environments on real time data processing systems. From this will follow fundamental demands for process control systems, and, especially, for programming languages used to develop real time software. Then, we shall make an inventory of the real time elements as provided by the major languages for this area of application. Subsequently, it will be discussed how these languages fulfill our fundamental demands, giving rise to a synopsis of important but not yet or only seldom realised real time features.

A two-part comparative survey of high level real time programming languages, both actually used, proposed and experimental, is carried out in Chapter 2. The survey reveals the degrees of inadequacy of these languages to meet their real time requirements. Two languages are identified for further consideration: Real-Time Euclid and PEARL. Real-Time Euclid is a language designed specifically with predictable and schedulability analysable real time software in mind. However, while it serves as a valuable research contribution, Real-Time Euclid has so far only been implemented and used in a research environment. PEARL, on the other hand, is standardised and widely utilised. Among industrially used languages, PEARL represents the closest match with respect to the identified real time requirements. On the basis of the ideas introduced by Real-Time Euclid and the real time needs not yet addressed, PEARL extensions are proposed.

Currently, real time systems programmers perform schedulability analysis in a manual, non-systematic, error-prone way. Attempts to systematise schedulability analysis have so far resulted in techniques which can adequately model and analyse only simple real time systems. When applied to realistic real time systems, these techniques yield overly pessimistic worst-case time bounds. This failure to produce tight bounds can largely be attributed to the lack of detail exploited. Practically all information about the language, its implementation, program organisation, and hardware configuration is not used or is reduced to a small number of parameters. In Chapter 3 we first describe a schedulability analyser, and then discuss how it can be used to analyse Real-Time Euclid and extended PEARL programs. The schedulability analyser consists of a partially language-dependent front end and a language-independent back end. Embedded in the code emitter of a real time language compiler, the front end extracts and prepares compilation-unit level schedulability information from a program. A stand-alone program, the back end reduces and analyses this information, generating schedulability statistics. The schedulability analysis is based on a new technique referred to as frame superimposition, that utilises knowledge on implementation and hardware details, and provides tight worst-case time bounds and other schedulability information. The analyser thus predicts accurately whether real time programs will meet their critical timing constraints.

Conventional architectures embody many features, such as hierarchical memories and DMA cycle stealing, that introduce formidable, sometimes insurmountable obstacles in the way of a priori assessment of predictable real time performance. Furthermore, architectural support is needed both to enable the implementation of various real time language constructs and generally to facilitate the building of predictable real time systems. In Chapter 4 we introduce a new hardware architecture, specifically designed for real time processing. It directly addresses such real time objects as tasks or deadlines, and supports earliest-deadline-first task scheduling. The architecture offers refinements to the traditional features DMA and hierarchical storage management, that have made predictable real time software development very hard if not impossible in the past. The refinements preserve the desired functionality of these features, while removing the source of unpredictable performance, such as DMA cycle stealing. Still in the architecture, process peripherals are provided, which perform their input/output operations at user-specified instants. The use of these peripherals ensures that the effects real time programs have on their external environments are delivered in a predictable fashion.

Whereas numerous high level language machines have already been defined or realised, there has been no architecture defined yet to support a real time language. In a constructive way it is shown, that this can indeed be done based on available technology. Thus, an architecture is described in Chapter 5, which integrates the hardware with the operating system kernel software. The kernel directly supports the real time features of extended PEARL, to close the "semantic gap" between the requirements of hard real time applications and the architecture. The hardware consists of a master-slave dual processor and special-purpose devices, specifically designed to support real time operating system functions. Application code is run on one processor, and the kernel code on the other. Both the hardware and the kernel operate predictably under all circumstances. Together with the architecture presented in Chapter 4, the kernel and its dedicated hardware comprise an effective platform for real time applications.

In Chapters 6 and 7 we report the results of an implementation and an extensive evaluation of Real-Time Euclid and its schedulability analysis techniques. Using a prototype implementation of the compiler, run-time kernel and analyser, two practical real time application programs have been written. The worst-case time bounds predicted by the analyser have been compared with the actual execution times, and found to differ only marginally. Thus, this study demonstrates the suitability of Real-Time Euclid for constructing real time applications with predictable behaviour. While no implementation of extended PEARL and its architecture exists yet, a qualitative evaluation is carried out, that establishes how a suitable implementation of its kernel and novel language features may be realised.

In Chapter 8 we conclude with a summary of the ideas presented, and an outlook for future work.

Chapter 2

Real Time Features of High Level Languages

The choice of the programming language plays a decisive rôle when building a computing system. Naturally, this general statement holds for real time systems as well. Therefore, it is the purpose of this Chapter to evaluate available languages, to compare them with the typical real time requirements, and to propose remedies for deficiencies, which impair the predictability of real time systems.

First, we consider real time programming in general, by working out a representative example, by outlining the development the corresponding languages have taken, and by compiling the requirements high level real time languages have to fulfill. Then, we review a number of representative languages, frequently used in real time computing. Since these languages are found to have inadequate real time features, we discuss experimental languages, designed to meet the real time language requirements that we defined. We present in detail Real-Time Euclid — the first defined[1], implemented (along with a schedulability analyser, a tool used to predict statically whether real time programs will meet their critical timing constraints) and evaluated schedulability analysable language.

---

[1]The essential ideas incorporated in Real-Time Euclid were also developed a few years earlier and independently as a proposal for the extension of PEARL [72]. However, the proposal was never implemented.

Real-Time Euclid clearly meets the real time language requirements we set forth, but as an experimental language it has never made it out of its laboratory.

As we are not satisfied with the result of our survey, we undertake another one, including this time both some other industrial languages and re-considering Ada and PEARL (two very widely-used languages that make some provisions for real time features) and Real-Time Euclid (to serve as a model). We now focus specifically on real time language features. The seven languages considered make better provisions for explicit real time constructs, than the average language in the first survey. However, the picture is still far from being perfect. It is clear that none of the industrial languages we have considered meets our requirements.

We then discuss in more detail the strong points and the limitations of Ada and PEARL, the two most widely-used languages. We report briefly on some current attempts to make Ada more real time, and propose a set of new language features for PEARL. The resulting PEARL dialect ensures predictable run-time behaviour and satisfies our requirements.

2.1   A Representative Real Time Application Design

Today's real time system programmer has a selection of hundreds of languages to choose from. Given these many choices, do we need to design another real time language? To answer this question we must try to do what real time programmers do — write a real time program — and show where the available languages fail.

Recall the X-29 fighter aircraft application described in Chapter 1. We shall now design and develop its control program, the way a programmer would. For simplicity, the only devices we consider are stick and pedals, control surfaces, and sensors. Moreover, we wish to concentrate only on the critical timing characteristics of the program. Thus, we make no attempt to address other important issues of our task. For instance, no attempt to make the program fault tolerant, beyond data and command comparison across the processors, is made.

Figures 2.1, 2.2, 2.3 and 2.4 contain a module/process level break-down of a possible design. *DeviceInterface* routines provide physical device access. *PilotData* and *SensorData* routines are for storage and retrieval of pilot and sensor input data, respectively. *ParameterCom-putation* routines use sensor data to derive speed, angular position, acceleration and angular velocity of the aircraft. *CommandComputation* procedures store the parameters computed in *ParameterComputation*, and determine control surface commands on the basis of these parameters. *Communication* routines arbitrate among the redundant X-29 computers. These routines suspend their callers until all sets of data or commands to be compared are available. The midvalues are then derived and returned.

The *StickDriver* process is activated when the pilot moves the stick. Stick position data are read, filtered, averaged and stored for future use. Since the pilot's reaction time is limited, *StickDriver* is activated no more often than once per this human reaction time limit. The *PedalDriver* process operates similarly to the *StickDriver* process.

The *PressureSensorDriver* periodically probes the pressure sensor. The sensor data is then reduced, averaged and stored. This process needs to be activated as often as is necessary to probe the sensor, and certainly no less frequently than once every 25 milliseconds [94]. The *TemperatureSensorDriver*, *SynchroDriver*, *AccelerometerDriver* and *Gy-roDriver* processes are similar to the *PressureSensorDriver* process.

The *SpeedComputer* process is activated when the pressure and temperature data — parameters needed to update the aircraft's speed — are available. The process retrieves the data, computes the speed and stores it for future use. *SpeedComputer* should be activated as often as *PressureSensorDriver* and *TemperatureSensorDriver* are activated. The *AngularPositionComputer*, *AccelerationComputer* and *AngularVelocity-Computer* processes operate similarly to the *SpeedComputer* process.

The *CanardCommander* process is activated when the parameters needed to compute the canard commands are available. The process computes the commands, averages them and sends the averaged commands to the canards. The frequency of *CanardCommander* should be the same as the frequency of the canard parameter computing processes. The *FlaperonCommander*, *StrakeFlapCommander* and *RudderComman-*

DeviceInterface
   GetStick
   GetPedal
   GetPressureSensor
   GetTemperatureSensor
   GetSynchro
   GetAccelerometer
   GetGyro
   SetCanard
   SetFlaperon
   SetStrakeFlap
   SetRudder

PilotData
   SetStick
   SetPedal
   GetStick
   GetPedal

SensorData
   SetPressureSensor
   SetTemperatureSensor
   SetSynchro
   SetAccelerometer
   SetGyro
   GetPressureSensor
   GetTemperatureSensor
   GetSynchro
   GetAccelerometer
   GetGyro

Figure 2.1: Modules of the X-29 control program.

ParameterComputation
    Speed
    AngularPosition
    Acceleration
    AngularVelocity

CommandComputation
    SetSpeed
    SetAngularPosition
    SetAcceleration
    SetAngularVelocity
    Canard
    Flaperon
    StrakeFlap
    Rudder

Communication
    ArbitrateData
    ArbitrateCommands

Figure 2.2: Modules of the X-29 control program (continued).

process *StickDriver*
>   — get stick data via *DeviceInterface.GetStick*
>   — filter the data
>   — get the reduced stick data midvalues via
>   *Communication.ArbitrateData*
>   — set the midvalues via *PilotData.SetStick*

process *PedalDriver* < similar to StickDriver >

process *PressureSensorDriver*
>   — get pressure sensor data via
>   *DeviceInterface.GetPressureSensor*
>   — filter the data
>   — get the reduced sensor data midvalues via
>   *Communication.ArbitrateData*
>   — set the midvalues via *SensorData.SetPressureSensor*

process *TemperatureSensorDriver* < similar to PressureSensorDriver >

process *SynchroDriver* < similar to PressureSensorDriver >

process *AccelerometerDriver* < similar to PressureSensorDriver >

process *GyroDriver* < similar to PressureSensorDriver >

Figure 2.3: Processes of the X-29 control program.

process *SpeedComputer*
  — get pressure sensor data via *SensorData.GetPressureSensor*
  — get temperature sensor data via
    SensorData.GetTemperatureSensor
  — compute the speed via *ParameterComputation.Speed*
  — set the speed via *CommandComputation.SetSpeed*

process *AngularPositionComputer* < similar to SpeedComputer >

process *AccelerationPositionComputer* < similar to SpeedComputer >

process *AngularVelocityComputer* < similar to SpeedComputer >

process *CanardCommander*
  — compute and get canard commands via
    CommandComputation.Canard
  — get the canard command midvalues via
    Communication.ArbitrateCommands
  — set the midvalues via *DeviceInterface.SetCanard*

process *FlaperonCommander* < similar to CanardCommander >

process *StrakeFlapCommander* < similar to CanardCommander >

process *RudderCommander* < similar to CanardCommander >

Figure 2.4: Processes of the X-29 control program (continued).

der processes are similar to the *CanardCommander* process.

It is now time to translate our program into a programming language. The translation takes place in two steps: first, at the higher module/process level, and second, at the lower declaration/statement level. The critical timing constraints of our design must be expressed at the higher level. Furthermore, these constraints must not be violated at the lower level. Finally, the timing constraints must be verified before the program is used operationally. While it is relatively easy to predict how much time each process will take to execute in isolation, predicting the amount of time the process will be delayed due to various forms of contention is a difficult endeavour.

The X-29 control program has fifteen processes and six modules. Five processes, namely *PressureSensorDriver, TemperatureSensor-Driver, SynchroDriver, AccelerometerDriver* and *GyroDriver*, are activated periodically. Periodic processes have predictable activation schedules. The timing behaviour of periodic processes is relatively simple to express and understand. To estimate CPU contention generated by periodic processes is thus straightforward to do.

Two processes, *StickDriver* and *PedalDriver*, are activated by pilot-generated interrupts. While neither process can physically be activated more often than human reaction permits, the time interval between any two consecutive activations can be arbitrarily long. *StickDriver* and *PedalDriver* thus display genuine aperiodicity. To predict accurately whether these processes will meet their timing requirements is hard to do.

The remaining eight processes are activated by processes conditional on the availability of data. These former processes depend on both periodic and aperiodic processes, as well as on conditions which occur depending on both periodic and aperiodic processes. Thus, these remaining eight are all aperiodic as well.

The six modules of the X-25 control program provide device and data access for the processes, and enable interprocess communication. Only one process accesses each device. Thus, *DeviceInterface* does not need to serialise access to the eleven devices it protects. Every other module has to serialise access to its data, to ensure consistent data states at all times. Access serialisation leads to device and data contention. The *Communication* module provides interprocessor communication. The access to this module's data has to be serialised as well, leading to communication contention. Predicting device, data and communication contention can be hard, especially if aperiodic processes are involved.

We have presented a solution of a real time application — an X-29 fighter control program — in order to demonstrate why languages with schedulability analysis provisions are needed in the field of real time software. The complete X-29 control program can be analysed at compile-time for the worst amount of time each statement, routine and process takes to execute. This systematic schedulability analysis is described in detail in Chapter 3. In Chapter 7, the analysis is demonstrated to be effective by running a prototype schedulability analyser on a set of realistic programs. These programs are similar to the X-29 control program presented here.

Having designed the high level structure of our program, the question now is: Which programming language do we translate it to? To choose an appropriate one, we present a sketch of the historical development these languages have taken, define our requirements for a real time language, and make a survey of the languages actually used in real time programming,

2.2 Historical Development of Real Time Languages

Until recently, the use of assembly languages has been prevalent in the programming of real time applications. The reason for this were the high prices for processors and memories enforcing optimal programming with respect to execution time and storage utilisation. The field of real time programming has lagged behind other programming fields in terms of languages and tools available. Surveys as late as those made in the late Seventies or early Eighties have reported that assembly and first generation high level languages were used, in program development environments that lacked even rudimentary debugging, testing and other support [69].

Yet, as it did in other fields of programming, the demand for high level language use in real time programming grew. The early designers of real time languages took the natural approach of augmenting existing languages with real time features. While these designers understood the model of real time computation desired by real time programmers, they provided but most rudimentary language features to support the model. For instance, to support periodic processes, most of the resulting languages incorporated delay statements, that could be placed at the end of loops. A single loop iteration thus became a single periodic process execution. The augmentation of existing commercial languages resulted in a large number of vendor-specific real time dialects of FORTRAN, BASIC and a few other languages.

The idea of creating new languages specifically for programming real time software was first realised in Britain in the Sixties. Two languages, CORAL 66 [44] and RTL/2 [19], the latter a version of the experimental prototype language RTL, were developed. However, rather surprisingly, neither language included features for real time programming. Other languages followed, including PROCOL [146], later replaced by LTR [41], in France, PEARL [53, 95] in Germany, PORTAL [133] in Switzerland, ILIAD [140] in the U.S.A., and Ada [86, 109, 1] in France and the U.S.A. Of these, some eventually became standardised nationally and internationally, and a number became widely used.

As new high level languages became available and popular in general systems programming, they also made their way into real time programming. While these languages, such as C, CHILL [36], Modula-2 [189] or PL/M, have but rudimentary or no real time features, they are very well known and very widely available.

In addition to the traditional high level languages, a number of application-class-specific, non-procedural higher level languages and "fill-in-the-blanks" template program generators are used in various real time application areas. Examples of the higher level languages include ATLAS [8] for automatic test systems or EXAPT [163] for machine tool controls. The program generators are generally vendor-specific and contain preprogrammed function blocks for measurement, control, and automation, which need to be configured and parameterised by the user. They are available for a number of distributed process control systems and programmable logic controllers, and have proven to be successful in their application area.

In this Chapter we shall be concerned with application level (high level) real time languages. Higher level, specification and logic languages, such as Esterel [26, 25] or Modechart [91], are outside the scope of the Chapter.

2.3   Requirements of a Real Time Language

Real time software must be guaranteed to meet its timing constraints [161, 183, 26, 70, 166, 46, 16, 15]. Therefore, we believe that a real time language must be designed such that its programs can be guaranteed to meet their deadlines at compile-time, i.e., to be schedulability analysable. This requirement is unique among programming language requirements in that it applies to real time languages only. To us, it is the most important requirement of all.

Real time programs must be very reliable in general. Thus, a real time language should be very secure[2]. Specifically, the language should have strong typing and structured constructs, and be modular. Moreover, a real time language should make provisions for error handling.

Real time software almost always involves multiprogramming. Thus, a real time language should include process definitions, as well as process synchronisation mechanisms, in other words support the task concept.

Many real time systems are quite large. Glass [69] reports a survey of twenty projects undertaken at eleven U.S. aerospace and defence companies. On the average, a project involved 30 programmers coding 150,000 instructions. Under such circumstances, a real time language must be very modular and allow separate compilation, thus enhancing "programming-in-the-large".

Real time software typically interfaces many different hardware devices. It is important, therefore, to provide constructs in the language to access hardware locations and handle interrupts directly in a flexible and yet secure way.

Real time systems have a long life expectancy, because so do the environments they control. It is well-known that the majority of the costs associated with such systems are maintenance costs. We therefore require that real time programs should be easy to understand, read and modify. This general maintainability requirement is greatly aided if the language is readable, well-structured, and not too complex.

In some real time applications, such as the X-29 fighter described previously, computer system response times are very short. Thus, even though compiler and run-time support system construction should, in theory, be independent of language design (and vice-versa), we say that a real time language should be designed to make an efficient implementation of it feasible. It seems that small, simple to understand, and

---

[2]The security we have in mind here is in the sense of reliability and robustness.

well-defined languages are easier to implement efficiently than are larger, more complex languages. Thus, a real time language benefits from being small, simple, and well-defined.

Having defined what we should like to see in a real time language, we now take a look at some existing ones.

2.4   Review of Existing Languages

2.4.1   Pseudocodes and Assembly Languages

Early real time software was written in machine pseudocodes. Quickly though, machine pseudocode use gave way to assembly language use. With assembly languages came a number of advantages, the biggest being, perhaps, the ability to write location-independent code[3].

Assembly language instructions operate directly on registers and memory locations, usually bit, byte or word at a time. Most contemporary assemblers also come with macro definitions, data block operations, and other advanced (from an assembly programmer's point of view) features. Despite being so low level, assembly language was still widely used in the late Seventies and even the Eighties. For example, half of the code of the twenty projects surveyed by [69] was written in assembly language, and the other half in FORTRAN, JOVIAL and other first generation high level languages.

The advantages of assembly programming are that the programmer has tight control over program efficiency, and direct hardware access is trivial. The disadvantages of assembly programming are as follows: no constructs to support schedulability analysis, very insecure, no process definitions, very hard for "programming-in-the-large", and very hard to maintain[4].

---

[3]This is code that did not depend at the time it was written on how it would be assembled and linked and where it was ultimately loaded into computer memory

[4]In the early Eighties, one of the authors attended a computer career seminar. One of the speakers was from Spar Aerospace. He told a story about one of their state-of-the-art flight simulators written entirely in assembly language. Despite its high quality, the simulator had to be scrapped once its original programmers were transferred or quit — no one else could maintain it.

2.4.2 FORTRAN

FORTRAN (*FOR*mula *TRAN*slator) [65] was the first high level language used[5]. It was aimed at expressing scientific and mathematical computing while allowing for efficient code generation. Originally, it was little more than a machine-independent assembler, but later evolved and incorporated structured loops, if-then-else, subroutines and other good "programming-in-the-small" features [9]. FORTRAN is widely used today and is likely to persevere for many more years to come.

The advantages of FORTRAN are its reasonable structure, separate compilation, and simplicity. FORTRAN programs are not too hard to maintain, and its compilers produce fast code. However, FORTRAN makes no provisions for schedulability analysis, error handling, multitasking, direct hardware access (other than through linking to assembly routines), and modularity.

2.4.3 JOVIAL

JOVIAL (*J*ules'[6] *O*wn *V*ersion of the *I*nternational *A*lgorithmic *L*anguage) [155] was created because the U.S. Air Force wanted its own standard, high level language. JOVIAL is ALGOL-based but also includes various features not found in ALGOL, such as assembly level inserts, records (though only one level deep), and arrays of records. The language is currently in use in many U.S. Air Force applications, but is likely to be replaced eventually by Ada.

The advantages of JOVIAL are that it is reasonably structured and has rudimentary typing, it allows for separate compilation and direct hardware access, and it is readable and simple. JOVIAL compilers produce fast code. While many tools have been built for JOVIAL, such as the one presented in [66] and used for conventional syntax and structural analysis, and instrumentation on the source code, no schedulability analyser for JOVIAL exists since the language makes no schedulability analysis provisions. In addition, JOVIAL has no exception handlers, has no multitasking, and is not modular.

---

[5]Zuse's Plankalkül [192] was the first high level language defined and published.
[6]after Jules Schwartz, the language's designer

2.4.4 RTL/1 and RTL/2

RTL/2 (*Real-Time Language/2*) [19] and its experimental prototype RTL/1 [18] were designed to be used in industrial process control. The languages are ALGOL-based and fairly well-structured. They allow for separate compilation and have rudimentary modules (stack, data and procedure combinations). The languages have a standard set of kernel interface procedures (callable from RTL/1 and RTL/2 programs, and used for I/O and tasking) and low level error handlers (kernel procedures, which the user can actually redefine). The implementations of the languages even try avoiding certain unpredictable timing delays. These delays manifest themselves in the cases of conventional garbage collection and dynamic stack management. RTL/1 and RTL/2 are small and readable, and their programs are maintainable.

However, both languages are weakly typed, enforce no intermodule type checking and information hiding, and make no provisions for schedulability analysis or direct hardware access. RTL/1 was never used on a non-experimental basis, while RTL/2 was and still is used in Britain and elsewhere for programming mainly small real time systems.

2.4.5 PEARL

PEARL (*Process and Experiment Automation Realtime Language*) [53, 95] was designed in the early Seventies by a group of German researchers from a dozen research institutes and industrial firms. Despite the large number of participants, this language, now widely used in Germany [127], is an example of a fine design and does not look like a designed-by-the-committee language.

PEARL is well-structured and has strong typing, modules with export and import constructs, and proper process definition. The language has constructs for time and/or event related process activation, suspension and termination. PEARL is readable and allows for direct hardware access and separate compilation. The disadvantages of PEARL are the insufficiency of its schedulability analysis provisions, the absence of structured exception handlers, and unstructured (semaphore-based) process synchronisation.

2.4.6 ILIAD

ILIAD [140] was designed at the Department of Computer Science of General Motors' Research Laboratories in order "to create a language in which application programmers can write well-structured programs". The language is now used at General Motors for such applications as data acquisition, parts inspection, and assembly line monitoring [104].

ILIAD is PL/I-like, well-structured and has strong typing. It also has process definitions, error handling through a user defined (one per system) error process, critical regions for process synchronisation, time and/or event dependent process delays, and direct hardware access constructs. ILIAD allows for separate compilation, and its programs are easy to maintain. However, the language makes no provisions for schedulability analysis, is not modular, and lacks structured exception handlers and process synchronisation primitives.

2.4.7 Modula and Modula-2

Modula [187] is intended to be run on bare microprocessor systems, and provide facilities for both low and high level programming. The extent of its actual use is comparable to that of RTL/2, but is definitely nowhere near that of JOVIAL or FORTRAN.

Modula is a very well-structured, small language, with strong type checking, modules (hence the name) with *use* (import) and *define* (export) lists, interface modules (monitors), and device modules (dedicated device monitors). It allows for direct hardware access and separate compilation. Modula has processes synchronised through waits and signals. Modula programs can be very easily maintained, and its compilers produce fast code.

Unfortunately, Modula does not define language-level exception handling. Moreover, the notion of real time process execution and, in fact, the very notion of explicit real time, is overlooked in the language [144, 5]. The lack of explicit language-level provisions for schedulability analysis in Modula can be explained by Wirth's position stated in [188]. While the author argues that there are reasons for designing real time programs differently from non-real-time programs, since, for instance,

> ... certain processes — which are not programmable at dis-
> cretion, as they may be part of the environment — may fail
> to wait for synchronisation signals indicating completion of
> the co-operating partner's task ... Hence validation ... will
> depend on ... a lower bound on the interval between two
> consecutive ... signals.

he eventually concludes that:

> ... Whereas real time programming calls for no additional
> language facilities, a new requirement must be imposed on
> implementations: they must be able to provide accurate exe-
> cution time bounds for any compiled statement or statement
> sequence.

Modula-2 [189] is a widely-used dialect of Modula, aimed at systems implementation. The language drops Modula's concurrent processes synchronised via monitors, waits and signals in favour of quasi-
concurrent co-routines and explicit run-time scheduler invocations. This
change makes Modula-2 less suitable for "programming-in-the-large".
Othertchangesafrom Modula, such as Modula-2's treatment of I/O as
low level operations, have raised questions about program portability
and maintainability [128][7]. Like Modula, Modula-2 lacks provisions for
schedulability analysis and error handling.

2.4.8   PORTAL

PORTAL [133] was designed by H.H. Nägeli, A.K. Gorrengourt, H. Lien-
hard, R. Schild and R. Schönberger at the Landis and Gyr Zug Corporation of Zug, Switzerland, and the Swiss Institute of Technology of Zürich
to be used in system programming and real time process control. To the
best of our knowledge, the language is not used outside of the Landis
and Gyr Corporation and various Swiss institutes of higher learning.

PORTAL is quite similar to Modula. It is very well-structured, has
strong type checking, modules with use and define lists, monitors and

---

[7]In our opinion, though, Modula-2 addresses well the trade-off of program portability and direct device access.

device monitors. PORTAL has processes that synchronise through waits and signals. The language allows direct hardware access and separate compilation. To make PORTAL suitable for real time programming, the designers introduced device monitor priorities and wait timeouts into the language. PORTAL programs are easily maintainable, and its compilers produce fast code. PORTAL provides unstructured (*ON ERROR*) exception handling. Unfortunately, PORTAL makes insufficient provisions for schedulability analysis and structured exception handling.

2.4.9 Ada

Ada [1] was designed as the result of a procurement exercise by the U.S. Department of Defense. Ada's raison d'être is that the DoD was very much concerned with too much maintenance and other costs associated with using over 1000 various languages, and wanted to move towards using a single standardised one. Ada's is already very wide-spread, and it is expected to become (if it has not done so already) the most used real time language in the near future.

The advantages of Ada are that it is very well-structured, quite readable, and modular, and it has strong typing. It allows for direct hardware access and separate compilation. Ada has tasks (processes) synchronised through asymmetric rendezvous, good error handlers, and both system- and user-defined exceptions.

One major disadvantage of Ada is that it is very large and complex. Being a typical design-by-the-committee product, it includes just about every feature conceivable in a modern language. As a result of Ada's size and complexity it was found hard to learn and use, and it requires large amounts of run-time support which makes it difficult to produce efficient code [147]. Moreover, Ada makes hardly any provisions for schedulability analysis.

2.4.10 Forth

Forth [29, 30] was created by Charles H. Moore because, as he put it in the foreword to [29], "The traditional languages were not providing the power, ease, or flexibility that I wanted". The language is used today at a number of U.S. process control applications.

Forth differs from every other languages in our survey in that it is interpretive. Its advantages are its convenience of use and ease of direct memory access. The disadvantages of Forth are that it makes no provisions for schedulability analysis, only has rudimentary exception handling (through its **Abort** statement) and is not modular.

2.4.11   Languages for Programmable Logic Controllers

Most languages used to develop real time programmable logic controllers (PLCs) make at best rudimentary provisions for schedulability analysis. Since these languages (as well as computer-aided software development tools) for PLCs are presently available in vendor-specific form only, the International Electrotechnical Commission (IEC) has worked out a very detailed draft on the definition and standardisation of these languages [87]. The languages are apt for all performance classes of PLCs and for the front end part of distributed process control systems.

The draft defines a family of four system-independent languages, viz. two textual and two graphical ones:

IL   Instruction List
LD   Ladder Diagram
FBD / SFC   Function Block Diagram / Sequential Function Chart
ST   Structured Text

The IEC claims that the languages are equivalent and can be transformed into one another. A serious shortcoming of the IEC draft as it stands now is that none of its four languages provides symbolic input/output capabilities. The use of explicit hardware addresses renders the development of portable control programs almost impossible, since these programs are usually highly I/O bound. Another drawback is that the timing properties of the cyclic execution of control actions and the duration of individual process states are implementation dependent and not under program control. The only means of time control are to delay actions and to schedule tasks cyclically. There are, however, no capabilities for absolute timing and for the temporal supervision of activities.

2.4.12 Experimental Hard Real Time Languages

Over the last fifteen years there has been increasing interest in the design of languages suitable for programming hard real time applications. Currently, none of these languages is in widespread use, and none of them shows much promise to be widely used in the future. However small scale these real time language experiments are at present, they nonetheless represent various approaches to hard real time programming and are interesting for that particular reason.

Among the many experimental hard real time languages, a number meets or largely meets the requirements of Section 2.3. Most notably, these languages include TOMAL [99], DICON [110, 111], ORE [54], FLEX [120], Real-Time Mentat [71] and RTC++ [90]. Since we are interested in industrial languages, there is no need to consider all these experimental languages here. It suffices to present one that meets all real time language requirements, to illustrate our point.

Real-Time Euclid [101, 169] (originally known as Real-Time Turing [167]) was designed to meet all of the real time language requirements of Section 2.3. Real-Time Euclid, described in more detail in [101, 169], is a descendant of Concurrent Euclid [42], and also benefits from Turing Plus [84].

Real-Time Euclid programs can always be analysed for guaranteed schedulability. This is achieved through (1) time-bounding loop and suspension constructs, (2) disallowing recursion and dynamic storage allocation, and (3) specifying timing information for each process.

An interesting part of Real-Time Euclid's design are its structured exception handlers with three severity-based classes of exceptions. While the language is statically scoped in general, exception propagation and recovery is single-thread *dynamic*. To ensure schedulability analysability of exceptional code, the language forces the length of each potential chain of exceptions to be statically bounded.

The language is well-structured, modular and strongly typed. It has

Requirement^Language	Assembly	FORTRAN	JOVIAL	RTL/1 and RTL/2	PEARL
Schedulability	No	No	No	No	Some
Security	No	No	No	No	Some
Concurrency	No	No	No	Some	Yes
Modularity	No	No	No	Some	Yes
Hardware Access	Yes	No	Some	No	Yes
Maintainability	No	Some	Some	Some	Yes
Efficiency	Yes	Yes	Yes	Some	Yes

Table 2.1: The Results of The Language Survey.

Requirement^Language	ILIAD	Modula and Modula-2	PORTAL	Ada
Schedulability	No	No	Some	No
Security	Some	Yes	Some	Yes
Concurrency	Yes	Yes	Yes	Yes
Modularity	No	Yes	Yes	Yes
Hardware Access	Yes	Yes	Yes	Yes
Maintainability	Yes	Yes	Yes	Maybe
Efficiency	Yes	Yes	Yes	Some

Table 2.2: The Results of The Language Survey (continued).

static processes synchronised through monitors, waits and signals, and direct hardware access mechanisms. Real-Time Euclid allows separate compilation of modules and subroutines.

Real-Time Euclid and its schedulability analyser have been defined, implemented and evaluated [169, 170, 137, 100, 138, 179]. To the best of our knowledge, this makes Real-Time Euclid the first defined and implemented, along with its analyser, schedulability analysable language. Our experience with Real-Time Euclid [169]) indicates that its programs run fast, and are easily maintainable. Like most other experimental languages in this survey, however, Real-Time Euclid has never made it outside the laboratory.

2.4.13 Survey Summary

We have defined what, in our view, were the requirements of a real time language, and we surveyed a number of existing real time languages. Tables 2.1, 2.2 and 2.3 contain the results of our survey.

None of the languages actually used in real time programming satisfies the above requirements entirely. Assembly languages meet prac-

Requirement^Language	Forth	PLC Languages	Real-Time Euclid
Schedulability	No	No	Yes
Security	No	Probably	Yes
Concurrency	Some	Some	Yes
Modularity	No	Yes	Yes
Hardware Access	Yes	Maybe	Yes
Maintainability	Yes	Yes	Yes
Efficiency	Some	Maybe	Yes

Table 2.3: The Results of The Language Survey (continued).

tically none of them. FORTRAN, JOVIAL and Forth do not address
the issues of schedulability analysis, modularity, structured error handling, and multitasking. RTL/1 and RTL/2 have the same flaws as
FORTRAN and JOVIAL do, except that the former two have rudimentary modules. PEARL, ILIAD, Modula and Modula-2 and PORTAL
make no provisions for schedulability analysis. Moreover, ILIAD is not
modular, Modula and Modula-2 have no exception handlers, and POR-
TAL has only unstructured exception handling. Ada does not meet the
schedulability analysis requirement. Moreover, Ada's large size and complexity make efficient implementation and, possibly, easy maintenance
improbable. The proposed standard languages for PLCs appear to satisfy some of our requirements, though failing in schedulability analysis.
As these languages remain to be implemented, little can be said about
their efficiency.

Thus, none of the industrial languages in our survey makes sufficient
schedulability analysis provisions. This sad state of affairs is well summarised by Berry:

> ... paradoxically, one can verify that the current so-
> called "real time programming languages" do not
> provide any explicit means of correctly expressing
> time constraints. A fortiori, they provide no insur-
> ance that the constraints would be respected when
> executing the program.[26]

Designing languages to be real time schedulability analysable is the only requirement of the ones above which is exclusive to real time languages. We consider this to be the most important requirement of all.

Real-Time Euclid is an experimental schedulability analysable language. Given our experience with Real-Time Euclid (see Chapter 7), we feel that it meets every one of the real time language requirements, and is thus unique in our survey of languages.

2.5   Taking a Closer Look at Real-Time Euclid

Of the languages considered in our survey, only Real-Time Euclid satisfies all requirements of a real time language. Real-Time Euclid is a procedural language. It is a descendant of the Pascal [186], Euclid [85], Concurrent Euclid [42] and Turing [83] line of languages. It has been specifically designed for real time applications.

2.5.1   Language Structure

Real-Time Euclid programs consist of modules. The modules are used to package data together with processes, procedures, and functions that use the data. A module may *export* a list of entry subprograms, types and constants declared inside the module that are to be accessed outside of it. Variables and modules cannot be exported. Exported identifiers may be accessed outside the module using the dot operator. Unexported identifiers cannot be referenced outside the module. Similarly, a module may *import* a list of identifiers declared outside of it that are to be accessed inside the module. Modules may be nested. Modules and subprograms can be compiled separately. To use separately compiled modules and subprograms, they must be declared **external** in the modules that use them. Strict type checking is enforced in all external references.

A Real-Time Euclid program executes in two stages: first the **initially** sections (sequential code to perform initialisation of data, at most one section per module) of all the modules are executed, and then the processes begin to execute. The program terminates when all the processes in the program have terminated.

Real time applications often involve scheduling of real time processes, some of which are executing concurrently. There are three essential facilities in Real-Time Euclid which are used to express the concurrent execution of several tasks, viz., processes, monitors, and synchronisation primitives.

A process consists of sequential code that is intended to be executed concurrently with other processes. Monitors are modules which allow only one process at a time to be active inside them. Processes synchronise their activities inside a monitor by using **signal** and **wait** statements [82]. These apply to **condition** variables, which are queues of processes.

We do not intend to describe the language exhaustively. Instead, we concentrate on those language features that satisfy the real time language requirements given in Section 2.3.

2.5.2   Real Time Units and Time Functions

In a real time system, it is desirable to know, inside the system, what time it is in real time units. In real time applications, the time is usually measured in seconds or fractions thereof, as opposed to machine cycles or years. We offer to the programmer the ability to define the time in real time units in a flexible way.

A Real-Time Euclid program is:

realTimeUnitCall
moduleDeclaration

where *realTimeUnitCall* is:

RealTimeUnit (*timeInSeconds*)

The *realTimeUnitCall* must be present in the beginning of each program, and is used to define one real time unit to be *timeInSeconds* seconds. **RealTimeUnit** is a built-in function, and *timeInSeconds* is a non-negative integer expression. For example, the statement:

RealTimeUnit (*25e-3*)

defines one real time unit to be equal to 25 milliseconds.

The built-in function **Time** returns the time elapsed from the startup of the system to the present in real time units.

2.5.3   Absence of Dynamic Data Structures

Many languages permit the use of dynamic arrays, pointers, and arbitrarily long strings. The presence of these features in Real-Time Euclid would make it very hard, if not impossible, to bound at compile-time the time required to allocate/deallocate these structures. Also, we have to guarantee before the execution begins that there is sufficient amount of memory for the processes to execute. With dynamic arrays and pointers eliminated, a *variableDeclaration* is one of:

  a. **var** *id {,id}: typeSpec [:= expn]*
  b. **var** *id {,id}:= expn*
  c. **var** *id {,id}: typeSpec :=*
     init (*initializing Value {,initializing Value}*)
  d. **var** *id {,id}:* **array**
     compile TimeIntegerExpn..compile TimeIntegerExpn
     {*,compile TimeIntegerExpn..compile TimeIntegerExpn*}
     of *typeSpec*

Type string is one of the *standardType typeSpecs* (along with integers, Booleans, and reals) and is defined as follows:

  string[*(compile TimeIntegerExpn)*]

An implementation bounds the lengths of all strings. Strings declared without a *compile TimeIntegerExpn* have a default maximum length, which is 255 or shorter if the implementation so requires.

A limited form of dynamic arrays and strings is permitted as formal parameters to procedures or functions. A *parameterType* is one of:

  a. *typeSpec*
  b. **array** *compile TimeIntegerExpn..**
     {, *compile TimeIntegerExpn..**} **of** *typeSpec*
  c. **string** (*)
  d. **array** *compile TimeIntegerExpn..**
     {, *compile TimeIntegerExpn..**} **of string** (*)

In forms (b) and (d), the upper bounds of the index types of an array parameter are declared as *. In this case any array whose element type and index type's lower bounds are equivalent to those of the formal parameter can be passed as an actual parameter. The compiler in that case emits information to the schedulability analyser to indicate that as much storage may be needed to pass the parameter, as it takes to accommodate the largest array that can be passed. This information is used by the analyser to bound the storage a procedure call may need. When the procedure is called at run-time, the amount of storage allocated to pass the parameter corresponds to the size of the actual parameter. Similarly, in forms (c) and (d), the maximum length of a dynamic string is declared as *. The compile-time size bounding and run-time allocation of a string parameter takes place in the same way as in the case of an array parameter.

As a convenience to the programmer, the predefined function *upper* accepts an array and returns the upper bound of the array. The function also accepts a string and returns its maximum length.

2.5.4 Time-Bounded Loops

Like other high level languages, Real-Time Euclid has a loop construct which repeatedly executes a set of statements until some Boolean condition becomes true. However, in a real time language, execution times of all program segments must be known at compile-time. Consequently, the loops are allowed to iterate no more than a compile-time known number of iterations. The iteration construct in Real-Time Euclid has the following form:

> **for** [decreasing] *[id]*:
> > *compileTimeIntegerExpn..compileTimeIntegerExpn*
> > *declarationsAndStatements*
> > [**invariant** *BooleanExpn*]
> **end for**

The statement of the form

> **exit** [**when** *BooleanExpn*]

causes an immediate exit from the nearest enclosing **for** construct. The optional Boolean expression makes the exit conditional.

2.5.5   Absence of Recursion

The compiler prohibits recursive calls. Forbidding recursion altogether is the simplest remedy against arbitrarily long chains of recursive calls. If unrestricted arbitrarily long chains of recursive calls were permitted, the schedulability analyser would have no way of determining the execution time of subprograms involving recursion, nor how much storage would be required during execution.

2.5.6   Processes

The **process** declaration is like the one in Concurrent Euclid. Thus, the declaration instantiates a process, and is not a process template. The reason we do not declare process templates, as is the case in Concurrent Pascal [28] or Turing Plus [84], is to disallow dynamic instantiation of processes. Dynamic process instantiation would make it difficult, if not impossible, to analyse the processes for schedulability. Fortunately, most real time applications consist of a fixed number of process control or other physical tasks.

Real-Time Euclid processes have been designed to reflect the nature of physical real time tasks. As we saw in Chapter 1, some of these tasks are periodic and some are aperiodic. Thus, Real-Time Euclid processes can be declared periodic or aperiodic. Physical aperiodic tasks activate their corresponding processes by interrupts. Processes can also be activated by other processes or by the timer.

The syntax of the process declaration is:

> **process** *id* : *activationInfo*
> > *[importList]*
> > *[exceptionHandler]*
> > *declarationsAndStatements*
> **end** *id*

The *activationInfo* is one of:

> a. **atEvent** *conditionId frameInfo*
> b. **periodic** *frameInfo* **first activation** *timeOrEvent*

The *activationInfo* (required for every process) is used by the schedulability analyser to determine if the entire system of processes is schedulable, and by the run-time system to activate/schedule/deactivate the processes.

The information about each process's frame can be given in absolute real time units, or as an integer relative to frame sizes of other processes. The two types of frame declarations are mutually exclusive. Note that if the frame information of each process is declared relative to frames of other processes then the schedulability analyser will provide a set of frames in absolute real time units. Each frame will be as tight as possible (see Section 3.2.3.6).

The syntax of *frameInfo* is one of:

    a. **frame** *compileTimePositiveIntegerExpn*
    b. **relative frame** *compileTimePositiveIntegerExpn*

A process may be activated for the first time in the following two ways:

1. The process declaration specifies a real time expression indicating when the process should be activated.

2. An interrupt is raised which activates the process. An active process may activate another active process by issuing a broadcast on an appropriate condition variable.

The syntax for the *timeOrEvent* is one of:

    a. **atTime** *compileTimeNonNegativeIntegerExpn*
    b. **atEvent** *conditionId*
    c. **atTime** *compileTimeNonNegativeIntegerExpn*   or
       atEvent *conditionId*

Once activated, the process must complete its task before the end of its current frame. A process cannot be activated more often than once per frame.

2.5.7 Condition Variables

Real-Time Euclid has two types of conditions: *outsideMonitorCondition* and *insideMonitorCondition*.

The variables of the *insideMonitorCondition* type are declared only inside monitors, and they may be used by various processes to synchronise access to the data being protected by the monitor.

The variables of the *outsideMonitorCondition* type are declared only outside monitors. Outside-monitor-condition variables add no power to the set of synchronisation primitives already containing inside-monitor-condition variables, monitors, waits and signals (to be presented shortly). They do, however, allow for simpler and more efficient solutions to an important class of concurrency control problems. Outside-monitor-condition variables are used (1) to handle process synchronisation in cases where no data needs to be shared, a situation where using monitors would be inefficient [96, 63], and (2) to activate/deactivate processes.

We demonstrate the use of outside-monitor-condition variables by means of the following example. Suppose each of a set of processes is to perform a subtask (the subtasks forming a bigger task) concurrently with its peer processes. It makes sense then to wake up the entire set of processes simultaneously. Such a wakeup is best performed via a *broadcast* (to be presented in the next Section) on an outside-monitor-condition variable [166]. The monitor, wait and signal solution, a cumbersome and inefficient cascade, is inferior to the broadcast solution.

A *conditionDeclaration* is one of:

    a. **var** *conditionId*:
       [**array** *compileTimeIntegerExpn..compileTimeIntegerExpn* **of**]
       insideMonitorCondition
    b. **var** *conditionId*:
       [**array** *compileTimeIntegerExpn..compileTimeIntegerExpn* **of**]
       outsideMonitorCondition

Where *insideMonitorCondition* is:

    [**priority**] [**deferred**] **condition** [**atLocation** *interruptAddress*]
    noLongerThan *compileTimePositiveIntegerExpn* :
    timeoutReason

The keyword **deferred** means that a **signal** applied to this condition leaves the signaler running, while making the signaled process ready to re-enter the monitor when it becomes unoccupied. This is as opposed to an immediate (non-deferred) condition, in which a **signal** statement immediately wakes up a sleeping process [82]. The idea of deferred condition variables has been borrowed from Turing Plus.

An *outsideMonitorCondition* is one of:

   a. **activation condition** [**atLocation** *interruptAddress*]
   b. **condition** [**atLocation** *interruptAddress*] **noLongerThan**
      compileTimePositiveIntegerExpn : timeoutReason

The optional **atLocation** clause is a machine dependent feature. It means that an interrupt specified by the *interruptAddress* will signal the condition. If this clause is present, the condition is called an *interrupt* condition. In a computer with vectored interrupts, the *interruptAddress* can give the address of the interrupt's vector location. A **signal** statement can signal an interrupt condition. A timeout is treated as an exception, and the *timeoutReason* is passed to the exception handler of the process that executed the wait. Exception handlers are discussed in Section 2.5.9.

2.5.8 Monitors, Signals, Waits and Broadcasts

Real-Time Euclid monitors, signals, and waits are those described in [82], except that the **wait** statement is extended to specify a time bound. The **signal** and **wait** statements are used in conjunction with monitors to provide exclusive access to shared data and monitor process synchronisation.

A new statement called **broadcast** is added for the purpose of simultaneously waking up all processes blocked on a given outside-of-monitor condition variable queue.

The three statements that operate on conditions have the following forms:

   a. **signal** *conditionId [(subscriptExpn)]*
   b. **wait** *conditionId [(subscriptExpn)] [, priorityExpn]*
      [**noLongerThan***compileTimePositiveIntegerExpn :*
      timeoutReason]
   c. **broadcast** *conditionId [(subscriptExpn)]*

If the time bound for the **wait** statement is not specified, then the schedulability analyser takes the time bound to be that with which the condition variable was declared. If a wait times out, an exception is raised and its *timeoutReason* is passed to an exception handler. If the wait does not specify a *timeoutReason*, then the *timeoutReason* specified in the condition variable declaration is used. After the timeout is handled and if the process is not deactivated or killed, the process has to re-queue for the monitor. After going through the queue, the process resumes execution right after the wait statement. The programmer is urged to keep the monitor invariant satisfied just before each wait statement.

2.5.9   Exception Handling

In order for a real time system to be robust, some sort of exception handling may be needed. Empirical studies indicate that introduction of even basic fault tolerance into the software results in much more reliable real time systems [75]. Exceptions may arise for various reasons, which may or may not have something to do with missed deadlines. For example, a division by zero raises an exception but this exception would have existed in non-real-time systems as well. In Real-Time Euclid there are also exceptions which are raised in the case of timeouts (when there is a danger of missing a deadline if the process continues to wait too long), in the case of premature activation of processes, and the like.

Exception handling in Real-Time Euclid is introduced via two different but related features. These features are:

1. the **kill, deactivate**, and **except** statements;
2. the **handler**, which is a block of declarations and statements located (optionally) at the beginning of a subprogram, a process, or an **initially** section.

The **kill** statement explicitly causes a real time process, possibly itself, to raise an exception and terminates it. If the victim process is inactive (i.e., has completed a frame) but has not yet started another frame, then the victim would not be able to handle the exception and thus no exception is raised. The process is nevertheless terminated. A process that was terminated through a **kill** cannot be reactivated.

The **deactivate** statement is used to raise an exception and terminate a process, possibly itself, in the current frame of that process. If the victim process is inactive when a **deactivate** is executed, then the statement has no effect. The victim process may be reactivated when its current frame expires, and, if the process is periodic, then it is reactivated automatically at that time.

The **except** statement is used to raise an exception in the process, possibly itself, without terminating the process or even its current frame. Once an exception raised by this statement is serviced by the exception handler, the process returns where it left off, and resumes execution in the same frame.

The syntax of the three statements follows below:

> **kill** *processId : killReason*
> **deactivate** *processId : deactivateReason*
> **except** *processId : exceptionReason*

An *exceptionHandler* has the form:

> **handler** *(exceptionReason)*
>   **exceptions** *(exceptionNumber [: maxNumberRaised]*
>   *{, exceptionNumber [: maxNumberRaised] })*
>   *[import list]*
>   *declarationsAndStatements*
> **end handler**

If no exceptions occur, exception handlers have no effect. In Real-Time Euclid, we distinguish between three classes of exceptions on the basis of the degree of their severity.

Exceptions in the first class are raised by executing **kill** statements, and are referred to as *terminal exceptions*. A terminal exception is thus raised when a process outlives its usefulness. For example, the process in control of a sensor is no longer useful after the sensor breaks down.

Exceptions in the second class are raised by executing **deactivate** statements, and are called *frame-terminal exceptions*. A frame-terminal exception occurs, for instance, when a consistency check of an intermediate result fails. The rest of the computation is then useless. The process in charge of the computation is therefore aborted in its current frame, though it will be re-activated in the next frame.

The third class of exceptions consists of *frame-recoverable exceptions.* These are raised by executing **except** statements as well as by timeouts, overflows, divisions by zero, and the like.

Real-Time Euclid processes, subprograms, and **initially** sections may have pre- and postconditions. A precondition must be satisfied when the corresponding process/subprogram/**initially** is activated/called/started. A postcondition must be satisfied when the corresponding process/subprogram/**initially** deactivates/returns/completes, unless a terminal or a frame-terminal exception was raised while executing.

Each exception has an *exception number* (also referred to as an *exception reason*), unique within the entire system. The uniqueness of the number is enforced at link-time. An exception number is explicitly specified in every **kill**, **deactivate**, **except**, and **wait** statement. Some exceptions may be raised when executing statements which do not explicitly specify an exception number. For example, an arithmetic operation may result in an overflow exception. These implicit exceptions are included in the implementation-dependent list of *standard exceptions*, and exception handlers treat them just like they treat explicit exceptions. A Real-Time Euclid implementation has a default system level exception handler to take care of each implementation-defined exception. Note that this does not preclude the programmer from handling some or all of these exceptions at the application program level as well.

A particular handler becomes ready to handle an exception when it is encountered during execution. By "encountered" we mean that the subprogram containing the handler is called, the process containing the handler is activated (i.e., begins a new frame) or the **initially** section containing the handler starts executing. The handler remains ready until the subprogram/process/**initially** in which it is located returns/deactivates/completes. Should an exception be raised the handler is given control. The handler then effectively replaces the subprogram/process/**initially** that contains the handler.

Exceptions will be handled in an orderly, consistent way by every implementation. If a process receives an asynchronous exception while in a monitor, the implementation will ensure that the monitor section will be completed before the exception is processed.

The remainder of this Section meticulously describes the way exception handlers operate in processes, subprograms, and **initially** sections.

If a process raises or receives[8] a terminal exception, then the handler of the process handles the exception and the process is terminated. If the handler of a process raises a terminal exception, then the exception is handled by the run-time system and the process is terminated. If a process raises a frame-terminal exception, then the handler of the process handles the exception. The process then is terminated in its current frame only, assuming the handler does not raise a terminal exception. If the handler of a process raises a frame-terminal exception, then the exception is handled by the run-time system. In this case the process is terminated in its frame only, assuming (1) the handler was not invoked because of a terminal exception, and (2) the run-time system does not decide to terminate the process for good, because of some other information unknown to the process's exception handler. If a process raises a frame-recoverable exception, then the handler of the process handles it. The process then resumes execution at the instruction following the one that raised the exception, assuming the handler does not raise a terminal or a frame-terminal exception. If the handler of a process raises a frame-recoverable exception, then the handler itself handles it. The handler then returns to the instruction following the one that raised the second exception, assuming no terminal or frame-terminal exception was raised.

Observe that it is possible to have a chain of frame-recoverable exceptions E_1, E_2, E_3, etc., where E_1 was raised by the process, E_2 was raised by the handler while handling E_1, E_3 was raised by the handler while handling E_2, etc. Such chains must be prevented from being arbitrarily long, for our processes are to be time-bounded. Each Real-Time Euclid exception handler has an **exceptions** clause (see the definition of a handler above) which lists all the exceptions handled by the handler along with optional compile-time evaluable numbers. These numbers corre-

---

[8]In what follows, when we say that a process raises an exception, we shall mean that the process either raises or receives an exception.

spond to the maximum number of times the exceptions can be raised in a chain of frame-recoverable exceptions. If no such number is specified for an exception, the default of one is assumed.

If an exception is raised whose number does not have a corresponding clause in the handler of the process, or if the handler is missing altogether, then the run-time system handles the exception. The subsequent action will depend on the kind of the exception, namely, whether it is terminal, frame-terminal or frame-recoverable.

Real-Time Euclid statically disallows **initially** sections from raising frame-terminal exceptions, because (1) **initially** sections have no frames as such, but execute only once at system initialisation time, and (2) no process starts executing until every **initially** section completes. The language also disallows **initially** sections from calling subprograms of other modules. This restriction is in effect because the modules are considered to be uninitialised until every **initially** section has completed. If an **initially** section raises a terminal exception, then the run-time system handles the exception and the entire program terminates.

Suppose a process or an **initially** section X calls a subprogram S_1 which calls a subprogram S_2 and so on until finally a subprogram S_N is called. Now, if S_N raises a terminal or a frame-terminal exception, then all of S_1 through S_N are aborted and the exception is passed to the exception handler of X. If X does not have an exception handler or if the exception handler of X does not handle this particular exception, then the exception is passed to the run-time system. If S_N raises a frame-terminal exception and X is an **initially** section, then the exception is ignored when it reaches X. S_1 through S_N are still aborted, since it is meaningless for **initially** sections to raise frame-terminal exceptions. If a procedure raises a frame-recoverable exception, then it is handled by the exception handler of the procedure.

2.5.10   Summary

In describing the Real-Time Euclid language, we have concentrated on those aspects of it that are dedicated to real time programming. Other Real-Time Euclid features, all borrowed from Concurrent Euclid, Turing and Turing Plus, are not important for the purpose of this book but are specified in [101].

Real-Time Euclid is a language with schedulability analysis provisions built-in. In Chapter 3 we shall present schedulability analysis techniques for Real-Time Euclid.

2.6 A Second Review — Focusing on Real Time Features

2.6.1 Selection of Reviewed Languages

In this second review of real time languages we focus on the real time features themselves. Therefore, in the sequel, we select for our considerations those languages offering a relative broad spectrum of real time typical constructs and disregards their actual availability and dissemination.

In [149] ALGOL 68 was considered in a comparison of real time languages. Although it allows parallel processing, we omit it here since it does not provide real time features.

The older British developments CORAL 66 and RTL/2 are designated as process control languages. The two languages, however, only comprise algorithmic elements and, as far as real time features, synchronisation, and I/O are concerned, they totally rely on operating system calls. Therefore, we do not consider them here.

Concurrent Pascal [28] and Modula [188] are operating system implementation languages, with but rudimentary real time elements. In particular, Modula incorporates no I/O or timing facilities, and does not provide language constructs to model a set of tasks upon a technical process and to control this task set accordingly. Instead, Modula allows one to write machine-dependent peripheral driver routines and the users' own timing, synchronisation, and resource sharing mechanisms.

Formulating real time application programs in Modula would therefore require a considerable amount of non-problem-oriented work and would yield non-portable software. The above statements on real time facilities hold even more for Modula-2 [189], especially with respect to tasking, since only the coroutine concept is implemented to express concurrency.

There are a number of dialects of BASIC (such as on reported in [31]) available incorporating a minimum of real time features aimed at scientific, not heavily used applications, where the control and evaluation of experiments is to be quickly programmed. Hence, these BASIC derivatives are also outside of our scope.

The language CHILL was developed by the Comité Consultatif International Telegraphique et Telephonique. Within the post administrations, its use is obligatory for telecommunication switching systems. Although it possesses some real time features, we do not consider it here for its rather limited application area and since it is better characterised as a system implementation language.

A number of experimental real time languages, referred to as *synchronous*, have recently been developed in France and elsewhere. These include Esterel and Lustre [34]. The design of the languages includes a key assumption, viz. that the execution of operations takes zero time, unless the operation specifies an explicit timing delay. While allowing one to reason about real time properties of programs in the abstract, this assumption does not address such prevalent, practical considerations as system resource contention, overhead and so on. We thus exclude synchronous languages from this survey of real time languages that may be used in a realistic industrial environment.

The languages Occam [88] and Occam2 [89, 152] support the communication and processor configuration in Transputer-based distributed systems. Parallelism can only be generated in a static way. Since the languages do not allow exception handling and only provide a non-deterministic guarded command feature for reacting to several possible events, they do not fulfill the predictability requirements of languages for hard real time systems.

Finally, the International Electrotechnical Commission is presently in the process of devising and standardising four languages [87] to be used in the software development for programmable logic controllers. One of them, namely, Structured Text, is an Algoloide high level language possessing the tasking feature. Otherwise, it falls very short of real time elements, although PLCs are widely used in this application domain. It is hoped that these shortcomings will be eliminated before the language becomes a reality through international standardisation.

In the main part of this Section, we consider seven languages that all have incorporated a number of real time features. These are not the only languages of this kind, but together they depict a fair perspective of the industrial real time language scene. The languages are: Ada, Industrial Real-Time FORTRAN, HAL/S, LTR, PEARL, PL/1 and Real-Time Euclid. With the exception of Real-Time Euclid, all the languages in the list have originated in industry and are available for industrial use. Real-Time Euclid is included in the survey as an experimental example that demonstrates how a language may be designed that ensures that all its programs can be analysed for predictable real time behaviour.

2.6.2 A Survey of Real Time Features Supported

In Table 2.4, we have compiled information on the availability of real time features of the seven languages under consideration. This information has been gathered from the relevant language manuals and references [86, 109, 1, 7, 20, 53, 95, 102, 41, 136, 149, 154, 101, 169].

The first category of features listed comprises language elements of conventional nature, required in real time applications. Typically, these features are supported through operating system device drivers, similarly to the way standard I/O is supported. All languages make adequate provisions for these conventional features.

In all languages considered, parallel processing is organised on the basis of tasks or parallel processes. These can be hierarchically ordered in Ada, HAL/S, and PEARL. Each language defines a different model of task states. In most cases, it is not possible to ascertain which state a task is presently in. Only Ada and PL/1 make it possible to determine whether a task is active or already terminated.

To control the execution of tasks and their state transitions, tasking operations are provided as language features. PEARL, FORTRAN, and Real-Time Euclid offer a wide range of such tasking operations, that may even be linked to interrupt occurrences and temporal schedules

Table 2.4: Survey on Real-Time Elements in Ada, Industrial Real-Time FORTRAN, HAL/S, LTR, PEARL, Real-Time PL/1, and Real-Time Euclid.

Category	Feature	Ada	FORTRAN	HAL/S	LTR	PEARL	PL/1	Euclid
Conventional elements	Bit processing	(n) (1)	y	y	y	y	y	y
	Reentrant procedures	y	n	y	y	y	y	y
	File handling	y	y	y	y	y	y	y
	Process I/O	y	y	n	y	y	y	y
Tasking	Hierarchy of tasks	y	n	y	n	y	n	n
	Task stati available	2	n	n	n	n	3	n
	Task scheduling	y	y	y	y	y	y	y
	Controllability of tasks	poor	complete	limited	limited	complete	poor	complete
	Exception handling in tasks	y	n	y	n	y	y	y
	Implied scheduling strategy	prio, fifo	—	prio.	pre-emp. prio.	prio.	prio., os-dep.	pre-emp. deadline
	Usage of priorities	y	n	y	y	y	y	y
	Changeability of priorities	y (2)	n	y	n	y	y	y
Synchronisation	Semaphores	y (2)	y	n	y	y	n	n
	Further synch. means	rendezvous signal (2) shared variable	resourcemark	compool lock	blockstruct.	bolt blockstruct. implicitly	shared obj. lock	monitor event
	Resource reservation	y	y	y	y	y	y	y
	Resource stati available	y	y	n	y	n	y	y
	Resource alloc. strategy	fifo	os-dep	prio.	prio	prio., os-dep.	prio.	deadline, prio.
	Deadlock prevention support	n	n	n	n	n	y	n
Events	Interrupt handling	y (1)	y	(y)	y	y	y	y
	Enable/disable interrupt	n (1)	y	(y)	(n)	y	y	y
Timing	Date/time available	y (2)	y	y	(y)	y	y	y
	Cumulative run-time avail.		n	(y)	n	n	n	
	Forms of time scheduling	delay	various	various	delay cyclic	various	delay fixed date	various
	Timing control of synch. operations	y	n	n	n	n	y	y
Verification	Testing aids	raise exception call int. entries	set eventmark	simulation run-time deter. trace	mapping trace flag display	induce event trigger int.	n	raise exception assert

(1) Only indirectly possible in the Ada version ANSI/MIL-STD-1815A-1983
(2) Not available in the Ada version ANSI/MIL-STD-1815A-1983.

in PEARL. In Ada and PL/1, it is only possible to activate and abort tasks, whereas additionally a wait operation may be requested in HAL/S and LTR. Furthermore, the latter two languages allow task activations to be scheduled for the occurrence of simple timing and other events. After the schedules for their initiation are met, the tasks compete for resources, including main processors. All language definitions, except that of FORTRAN, imply that the appropriate dispatching decisions are then made on the basis of a strategy. All languages but LTR use task priorities that may be dynamically changed. According to [86] an operating system supporting Ada at run-time may also utilise the first-in-first-out policy for task scheduling. Only Real-Time Euclid employs the more appropriate concept of deadlines to schedule tasks.

All languages considered provide means for the synchronisation of task executions and for the reservation of resources to be used exclusively. The most common synchronisation feature is the semaphore. In addition, various other concepts are realised in the different languages. The availability of resources can be checked in all languages except in HAL/S and PEARL. The employed resource allocation schemes are mostly either priority-based or operating-system-dependent. Real-Time Euclid allocates resources by deadline, or by priority, dependent on the nature of the resources. Only Ada systems use the first-in-first-out policy. Deadlock prevention as objective of the language has only been found in PL/1.

Tasks may communicate with each other in all seven languages via single bit messages or events. Associating events with interrupts is common. In Ada, interrupts cannot be enabled or disabled.

As we shall see later, all languages lack some timing features. The cumulative run-time of a task, which must be known to perform deadline driven scheduling, is only available in the preliminary version of Ada and in Real-Time Euclid. For simulation purposes, this information is made available, in terms of machine cycles, in HAL/S. Whereas the capabilities of Ada, PL/1, and LTR for time-constrained scheduling of task executions and operations are very limited, the former two languages as well as Real-Time Euclid allow forcing synchronisation operations to complete within predefined time frames.

Real-Time Euclid is unique in this comparison of languages in that it is schedulability analysable. This means, given a Real-Time Euclid program, it can always be ascertained statically whether it will meet its timing constraints. To allow for schedulability analysis, Real-Time Euclid has no constructs that take arbitrarily long to execute, the number of tasks in the system may not be arbitrarily high, and the timing and activation/deactivation constraints of each task are expressed explicitly.

Only HAL/S provides run-time determination and simulation facilities to aid the verification of real time software. In the other six languages, one has to implement support for run-time determination and simulation explicitly, through generating events under program control.

As far as the state of implementation and availability is concerned, the situation varies for the considered languages. There is a vast number of Ada compilers available, whose target systems include all major microcomputers. Various dialects of FORTRAN and PL/1 with a broad range of different real time capabilities are on the market. Suitable for consideration in a language comparison, however, are only the corresponding proposals for standardisation [102, 20] comprising the experience with former implementations and providing the widest spectra of features. Of the subroutine package constituting Industrial Real-Time FORTRAN, only subsets have so far been experimentally implemented. HAL/S compilers exist for IBM/360 and /370 systems. LTR can be employed on SEMS' line of Mitra computers. PEARL programming systems are commercially distributed for some 50 different target computers, ranging from microcomputer to mainframe systems. These implementations are based on some 10 compilers and corresponding real time operating systems, providing the required features. Single board microcomputer systems, either containing complete PEARL programming environments or only object programs generated from PEARL sources, are shipped in large quantities and used in industrial, scientific, and military applications. Real-Time Euclid has been implemented at the University of Toronto. The implementation, targeted at a distributed microprocessor system, includes a compiler, a schedulability analyser, and a run-time kernel. Real-Time Euclid has been used in a research environment only, and is not commercially available.

2.6.3 A Discussion of Additional Real Time Features Needed

As we have seen in the surveys of existing real time languages, these languages lack many features needed to produce predictable real time software. We have tabulated these desirable features in Table 2.5. The features are organised into three groups. In the first group are language elements facilitating the construction of application software. The basic task control operations, including those of synchronisation and resource access are also in the first group. The second group consists of run-time language system services, needed for predictable and reliable real time software performance. Some of these services may need to be explicitly invoked, through language constructs or library calls, and others may be supported implicitly, in the run-time implementation. Finally, software verification and analysis mechanisms comprise the third group. The last requirement listed, namely the schedulability analysability, is an overall, very important feature.

These features, if made available in a real time language, would greatly facilitate the construction of predictable, reliable real time software. The language constructs and run-time system mechanisms called for are robust and safe. The use of these constructs and mechanisms would make expressing explicit timing constraints in the native application domain both easy and natural. The very paradigm of programming would change from that of the traditional, all-too-general, non-real-time, to one that reflects the way real time applications inherently and naturally are.

The leading idea behind all the proposals mentioned is to facilitate reliable, predictable, and fault tolerant program execution by providing robust and inherently safe language constructs, which generally aim to prevent software malfunctions. All this is a prerequisite for the safety approval of software in hard real time environments. This approach is oriented at the objective of modern quality assurance, viz., not the detection of faults but their systematic prevention is to be achieved.

The languages considered in our surveys lack, to a significant degree or entirely, the features listed in Table 2.5. With the exception of Real-Time Euclid, a language that has not made it out of a laboratory,

Application-oriented synchronisation constructs
Surveillance of the occurrences of events within time windows
Surveillance of the sequences in which events occur
Timeout of synchronisation operations
Timeout of resource claims
Availability of current task and resource states
Inherent prevention of deadlocks
Feasible scheduling algorithms
Early detection and handling of transient overloads
Determination of entire and residual task run-times
Task-oriented look-ahead hierarchical storage management
Accurate real time
Exact timing of operations
Dynamic reconfiguration of distributed systems when a failure occurs
Support of software diversity
Application-oriented simulation of the operating system overhead
Interrupt simulation and recording
Event recording
Tracing
Usage of only static features if necessary
Schedulability analysability

Table 2.5: Desirable Real Time Features.

no language allows one to specify completion deadlines for task executions. Yet, main processors ought to be scheduled using algorithms capable of guaranteeing the observation of the tasks' deadlines. This goal cannot generally be achieved through programmer controlled dynamic priority schemes, as is common among the languages considered. These scheduling algorithms also allow for the early detection of violated timing constraints. Should a violation be detected, some task or tasks should either not be activated or be terminated. In order to carry out this load reduction or premature termination in an orderly and predictable manner, the language should allow one to specify which tasks could be terminated or possibly replaced by substitute tasks with less stringent processing requirements.

To analyse a real time program for predictable, timely performance, one must ascertain the amount of time the program's tasks may take to execute. Accurate determination of task run-times is, however, very difficult, especially when resource contention, hierarchical memory effects and interference are taken into account. Strict resource access rules, task-based storage management, language level explicit timing directives, and other such mechanisms simplify ascertaining task run-times, entire or residual.

Here, the stealing of memory cycles by direct memory access devices becomes a problem. However, in Chapter 4 it will be shown that this problem can be solved, and task scheduling schemes that meet the requirements of a reliable and predictable software behaviour in hard real time environments can be provided.

To provide information about date and time, existing real time systems and languages rely on conventional interval timers and corresponding interrupt handlers. Variations in interrupt service time, stacked interrupts, and other unpredictable system overhead may lead to delays in time updates, or even to missed logical clock ticks. Such delays tend to accumulate, and, unless the logical clocks are periodically compensated, become intolerable. One way of overcoming this problem is to provide highly accurate real time clocks, as hardware components. Ideally, a clock should be dedicated for each future time-critical event. At the very least, the next time-critical event should be associated with a clock.

Once accurate real time clocks are available, language features, explicitly describing timing constraints, should also be provided. When compiled, these features should then be associated with the clocks. For instance, timing requirements may need to be expressed, specifying that events occur within given time frames or in predefined sequences. As we have seen in the survey, Ada, PL/1, and Real-Time Euclid already provide, to different degrees, such language features. Yet, much more work needs to be done in this direction. With respect to Ada, for instance, it is found in [123] that "Ada multitasking seems to assume that a calling task requesting a resource can wait until that resource is available", in other words, indefinitely.

When developing real time software, it is not sufficient to merely ascertain that the software performs its function correctly, in the traditional program correctness sense. It is equally important to ensure that the software behaves in a predictable, *timely* manner. Correctness and timing verification, and analysis of real time software, in the context of multiple tasks, interacting with an external environment, are an integral part of real time software development. One way to enhance this verification and analysis process is through application-oriented simulation. Another possibility is to perform a schedulability analysis, which is a static, worst-case scenario prediction of real time program behaviour.

A third method is through software testing. No matter which approach is taken, in isolation or combined with others, it is important not to oversimplify the problem considered. Too often are time-critical systems built with the implicit assumptions that "the computers are fast enough to take on any workload", or that "this combination of events is so rare, that it will never happen". Another common assumption, inherited from non-real-time languages, is that task state transitions are "instant" [26, 25, 102]. While correctness of a non-real-time program is traditionally established *independently* of task timing constraints, the correctness of a real time program *is* time-dependent.

To verify and analyse a real time program for predictable performance, all issues, with a direct or indirect timing effect, have to be addressed. Thus, timer overhead, interrupts, task queue operations and so forth should all be considered.

All relevant events should be logged in a way that is suitable for subsequent timing error analysis and recovery. Errors, inherent in task and resource scheduling should be prevented or corrected. Thus, the traditional treatment of deadlock, starvation, and similar conditions should be included and extended, to ensure the treatment occurs in a predictable, timely manner.

It is easier to guarantee predictable, timely program behaviour when every task is expressed in terms of static language elements. Otherwise, the language should be used in conjunction with a programming discipline that dictates how each construct should be used, to make guaranteeing predictable, timely behaviour easier or even possible.

2.6.4 Summary

The seven languages compared above support relevant real time requirements to different extents. This is quite natural, for each language considered has been designed under different constraints and conditions. Some languages have been designed by a small number of people and others by large committees. Some languages are products of academic research and others have come about as industrial market-driven efforts. It is not surprising that those languages designed in an environment of fewer constraints, include more in the way of real time features.

It is not the purpose of this summary to rank the languages. Rather, we now ascertain the pragmatics of the real time language scene. Ada and PEARL have been implemented on a wide range of computers including the major 16- and 32-bit microprocessor series, on which most contemporary process control computers are based. Thus, Ada and PEARL are the only high level real time languages readily applicable in industrial control environments. For this reason, we earlier took a closer look at the two languages.

In the past, to enable implementation under existing environments, and to conform to the traditional, non-real-time paradigm of computing, serious design concessions have been made in real time languages. Even when an entirely new language, such as Ada, was being designed, the natural real time paradigm of predictable, timely program behaviour has given way to a more conventional, general concurrent language model.

Yet, there is a genuine, fast growing need for better means of building real time systems. The use of appropriate real time languages, enhanced with schedulability analysers and other relevant tools, would provide real time system builders with such better means.

In this survey Section we have looked at a number of representative languages, used in real time programming. The attempt has been to ascertain if not the state of the art then the state of the technology. It is a sad fact that none of the languages actually used in industry are genuinely real time. Even when a program is written in Ada or PEARL, the two most prevalent of the languages surveyed, it is still impossible to ascertain to what extent, if at all, the program will exhibit predictable, real time behaviour.

Finally, we have speculated on what features need to be introduced into the existing languages and their run-time environments, to advance this inadequate state of affairs. Most of the issues mentioned are still open for research, both fundamental and experimental. We hope that in the near future, and certainly before real time systems become omnipresent, significant advances will be made.

2.7   Taking a Closer Look at Ada

The programming language Ada has emanated from an effort of the U.S. Department of Defense to make available a software production tool suited to program embedded systems. Ada is supposed to save considerable software costs by replacing the vast variety of languages presently in use in DoD projects. The evaluation of the latter gave rise to requirements for a common DoD language. The language and its requirements have been refined several times, resulting in the present definition of Ada.

Military and other real time applications, such as Grumman's X-29 aircraft [94], are well known for their hard time-critical properties. Often, these applications require the observation of tight timing constraints with only small tolerances. Ada is meant to be a language well-suitable for real time applications. Thus, one would expect that Ada would embody features to enable safety, reliability, and predictability of program behaviour in the context of critical timing constraints.

2.7.1 Ada's Limitations

Unfortunately, Ada's design has a number of limitations, that make its acceptance as a real time language difficult. In this Section we list some of these limitations.

Although Ada is intended to support the development of large software systems in a well structured way, some users report that it "does not have the adequate capabilities to express and to enforce good system design" [57]. The reason for this may be that a language must reflect the users' way of thinking, and the Ada users generally are engineers and technicians, and not computer scientists. Ada's features, although elegant from a computer-theoretic point of view, are not easy to understand.

The semantics of Ada imply that processors are dispatched on the basis of priorities and all other resources are scheduled first-in-first-out. Initiation and termination are provided as sole tasking elements. Many feel that these are insufficient. For instance, in [181], the provision of language extensions allowing rapid mode shifting of tasks is demanded.

The only way for expressing time dependencies in Ada is to delay the executions of tasks by specified periods. Absolute time specifications are, however, impossible. Hence, an Ada programmer is forced to hand-tune task timing dependencies: a feat that is made virtually impossible given typical external-event-driven demands. An interrupt may reactivate but a single task. The operations of enabling or disabling interrupts are not contained in the language. Furthermore, the prevention of deadlocks is not supported. Thus, Ada's multitasking model does not fit the model of predictable real time task execution. As one user put it [123],

> The Ada view of multitasking represents a radical departure
> from the traditional "cyclic executive" approach to real time
> operating systems. ... it would be unrealistic to expect an
> abrupt change of this magnitude in engineering practice.

Another design goal of Ada is to support distributable and dynami-

cally reconfigurable applications. Some feel that the language does not
provide sufficient expressive means for this purpose [181, 48], and that
it is hard to formulate distributed software within Ada's framework.

Ada embodies an elegant task synchronisation concept, the *rendezvous*. Rendezvous may be set to be time-bounded. Current experience shows [124], however, that the rendezvous takes too much time to
be carried through. Moreover, the non-deterministic selection of an entry call by select statements, in case several calls are possible, introduces
unpredictability into the program execution.

When comparing the current Ada definition [1] with its preliminary
specification [86, 109], one finds that Ada's feasibility for real time programming has been impaired by abolishing several significant features.
Thus, the **initiate** statement has been deleted. Tasks are immediately
activated when their declarations have been elaborated. Priorities may
be assigned only once, and may never change dynamically. Semaphores
and signals, as predefined synchronisation mechanisms, have been relin-
quished. Finally, the cumulative processing time of tasks is no longer
available.

Although Ada is intended for real time applications, there is nothing
in the language definition that ensures that Ada programs will provide
the performance necessary to accommodate critical real time constraints
of their applications. Consequently, Ada makes insufficient provisions
for schedulability analysis, and the performance issues of particular applications are left to supplemental measurements such as benchmarking
[40].

2.7.2   Changing Ada

The limitations of Ada, summarised in the previous Section, have been
widely recognised. In the panel discussions of the 5th IEEE/USENIX
Workshop on Real-Time Software and Operating Systems, Washington,
D.C., 12 – 13 May 1988, for example, some developers of large, embedded
real time systems even expressed their concern that Ada cannot be called
a real time language. The prevailing opinion is well-summarised by
Burns and Wellings [32]:

Although the Ada programming language was designed to address many of the real time issues within a single-language framework, it is now widely accepted that it has not totally succeeded in achieving its stated design goals. Ada, with an appropriate project support environment, has successfully addressed many of the software engineering issues associated with the production of soft real time software. It has failed, however, to cope adequately with most of the hard (and real) real time problems....

Hence, the Ada Joint Program Office of the U.S. Government initiated an official revision process for Ada [35]. In its first phase, revision requests submitted by the interested public were compiled. Furthermore, there is a number of conference series in progress, such as the Ada-Europe International Conferences [6] or the International Workshops on Real-Time Ada Issues [2, 3], which discuss ways of appropriate remedies. The goal is a substantial revision of Ada, called Ada 9X, to take effect in the late Nineties.

Since the new Ada standard is still far away, there are now efforts to make Ada more suitable for real time applications through its run-time environment, while still adhering to the definition of the language. Baker's [13, 14, 16, 15] and Jeffay's work [17] on Ada is a good example. As a first step, Baker and Jeffay introduced constraints into Ada at the package level. The constraints made Ada task scheduling more deterministic and thus easier to analyse for guaranteed schedulability. Baker intends to explore the ways in which real time Ada software can be reduced systematically to be provably schedulability analysable. Another example of such work is due to Sha and Goodenough [156]. Sha and Goodenough's project aims to cope with the priority inversion problem (due to Ada's native synchronisation) by modifying the Ada run-time scheduler, to both minimise the time a higher priority task is blocked by a lower priority task, and prevent related deadlocks from occurring.

2.8   Taking a Closer Look at PEARL

Although conceived a decade earlier, the language PEARL provides
more expressive power for formulating real time and process control
applications than does Ada. The reason may be that the language has
been defined by electrical, chemical, and control systems engineers, on
the basis of their practical experience in industrial automation problems
and devoting special attention to the timing aspects of the applications.
Sponsored by the Ministry of Research and Technology of the Federal
Republic of Germany, the development of PEARL has begun in the late
Sixties. There are two versions of PEARL: Basic PEARL and the su-
perset Full PEARL. Both versions have been standardised nationally
through DIN.

2.8.1   An Overview of Basic PEARL

PEARL includes all conventional elements of Pascal and Pascal-like languages, and extends the basic data types with the additional data types
clock and **duration**, and their corresponding operations.

To support modular construction of complex software systems,
PEARL programs are composed of separately compilable modules. A
module may contain a system division and a number of problem divisions. A system division encapsulates and isolates hardware and other
environment dependencies. Such a division contains complete information necessary to run the module, relinquishing the need to describe the
environment in a job control language or otherwise outside of PEARL.
User defined identifiers are associated with hardware devices and addresses in the system division. These identifiers and not the actual
devices are referenced in the subsequent problem divisions. Problem
divisions are thus dedicated to expressing the algorithmic logic of the
program, in a way that is environment-independent.

Besides high level file-oriented I/O statements, PEARL also provides
low level constructs to exchange information with process peripherals.
These constructs do not communicate with the peripherals directly, but
rather go through virtual data station or **dations**, associated with the
actual peripherals in the system divisions.

PEARL features a comprehensive, application-oriented range of features supporting task scheduling and control, and the expression of time-constrained behaviour. In particular, there are simple schedules depending on temporal events or interrupt occurrences:

single-event-schedule::=
    at clock-expression | **after** duration-expression |
     when interrupt-name

as well as general, cyclically repetitive ones:

schedule::=
    at clock-expression **all** duration-expression
     until clock-expression |
    after duration-expression **all** duration-expression
     during duration-expression |
    when interrupt-expression **all** duration-expression
     {**until** clock-expression | **during** duration-expression}

Five statements are provided for the control of task state transitions. Their actual execution can be linked to schedules. A task is transferred from the dormant to the ready state by an activation, in the course of which also the task's priority may be changed:

[schedule] **activate** task-name [**priority** positive-integer];

The operation inverse to this is the termination:

terminate task-name;

Running or ready tasks can temporarily be blocked with the help of

suspend task-name;

which is reversed by

[single-event-schedule] **continue** task-name;

Applied to the calling task itself, the last two operations are combined into

single-event-schedule **resume**;

All scheduled future activations of a task are annihilated by the execution of

> **prevent** task-name;

PEARL combines the advantages of general purpose and of special purpose synchronous real time languages [24]. The language avoids such Ada's problems as non-determinism in synchronisation and communication, and lack of means for immediate task abortion.

2.8.2   PEARL's Limitations

Nevertheless, PEARL has a number of shortcomings. One significant limitation is the lack of well-structured synchronisation primitives with temporal supervision. PEARL's exception handling facility is unstructured. The language lacks the means to interrogate task and resource states. It is possible to construct a PEARL program that will take arbitrarily long to execute, in a single task activation. Thus, the language makes insufficient provisions to enable schedulability analysis of its programs.

An effort to enhance the PEARL standard is currently under way. The features to be included in the new language version, presently referred to as PEARL 90, include minor modifications of some non-real-time language elements, addition of process graphics facilities, a provision for deadline-driven task scheduling, support of fault tolerance through a comprehensive, structured exception handling mechanism, and addition of the distributed-system features discussed in the next Section.

2.8.3   An Overview of Distributed PEARL

Distinguishing it from all other available real time languages, in 1989 a third part of PEARL has been standardised in Germany [53], which allows for the programming of distributed applications and for dynamic system reconfiguration. These, "Multiprocessor-PEARL" language extensions include elements for describing the hardware configuration of a multiprocessor system. Among these, the nodes or **stations** and the external peripherals are described, as well as the physical communication network that connects them. The distribution of software units among the nodes is described, as are the logical communication channels, transmission protocols, and failure recovery procedures.

Multiprocessor-PEARL programs are structured by grouping modules in **collections**. The collections are distributed statically or dynamically among system nodes. Since collections may move among nodes, system divisions may not be contained in a collection. Instead, a single system division is provided for each station in a given configuration. In addition, there is a global system division to enable the access to devices attached to other nodes. To allow dynamic reconfiguration in response to system state changes, Multiprocessor-PEARL provides configuration divisions and corresponding executable statements for loading and unloading of collections and for the establishment and the discontinuation of logical communication paths:

```
configuration;
    initial-part
    [reconfiguration-part-string]
confend;

where

initial-part::=
    declarations load-clause-string connect-clause-string

reconfiguration-part::=
    state (Boolean-expression)
    begin
        disconnect-clause-string
        remove-clause-string
        load-clause-string
        connect-clause-string
    end;

load-clause::=
```

load collection-identifier **to** processor-identifier;

remove-clause::=
   remove collection-identifier **from** processor-identifier;

connect-clause::=**connect** port-id → port-id;

disconnect-clause::=**disconnect** port-id → port-id;

The configuration statement contains an initial part and may contain reconfiguration parts. The assignment of collections to the processors present in the system for undisturbed normal operation is specified in the initial part by a sequence of load-clauses. For an error condition represented by a Boolean expression in the state-clause of a reconfiguration part, the latter determines how the software is to be redistributed when the error occurs. This is carried out by specifying which collections are to be removed from certain processors and which ones are to be loaded to other ones with the help of remove- and load-clauses.

Communication among collections is performed through message exchange. The message exchange avoids referencing the communication objects in other collections directly, and decouples the communication structure from the logic of message passing. The exchange is supported through communication endpoints or **ports**. Ports represent interfaces between collections and the outside world. A collection may have an arbitrary number of them. There are input and output ports. In problem divisions of collections, messages are routed through the ports. The logical communication paths among collections in a certain configuration are established by executing language statements to connect ports. One-to-many and many-to-one communication structures may be set up. Logical transmission links may be mapped to physical links in three different ways: by selecting specific physical links, by specifying preferred physical links, or by leaving the selection to the network operating system. A message may be sent using one of three protocols: the asynchronous "no-wait-send", the synchronous "blocking-send", or the synchronous "send-reply". If a synchronous send or receive operation is selected, it may be executed with a timeout clause.

2.9   Proposal for an Extension of PEARL

Real-Time Euclid has been found to satisfy our language requirements, thus facilitating the writing of predictable real time software. Unfortunately, Real-Time Euclid, or any other such experimental language, have little if any chance of becoming a widely used industrial language. Even Real-Time Euclid's predecessors, such as Concurrent Euclid and Turing Plus, while more than just products of academic research exercises, have little chance making it outside of academia and a few industrial research centres. To bring the ideas introduced by Real-Time Euclid to the industrial real time software writer, to facilitate the writing of predictable real time programs where it really counts, we thus need to go beyond Real-Time Euclid.

A widely used industrial language, and well-defined by standardisation, PEARL already satisfies a considerable number of our requirements. Therefore, in this Section, we suggest an extension of PEARL, to satisfy the rest of the requirements.

2.9.1   Locks and Timeouts

On the one hand, PEARL provides but the very basic mechanisms of concurrency control, namely semaphores and bolts. Applying these mechanisms to ensure serialised usage of resources veils the nature of the operation to be performed, since there is no obvious and verifiable relation between the resource and the synchronised tasks. Furthermore, the compiler is unable to detect deadlocks and other concurrency control errors that may occur when requested resources are not released, since there is no syntactic relation between mutually inverse synchronisation operations applied to the same resource. On the other hand, sophisticated concepts like monitors or tasks to be accessed by rendezvous are also error-prone due to their complexity.

The access to shared objects, i.e., to shared variables and **dations**, can be protected with the help of implicit, "invisible" bolts to be generated by the compiler. To instruct the compiler to do so in the case of shared basic objects, arrays, and structures, we introduce the optional attribute

shared

as part of the pertaining declaration syntax. This feature has been adapted from PEARL's dataway synchronisation providing such a control upon opening. Since synchronisers are constituents of shared objects, the prevailing rules need to be observed. So they must be declared on module level. As data types of shared variables, array elements, and structure components, respectively, only basic ones are admitted, because sharing others either leads to difficulties or is meaningless.

To both provide and encapsulate serialised access to protected resources and to enforce the release of synchronisers, we introduce a **lock** statement similar to the structures considered in [20, 58, 59, 60], and with a timeout clause as proposed in [64] in a different context:

> **lock** synchronisation-clause-list [**nonpreemptively**]
>   [timeout-clause] [exectime-clause]
> **perform** statement-string
> **unlock**;
> where
> timeout-clause::=
>   **timeout** {**in** duration-expression | **at** clock-expression}
>   **outtime** statement-string **fin** ,
> exectime-clause::=**exectimebound** duration-expression ,
> synchronisation-clause::=
>   **exclusive**(shared-object-expression-list) |
>   **shared**(shared-object-expression-list)
> shared-object::= shared-variable | dation

The task executing a **lock** statement waits until the listed shared objects can be requested in the specified way. By providing a **timeout** attribute, the waiting time can be limited. If the **lock** cannot be carried through before the time limit is exceeded, the statements of the **outtime** clause will be executed. Otherwise, control passes to the statement sequence of the **perform** clause as soon as the implied request operations become possible. The corresponding releases will be automatically performed upon reaching **unlock**, or when terminating the construction with the help of the

> **quit**;

statement. For reasons of program efficiency, seized resources ought to be freed as early as possible. To this end, the instruction

unlock shared-object-expression-list;

can be applied before actually reaching the end of the surrounding **lock** statement, where the remaining releases will be carried through.

The optional **exectime** clause is introduced to enhance the predictability and safety of real time systems. It limits the time, during which a task is in a critical region. Thus, the clause prevents the critical section from executing arbitrarily long, thus causing an arbitrarily long logical [9] blockage elsewhere in the system. In order to handle a violation of a **lock**'s execution time bound, a signal[10] must be introduced.

The optional attribute **nonpreemptively** serves for the improvement of performance. By specifying it, the operating system is instructed not to pre-empt the execution of the locked critical section due to reasons of the applied processor scheduling strategy. Thus, superfluous and time-consuming context-switching operations can be saved in the case, where a more urgent task requesting one of the locked resources commences execution before termination of the **lock** statement.

For shared objects of type **dation**, their reference in a synchronisation clause of a **lock** statement is equivalent to executing an **open-close** statement pair with a corresponding dataway synchronisation control. Except for their appearance in synchronisation clauses, shared objects may only be referenced within the scope of the corresponding **lock** statements. The objects must be locked for exclusive access if they are used in any assignment context or if they are passed as parameters to procedures with the identical mechanism.

The **lock** synchronisation mechanism solves [73], when used in combination with deadline-driven task scheduling, the uncontrolled priority inversion problem [141] in a very simple and elegant way. Moreover, deadlock prevention schemes can be very effectively implemented using the mechanism, as will be shown below.

The **lock** mechanism replaces PEARL's six unstructured synchro-

---

[9] Physically, other tasks requesting the same resources will timeout.
[10] Signals are PEARL's realisation of the exception concept.

nisation statements. Consequently, semaphores and bolts are removed from the language. The rôle semaphores are playing in the framework of the **activate** statement's optional **using** clause, viz. the formulation of task precedence relations, is taken over by the **parallel** statement introduced below.

2.9.2   Timed Synchronisation

The resource access synchronisation schemes, as provided by multi-tasking programming languages and operating systems — including the just defined **lock** — are rather primitive in comparison with the methods which are applied in everyday life for synchronisation purposes, or to reserve resources. What is lacking is a means to specify the actual time when synchronisation is to take place. This is, for instance, the fundamental difference between an Ada rendezvous and its real life counterpart. We now show how this deficiency can be eliminated easily.

Once allowed by the program logic, tasks specify future points in time when they will need certain resources. The operating system then assigns future time slots to these resource requests, in accordance with resource characteristics. The time-slotted requests are maintained in individual resource queues. The operating system can immediately check whether the period between two subsequent requests is compatible with the capabilities of the resource. If this is not the case, the requests must be rejected. Synchronisation conflicts can arise, when the time slots corresponding to the requests of different tasks overlap. These conflicts are then handled by evaluating the tasks' relative urgencies. One side-effect of the conflict resolution is that the requests of tasks with low urgency may not be granted. Then, the operating system offers to these tasks the next available or other suitable time slots. It is also possible that a task requests a time slot which was earlier assigned to another task, but with lower importance. Then, the time slot is withdrawn from the original owner and assigned to the more urgent task. In the course of this process, the operating system also raises an exception in the task that held the time slot originally. The main function of the corresponding exception handler is to select and reserve another time slot amongst those offered by the operating system. It is possible that none of the alternative slots are appropriate. Once the choice of the new time slot (if any) is made, the exception handler can initiate the re-evaluation of the task's (control) algorithm, taking the new delay into account, or it can take other appropriate action.

To support time-slot-based resource access synchronisation, we define the following set of operating system functions. A cyclic resource access schedule is requested by calling

seize

Cyclic time schedules are represented by three parameters, viz. first instant of a schedule, increment between the instants, and last instant. If only single points in time need to be specified, the same value is provided for the first and the last instant and the increment is set to zero. These three quantities are supplied as parameters to both the procedures **seize** and its inverse, which releases time slots requested earlier:

free

When a resource may not be reserved as requested, due to impossible time constraints or a conflict with an existing reservation, or when the operating system cancels an existing reservation, corresponding exceptions are raised and exception handlers are triggered. To select new, alternative time slots, the exception handlers call the following two functions

free_after
next_slot_available

which both yield values of type **clock**. The first function provides the time from which on the specified resource will be totally unreserved, and the second one gives the i-th available time slot, where i is one of the input parameters.

Time-based synchronisation schemes as specified above are considerably more problem-oriented than the existing ones are. Moreover, proper use of these schemes' potential eliminates indefinite delays. Finally, the schemes also enhance reliability and predictability of program execution, because the operating system is enabled to perform a variety

of checks detecting well in advance the cases in which correct operation
cannot be verified. Tasks are notified as early as possible about possible
synchronisation conflicts, thus enabling the tasks to take appropriate
remedial action and to participate actively in the conflict resolution.
Derived from analogies and experience in everyday life, time-based synchronisation reflects the user's way of thinking, and provides a strong
foundation for real time resource scheduling.

2.9.3   Time-Bounded Loops

The number of times the instructions in a **repeat** statement are performed generally depends on the values of variables and is, therefore, not
known a priori. To enable schedulability analysis for loop statements,
we augment the loop construct with the following clause:

  maxloop fixed-literal **exceeding** statement-string **fin**.

If the number of iterations exceeds the limit set by this clause, the loop
execution is terminated and the statements specified after the keyword
exceeding are carried out in place of the remaining iterations. Having
completed this action, the control is transferred to the statement following the end of the loop. Thus, no loop will execute arbitrarily long, thus
also precluding infinite loops and related system hang-ups.

   The idea of limiting the number of loop repetitions for real time
safety purposes is very similar to that in Real-Time Euclid, and was
first demanded by Ehrenberger [55].

2.9.4   Status Operators

In this section we define functions that provide status information on
tasks and shared objects. The functions yield results of type **fixed**.
Given a certain model of task states together with an appropriate num-
bering of these states, the

  tstate task-identifier

operator returns the number corresponding to the parameter's current
status.

The stati of shared objects can similarly be inquired with the operator

sync shared-object

where **sync** returns the values of 0 or -1 if the shared object is in the unreserved or exclusive access state, respectively, or the current number of tasks having shared reading access to the specified object, otherwise.

2.9.5 Surveillance of Event Occurrences

For the surveillance whether and in which sequence events occur, in this Section we propose a new language feature. In this context we use the term *event* very broadly to include

- interrupts,
- signals,
- time events,
- status transfers of synchronisers and tasks, and
- the occurrence of a specified relation among shared variables.
- the assumption of certain relations of shared variables to given values.

Events may be expressed according to the following syntax rules:

event::=
    when interrupt-expression |
    on signal-expression |
    at clock-expression |
    after duration-expression |
    status-function-call relational-operator expression |
    shared-variable-reference relational-operator expression |
    bit-type-shared-variable-reference

where status-functions are the ones introduced in the previous Section. In the case of the last three of the above alternatives, the events are raised when the corresponding Boolean expressions turn true. Now the new language element is defined by

> **expect** expect-alternative-string **fin**;
> where
> expect-alternative::=**await** event-list **do** statement-string.

When the program flow of a task reaches an **expect** block, the expressions contained in the event specifications are evaluated and the results are stored. The task is suspended until one of the events specified in the **await** clauses occurs. Then the statement string following the associated **do** keyword will be executed. When several events listed in different **await** clauses occur simultaneously, the corresponding **do** clauses will be performed in the order in which they have been specified. When the operations responding to the just occurred event(s) have been executed, the task is once again suspended, until further events occur. To terminate an **expect** block and transfer the control to the statement following the block's **fin**, the

> **quit**;

statement may be included in a **do** clause(s). When this has been done, there will be no further reaction to the events mentioned in the **expect** feature.

Nesting **resume** statements, **on** reactions, or other **expect**s into the alternatives is not necessary, since the corresponding functionality can be formulated employing just one **expect** structure. A single, unnested **expect** block is sufficient to handle any sequence of events. Thus, in accordance with our overall quest for simplicity, we forbid nesting **expect**s, as well as including **resume**s or **on**s in **expect** blocks.

Observe that the scheduled **release** requested in [68, 148] can be expressed using **expect**, since the latter construct allows the formulation of the surveillance of input/output operations' execution and time behaviour. Finally, it should be stated that while **expect** is similar to Ada's **select**, unlike the latter, the former has deterministic semantics, and is thus suitable for predictable real time systems.

2.9.6 Parallel Processing and Precedence Relations of Tasks Sets

Although parallelism can be expressed and realised with the task concept, it is sometimes necessary to request parallel execution of certain activities in a more explicit and specific way. That is the rationale to introduce the following language feature:

> **parallel** activity-string **fin**;
> where
> activity::=**activity** statement-string.

Naturally, **parallel** language elements may be nested and applied in sequence. Then, by including task activation statements in **activity** strings, task executions can be grouped and precedence relations (allowing a statically known, arbitrary number of predecessors and successors) among task sets can be expressed.

2.9.7 Expressing Timing Constraints

Processors ought to be scheduled through procedures that guarantee the observation of strict deadlines associated with software tasks. This goal, however, can generally not be achieved by conventional priority schemes, either operating system or programmer controlled. To support the implementation of appropriate scheduling algorithms, such as earliest-deadline-first (which is feasible and optimal for single processor systems), we introduce language elements that specify due dates and total and residual run-times or their least upper bounds, on a per task basis. Furthermore, such scheduling algorithms allow the early examination whether it is possible to process a task set in time. Otherwise, parts of the workload have to be discharged. In order to carry this through in an orderly and predictable manner, it should be possible to state in the source program, which tasks could be terminated or at least be replaced by ones with shorter run-times, when required by an emergency or an overload situation.

We begin with replacing the **priority** clause by an optional deadline of the form

due after duration-expression

in task declarations and in the **activate, continue,** and **resume** statements. When the condition for a task's (re-) activation is fulfilled, the specified duration is added to the actual time yielding the task's due date. As additional parameter, the deadline-driven scheduling algorithm requires the task's (residual) run-time which is stated in its declaration in the form

runtime {duration-expression | **system**}

In general, the given duration can only be an upper bound for the required processing time. If the latter is not known, the programmer can instruct the compiler to supply one (by running schedulability analysis as described in the next Chapter) by specifying the keyword **system**.

Three additional fields are defined in the task control block T. The fields, both used by the scheduling algorithm and accessible in the program as special variables, are as follows. The due date is stored in

T.due

an object of type **clock**. The other two variables are of the type **duration** and must be continuously updated while the task is being executed:

T.time

is initially set to zero and contains the accumulated execution time, whereas

T.residual

is initialised with the **runtime** parameter, and is decremented to provide the residual time interval needed to complete the task properly.

As we shall see in the next Chapter, to compute a task's run-time exactly is quite hard. Hence, we have to content ourselves with estimations. However, it will often be possible to improve the estimation of a task's residual run-time in the course of its execution, such as for instance, when the control reaches a point where two alternative program sequences of different lengths re-join. To this end, the statement

update task-identifier.**residual**:=duration-expression;

is introduced for setting the residual run-time to a new and lower value.

2.9.8   Overload Detection and Handling

When the due dates and execution times of tasks are available a priori, using the sufficient conditions as specified in Chapter 4, a feasible scheduling algorithm is able to detect whether a task set given at a certain time instance can be guaranteed to meet its specified deadlines.

If the conditions are violated, a (transient) overload results that must be handled. In order to carry overload handling through in an orderly and predictable manner, all interrupts will be masked, all tasks will be terminated, and schedules of further activations of these tasks will be deleted, unless a task declaration contains the optional

keep

attribute. The tasks that specify **keep** will remain, and will be processed, along with the emergency tasks that will handle the overload.

An overload, and the consequent discharge of load, may also result from error recovery. Since error recovery requires extra time, the set of ready tasks may lose its feasible executability. The **keep** attribute provides the appropriate means to cope with such a situation and to implement a fault tolerant software behaviour.

The overload handling scheme presented here is suitable for and is aimed at industrial process control applications. In contrast to this, the method outlined in [27] tries to cope with transient overload situations by sharing the load in a distributed system. Besides its disadvantages that some tasks may still not be completed in time if at all, and that such task completion failures are not handled, the latter method is unrealistic, since load sharing is usually impossible due to hard-wired connections of process peripherals to specific processors.

2.9.9   Hierarchical Deadlock Prevention

The **lock** construct introduced earlier allows for compiler verifiable application of the well-known deadlock prevention scheme that requires all needed shared resources to be reserved en bloc and before entering the critical region where the resources are used. The scheme is easily implemented by specifying the resources in the synchronisation-clause-lists of the corresponding **lock**. To ensure a deadlock free operation, the compiler has only to ascertain that no further resource requests appear within the **perform** clause.

To extend the scheme to support nested **lock**s, a resource hierarchy (ordering) of shared objects is provided, at the module level. The hierarchy is defined through the following new construct

> **resource hierarchy** shared-object hierarchy-clause-string;
> where
> hierarchy-clause::=>shared-object

Nesting of **lock** statements can then be allowed, as long as the sequence in which the resources are claimed complies with the predefined hierarchical ordering.

2.9.10   Support of Task-Oriented Hierarchical Storage Management

We defer a detailed discussion of predictable hierarchical storage administration until Chapter 4. A brief mention of the concept is nevertheless needed here, for the purpose of introducing related extended PEARL constructs. To manage hierarchical storage predictably, we introduce nearly optimal look-ahead algorithms, which transfer entire task bodies instead of arbitrarily derived pages, and which pay close attention to task deadlines. In these algorithms, the ready tasks are ordered in the increasing order of their response times. Thus, storage is managed as application-oriented working sets.

In this scheme, it is possible to include inactive (and not only ready) tasks. A more sophisticated look-ahead algorithm is used, which knows when the inactive tasks are activated, and where they will be inserted in the ready queue.

As will be shown in Chapter 4, the information needed to foresee future task activations is available in process control systems and can be derived by considering buffered task activations and the schedules for task activations and continuations. The calculation of the required parameters is straightforward for time-driven schedules. To enable a similar determination of future task (re-) activations in the case of interrupt driven schedules, the user must supply an average occurrence frequency for each of them. This can be achieved by augmenting the interrupt definition in the system division with a corresponding optional attribute:

> **interval** duration-literal.

This feature is also useful for specifying frames in the sense of Real-Time Euclid, and consequent schedulability analysis through frame superimposition.

A number of existing PEARL constructs can be utilised to provide further directives for the storage management. System data and shared objects with **global** scope should be placed together with parts of the operating system in a non-paged storage area. The same semantics may be assigned to the attributes **resident** and **reent** of tasks and procedures, respectively. The **module** concept in connection with permanent residency may be used to keep non-paged shared variables, procedures, and heavily used small tasks in one page.

2.9.11 Exact Timing of Operations

Although PEARL allows to specify time schedules for tasking operations, one cannot be sure when scheduled activities actually take place. Since this situation is unacceptable in many industrial and scientific applications, we provide the following optional language construct that requests punctual execution of tasking operations. For this purpose the optional

> **exactly**

attribute may be mentioned in time schedules.

2.9.12   Tracing and Event Recording

In industrial applications, run traces and logs are used on a regular basis: to find out whether the software works as intended, for performance measurements and so on. Earlier process control languages, such as FORTRAN [102] and LTR [41], provided comprehensive sets of special directives to instruct the compiler to generate additional code that would write specified traces into special files. We propose the same features for extended PEARL (the exact syntax is not relevant). Furthermore, to avoid frequent changes in the source code, we propose that depending on a compiler option, the features be treated as either compiler directives or non-executed comments.

To understand the temporal behaviour of real time software we propose that events be labelled as to be recorded. The events of relevance are:

- interrupts, signals, and changes of masking states,
- state transfers of tasks and synchronisation variables,
- reaching and actual execution of tasking and synchronisation operations.

These events, or specified subsets thereof, should be recorded on a persistent mass storage device. Such records are not only useful in the test phase but also during routine operation to enable post mortem analysis of software malfunctions.

2.9.13   Restriction to Static Language Features

The use of dynamic language elements may introduce unpredictability in both time and storage requirements. Thus, the use of variable array dimensions, dynamic variables and recursive calls may be optionally suppressed (as in Real-Time Euclid).

2.9.14   Application-Oriented Simulation

Once the constructs (or compiler directives) for tracing and event recording are introduced, the constructs may be used along with the existing

trigger and **induce** (these constructs generate external and internal events) to facilitate application simulation.

A program simulation may now be carried out as follows. A formal description of the requirements or of a benchmark test for the program is used to develop a test routine that will generate, according to worst-case conditions, simulated events. If need be, appropriate test data are provided as inputs. In case these data cannot be read in from the original devices, they could be made available by especially written (simulated) interfaces (in the sense of PEARL). Then, the test program and the software to be verified are processed jointly under control of the same operating system that is used in the production environment. When tracing and event recording are specified, all the results a simulation is expected to yield are automatically provided.

The simulation takes place under very realistic conditions, and should thus fulfill requirements of official safety licensing. In general, the time consumption of a simulation is greater than that of the actual process, due to testing overhead. Hence, it is necessary to stop the system clock whenever test routines are executed. To reduce the amount of time the simulation takes, however, the system time can be set to the next scheduled critical instant, whenever the processor turns idle. These are the only additional functions a simulation monitor could provide. Naturally, also a faster processor of the same kind may be applied instead of the target system.

2.9.15   Graceful System Degradation Using the Concept of Imprecise Results

Imprecise results are defined as intermediate results with the property that the more recent an intermediate result is the closer it approximates the final result (i.e., the idea only works in monotonically improving computations) [39, 119, 118, 122]. By making results of poorer quality available when the results of desirable quality cannot be obtained in time, real time services, possibly of degraded quality, are provided in a timely fashion. This approach makes it possible to guarantee schedulability of tasks while the system load fluctuates.

In order to utilise the imprecise computation approach, real time tasks need to perform their computations monotonically. The precision of intermediate computation results is then non-decreasing with the amount of time spent to obtain the results, and the results available when a task terminates normally are precise. External events such as timeouts and failures may cause a task to terminate prematurely. Intermediate results are saved when tasks terminate prematurely, in hope that the results may still be found sufficiently precise and, hence, acceptable.

Imprecise computation makes scheduling hard real time tasks significantly easier. Specifically, while a task should be guaranteed to meet its critical timing constraints when requesting enough time to compute its results precisely, a monotonic task may also be associated with the minimum execution request that is sufficient to compute the least accurate acceptable results. Then, should external events introduce unbearable load (a transient overload) on the system, the scheduler may choose to terminate a task any time after it has produced an acceptable result.

As already mentioned above, the prerequisite for employing the imprecise computation approach is that real time tasks possess the monotone property. Iterative algorithms, multiphase protocols, and dynamic programming are examples of methods that can be used to implement monotone tasks. Unfortunately, tasks found in process control applications seldom have the monotone property. We now present a modification of the imprecise computation approach, to make the concept feasible for control and automation applications. In order to detect and handle errors on the basis of diversity, the altered concept is also employed to provide graceful degradation of system performance in response to the occurrence of faults.

2.9.15.1   Transient Overloads

Despite the best planning of a system, there is always the possibility of a transient overload of a node resulting from an emergency situation. To handle such a case, many researchers have considered load-sharing schemes which migrate tasks between the nodes of distributed systems. In industrial process control environments, however, such schemes are generally not applicable, because they only work for computing tasks. In contrast to this, control tasks are highly I/O bound, and the permanent wiring of the peripherals to certain nodes makes load-sharing impossible. Therefore, we present a fault tolerant scheme, which handles overloads by degrading the system performance gracefully and predictably.

In addition to the overload handling scheme that uses the **keep** attribute, as described above, we now introduce a more sophisticated method based on the concept of imprecise results. The scheme's basic idea is that the programmer provides alternative executable bodies for each task. Specifically, the **runtime** attribute of a task declaration includes the following (third) possibility

> **runtime selectable**

and the corresponding task defines alternatives of different runtimes for its executable part with

> **task_body** body-alternative-string **fin;**
> where
> body-alternative::=
> > **alternative_with_runtime**
> > {duration-expression | **system**};
> > statement-string

The run-time parameters of each alternative are specified in the same form as that for tasks. The compiler stores the alternatives in decreasing order of their run-times. Thus, when a task with alternative bodies is activated, the task scheduler can select for execution the first task body alternative in the ordered list which allows feasible executability. Since the order generally conforms with decreasing quality and accuracy of the results produced by a task, this scheme represents a realisation of the requirement of graceful degradation of system performance when a transient overload occurs.

To appreciate the usefulness of the our approach to handling transient overloads consider the following example. Periodic sampling of analogue or digital external values is a common, frequent task in many process control applications. In the presence of a transient overload, the current value may be approximated through extrapolation from a few most recent measurements, instead of actually being measured. Since

no sensor driver code needs to be executed, the task's execution time
is reduced to a very small fraction. Nevertheless, acceptable results are
delivered and, thus, the effect of the overload is reduced.

2.9.15.2   Diversity Based Error Detection and Handling

Software diversity can be used to detect and to cope with programming
errors. In general, however, this approach is rather costly, because several different versions of a program module need to be executed either
in parallel or sequentially. Here, savings can be achieved by once again
employing the concept of imprecise results. Instead of having different
modules, which yield the same results, only one module is provided that
determines the results precisely, whereas the other modules provide imprecise (though still acceptable) results. The former module is typically
relatively complex and more time-consuming, compared to the latter
ones. We implement the concept with the following language construct:

> **diverse**
> diverse-alternative-string
> **assure** statement-string
> **fin**;
> where
> diverse-alternative::=**alternative** statement-string.

Each alternative constitutes a diverse software module. When all occurring alternatives are executed, the comparison of their results is carried
through in the **assure**-clause. Its function is to verify the precise results. If, however, an error is detected, imprecise results can be assigned
to the result variables, which will be used in the continuation part of the
program. The rationale behind this approach compounds the common
belief that diversity leads to at least some module(s) producing correct
results by also assuming that imprecise modules are more reliable since
these modules are less complex than the precise one.

Naturally, the above described semantics could also be implemented
with selector (if-then-else) statements. Unlike the selector, however, the
diverse construct may be parallelised, distributing individual alternatives among different processes.

In the example of the last section, the extrapolation routine could be run as a parallel alternative. Each extrapolated value could be used to verify the corresponding sampled external value. If the measured and the extrapolated values differ only within an acceptable predetermined margin, the **assure**-clause should return the sampled value as the result. Otherwise, the extrapolated value should be used, and an error in the external data source or its control software should be sought.

In the form described above, the concept of imprecise results can be employed to provide software diversity at relatively low cost combined with graceful degradation in the presense of errors.

2.9.16   Synopsis of PEARL Language Extensions

In what follows, we present a complete syntax list of the new PEARL extensions that have been presented throughout the previous Sections. The syntax description uses the symbols | and [ ] to denote alternatives and optional parts, respectively. To enhance readability the following two suffixes are employed:

- "-list" stands for one or more elements of appropriate type separated by commas and
- "-string" stands for the repetition of one or more elements of appropriate type.

Those non-terminal symbols that are not defined explicitly, are known from either the original PEARL syntax or from a previous informal description. Wherever the non-terminal *expression* is used, it is implicitly assumed to be of correct type.

> Status operators:
> **sync** shared-object
> **tstate** task-identifier
>
> basic-type-declare-clause [**shared**]
> array-declare-clause [**shared**]
> structure-declare-clause [**shared**]

```
task-declaration::=
task-identifier: task
[due after duration-expression runtime
{duration-expression | system | runtime selectable}]
[global] [resident] [keep];
[definitions]
{[statement-string] |
[task_body body-alternative-string fin]}
end;


body-alternative::=
    alternative_with_runtime
        {duration-expression | system};
    statement-string


repeat-statement::=
[for identifier]
[from expression]
[by expression]
[to expression]
[while expression]
repeat maxloop fixed-literal
        excceding statement-string fin [;]
[declaration-string]
[statement-string]
end;


quit-statement::=quit;


schedule::=
at expression [interval [duration]] [exactly] |
[when expression] [after expression]
[all expression [duration]] [exactly]
interval::=every expression | all expression
duration::=until expression | during expression


due-clause::=due after duration-expression
```

runtime-clause::=**runtime** {duration-expression | **system**}

Temporal task control block parameters:
T.due
T.time
T.residual

expect-statement::=**expect** expect-alternative-string **fin;**
expect-alternative::=**await** event-list **do** statement-string
event::=
    when interrupt-expression |
    on signal-expression |
    at clock-expression |
    after duration-expression |
    status-function-call relational-operator expression |
    shared-variable-reference relational-operator expression |
    bit-type-shared-variable-reference

activate-statement::=
[schedule-list] **activate** task-identifier [due-clause];

continue-statement::=
[single-event-schedule] **continue** [task-identifier]
[due-clause];

resume-statement::=
single-event-schedule **resume** [due-clause];

update-statement::=
update task-identifier.**residual**:=duration-expression;

lock-statement::=
lock synchronisation-clause-list [**nonpreemptively**]
    [timeout-clause] [exectime-clause]
perform statement-string
unlock;

timeout-clause::=
    timeout {**in** duration-expression | **at** clock-expression}
    outtime statement-string **fin**

exectime-clause::=**exectimebound** duration-expression

synchronisation-clause::=
    exclusive(shared-object-expression-list) |
    shared(shared-object-expression-list)

shared-object::= shared-variable | dation

parallel-statement::=**parallel** activity-string **fin**;

activity::=**activity** statement-string

diverse-statement::=
diverse diverse-alternative-string
assure statement-string
fin;

diverse-alternative::=**alternative** statement-string

unlock-statement::=**unlock** shared-object-expression-list;

resource-hierarchy-definition::=
resource hierarchy shared-object hierarchy-clause-string;

hierarchy-clause::= >shared-object

frequency-attribute::=**interval** duration-literal

Functions for time-slot-based resource synchronisation:
seize
free
free_after

next_slot_available

2.9.17 Summary

In the past, concessions have been made when designing real time languages, to enable their implementation under conventional, pre-existing operating systems. This approach is inappropriate, because operating systems ought to support language features in an inconspicuous manner, and to bridge the gap between language requirements and hardware capabilities. Hence, the development of a process control system should commence with the definition of a suitable language incorporating a host of features enhancing software reliability. Then the hardware architecture is to be designed, enabling the implementation of the language as easily and efficiently as possible, and thus keeping the operating system and its overhead relatively small. In cases where the aforementioned implementation and operating efficiencies of a real time system are in conflict with the efficiency and the safety of the process to be controlled, the latter criteria should take priority. In this Section, some shortcomings of presently available real time languages with regard to process control applications have been presented. New real time features have been proposed that overcome these shortcomings and make it possible to express all process control requirements in a high level language. The proposal has focussed on providing only such language constructs that are inherently safe and that facilitate the development of fault tolerant and robust software with predictable behaviour.

Chapter 3

Language-Independent Schedulability Analysis of Real Time Programs

Schedulability analysis is an integral part of the development process of predictable real time software. Real time software thus needs to be expressed in a schedulability analysable language, such as Real-Time Euclid or extended PEARL, and the software must be supported by an operating system and hardware environment that are also schedulability analysable. In this Chapter, we present language-independent schedulability analysis of real time programs, and then show how it applies to both Real-Time Euclid and extended PEARL.

A real time program is analysed for schedulability in two stages. The schedulability analyser program consequently consists of two parts: a partially language-dependent front end and a language-independent back end. The front end is incorporated into the code emitter, and its task is to extract, on the basis of program structure and the code being generated (thus, the front end may be as language-dependent as the code emitter), timing information and calling information from each compilation unit, and to build language-independent program trees. By "compilation unit", we mean anything that is separately compilable; i.e., a subprogram, a process or a module. The front end of the analyser does not estimate interprocess contention. However, it does compute the amount of time individual statements and subprogram and process bodies take to execute in the absence of calls and contention. These times, serving as lower bounds on response times, are reported back to the programmer.

The back end of the schedulability analyser is actually a separate, language-independent program. Its task is to correlate all information gathered and recorded in program trees by the front end, and to predict guaranteed response times for the entire real time application. To achieve this task, this part of the analyser maps the program trees onto an instance of a real time model, and then computes the response time guarantees.

The particular real time model we use satisfies the assumptions of Section 1.4 and consists of a commonly found distributed configuration where each node has a processor, local memory and devices. Processors communicate via messages or a mailbox memory. The response time guarantees are represented as a set of constrained sums of time delays. The delays in each sum are worst-case bounds of various types of execution times and contention delays. Each sum represents a guaranteed response time of a process.

The statistics generated by the schedulability analyser tell the programmer whether or not the timing constraints expressed in the real time program are guaranteed to be met. If so, the programmer is finished with the timing constraint verification process. Otherwise, the statistics help the programmer to determine how to alter the program to ensure that the timing constraints are guaranteed.

3.1   Front End of the Schedulability Analyser

Despite the major programming effort required to implement it, the front end of the schedulability analyser is a relatively straightforward tool to understand. Hence, we only present a high level description of this part of the schedulability analyser.

3.1.1 Front End Segment Trees

As statements are translated into assembly instructions in the code emitter, the front end of the schedulability analyser builds a tree of basic blocks, which we call *segments*, for each subprogram or process.

The various types of segments are as follows.

1. A simple segment corresponds to a section of straight-line code. The segment contains the amount of time it takes to execute the section. As each assembly instruction is generated in the straight-line section, the front end of the schedulability analyser adds its execution time to the segment time. Instruction execution time is computed, in a table-driven fashion, as a function of the opcode(s), the operands and addressing modes, following the procedure described in the appropriate hardware manual such as [134]. The front end of the schedulability analyser does not know the processor rates of the target implementation. All times are thus recorded in clock cycles instead of in absolute time.

2. An internal-call segment corresponds to an internal subprogram call. The segment contains the name of the subprogram. Each such segment is eventually resolved by substituting the amount of time it takes for the called subprogram to execute.

3. An external-call segment is similar to an internal-call segment, except that the former corresponds to an external subprogram call.

4. A kernel-call segment is similar to an internal-call segment, except that the former corresponds to a kernel subprogram call. If the call attempts to open or close a bracket, the name of the bracket (which may correspond to a semaphore name, a critical section label, a monitor number, a condition variable name and so on), and a pointer to the bracket record are recorded in the segment record. Furthermore, if the call is an open-bracket, then its **noLongerThan** time is recorded.

5. A communications segment is similar to a kernel-call segment, except that the former corresponds to a call that triggers interprocessor communications.

```
x := 5
if x > 7 then
    < statements >
end if
```

Figure 3.1: An if-statement with a vacuous condition.

6. A selector-segment corresponds to a selector (an if- or a case-) statement. The segment consists of n subtrees, where n is the number of clauses in the selector, and each subtree corresponds to a clause. A selector-segment is eventually resolved[1], and only the subtree which takes the longest to execute is retained.

An iterator (a loop) does not by itself generate any new segments. If the body of the iterator is straight-line code, then the iterator just contributes to a simple segment an amount of time equal to the product of a single iteration time and the maximum number of iterations. If the body of the iterator contains a call-, or a selector-segment, then the iterator is unwound into a segment chain. In other words, the body of the iterator is repeated the number of iterations times.

Logic analysis can certainly improve upon the schedulability analyser performance. For example, such analysis can be used to detect and reduce if-statements with vacuous conditions, such as the one on Figure 3.1. However, logic analysis falls outside the scope of the work discussed here, and remains open for future work. Thus, the schedulability analyser does not do any analysis of the program logic.

The reader familiar with execution graph software analysis will notice that the front end of the schedulability analyser builds segment trees similar to execution graphs. However, while execution graph program analysis typically computes *expected*, or *averaged* response times [160], our analysis is *worst-case*. To demonstrate how segment trees are built, let us consider the example of Figures 3.2, 3.3 and 3.4.

The high level statements H_1 and H_2 translate into assembly sections

---

[1]By "resolution" we mean the purging of subtrees until the segment (sub)tree becomes a segment list.

$$
\begin{aligned}
&H_1 \qquad x := y + z \\
&H_2 \qquad y := 2 * y \\
&H_3 \qquad B\ (x,y) \\
&H_4 \qquad \textbf{if } y > x \textbf{ then} \\
&H_5 \qquad\qquad z := z + 5 \\
&H_6 \qquad \textbf{else} \\
&H_7 \qquad\qquad \textbf{signal } (c) \\
&H_8 \qquad \textbf{end if} \\
&H_9 \qquad z := x * y
\end{aligned}
$$

Figure 3.2: A block of high level Real-Time Euclid statements.

$$
\begin{aligned}
&A_{01} \qquad <\textit{Add y and z and assign to x}> \\
&A_{02} \qquad <\textit{Shift y left one bit}> \\
&A_{03} \qquad <\textit{Push x,y on stack; Jump to B}> \\
&A_{04} \qquad <\textit{Restore stack}> \\
&A_{05} \qquad <\textit{Compare y and x}> \\
&A_{06} \qquad <\textit{If greater, jump to } A_{09}> \\
&A_{07} \qquad <\textit{Add 5 to z}> \\
&A_{08} \qquad <\textit{Jump to } A_{11}> \\
&A_{09} \qquad <\textit{Push c on stack; Jump to Kernel.Signal}> \\
&A_{10} \qquad <\textit{Restore stack}> \\
&A_{11} \qquad <\textit{Multiply x and y and assign to z}>
\end{aligned}
$$

Figure 3.3: The corresponding block of assembly statements.

A_{01} and A_{02}, respectively. H_3, a call to a procedure B, generates sections A_{03} and A_{04}. The procedure execution will take place right after A_{03}, a section comprising a push on stack of the variables x and y and a jump to B, and before A_{04}, a stack restore section. The if-test of H_4 results in a compare A_{05} and a conditional jump A_{06}. The assignment H_5 maps to A_{07}. The else H_6 becomes the unconditional jump A_{08}. The signal H_7 generates A_{09}, an assembly section encompassing a push on stack of the condition variable c and a jump to $Kernel.Signal$, the kernel routine supporting the signal primitive, and A_{10}, a stack restore section. The last assignment statement, H_9, generates section A_{11}.

The segment tree corresponding to the high level code block is formed as follows. A_{01}, A_{02} and A_{03} form a contiguous section of straight-line code. Thus, they comprise a single simple segment S_1. The amount of time A_{01}, A_{02} and A_{03} take to execute is recorded in the segment. The call to B forms S_2, an internal-call segment[2]. A_{04} and A_{05} form a simple segment S_3. Now we must form two branches. If the conditional jump A_{06} fails, then the sections A_{07}, A_{08} and A_{11} will be executed. The amount of time it takes to execute A_{06} if the test fails is thus combined with the times of A_{07}, A_{08} and A_{11} to form a simple segment S_4. If the test succeeds, then the sections A_{09}, A_{10} and A_{11} will be executed. The right branch is therefore formed as a list of three segments: a simple segment S_5 encompassing A_{06} (if it succeeds) and A_{09}, a kernel-call segment S_6 corresponding to the signal, and S_7, a simple segment comprising A_{10} and A_{11}. We have omitted a description of how the signal call maps to bracket open and close calls, and how the condition variable name and other supplementary information is stored. We shall address language-specific operations when we discuss how our language-independent schedulability analysis is done on Real-Time Euclid and extended PEARL programs, later in this Chapter.

---

[2]or an external-call segment. It does not really matter for the purpose of the example.

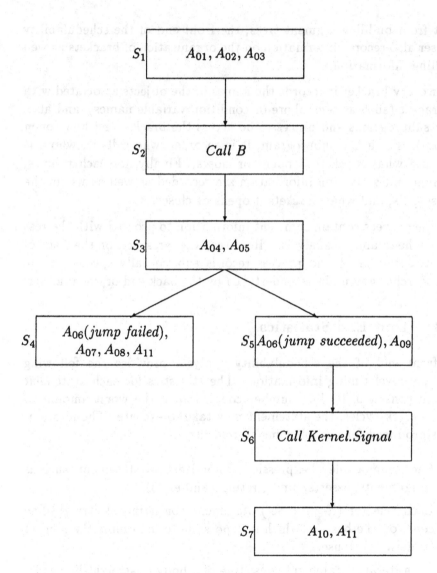

Figure 3.4: The corresponding tree of segments.

3.1.2 Condition, Bracket, Subprogram and Process Records

Apart from building segment trees, the front end of the schedulability analyser also records information on the organisation of brackets as well as calling information.

For every bracket it records the names of the objects associated with the bracket (such as semaphore or condition variable names), and also, which subprograms and processes do access the bracket and how (open or close). For every subprogram, it is recorded who calls it, whom it calls, and what brackets it opens or closes. Finally, for each process, its frame and activation information are recorded as well as whom the process calls, and what brackets it opens or closes.

Segment trees contain sufficient information to proceed with the rest of the schedulability analysis. However, the presence of the lists of bracket, subprogram and process records substantially speeds up the many searches and updates undertaken by the back end of the analyser.

3.1.3 Front End Statistics

The front end of the schedulability analyser provides the following statement-level timing information. The statistics for each statement involved consist of its line number coupled with the worst amount of time, in clock cycles, the statement may take to execute. The information is produced for the following statements.

1. Each language-level expression or non-iterative statement (such as assignments, asserts, binds, returns and exits).

2. Each selector (if- or case-) statement consisting of straight-line code, on the basis of which it is possible to determine the longest (time-wise) clause.

3. Each iterator-statement consisting of a body of straight-line code.

The programmer can use this statement-level information to determine which statements and groups of statements run longer than he expects. The information can also be used at a later stage, when the rest of the schedulability information, such as guaranteed response times, becomes available. Then the programmer can decide which process parts have to be re-written to increase their speed.

3.2   Back End of the Schedulability Analyser

The back end of the schedulability analyser derives the parameters of the schedulability analysable real time model, presented shortly, from the front end segment trees, and solves the resulting model.

3.2.1   Resolving Segment Trees

The back end of the schedulability analyser starts off by resolving segment trees built by the front end. All segment trees and bracket, subprogram and process records are concatenated into one file, including the segment trees and records pertinent to predefined kernel and I/O subprograms. All non-kernel calls are recursively resolved by substituting the corresponding subprogram segment trees in place of each call-segment. As many selector-segments as possible are resolved. A selector-segment cannot be resolved when two or more of its subtrees result in a delay segment (see the next Section).

3.2.2   Converting Process Trees

After all non-kernel calls are resolved, only process[3] segment trees are left. These trees are converted to different segment trees, where each possible segment is one of the following.

1. An interruptible segment corresponds to an interruptible section of code, that is a section of code executed with interrupts enabled. The segment contains the amount of time it takes to execute the section.

2. A non-interruptible segment corresponds to a non-interruptible section of code, which we assume is found only in the language

---

[3] As opposed to both process and subprogram segment trees.

run-time kernel. The segment contains the amount of time it takes
to execute the section.

3. A specified-delay segment corresponds to a delay specified in a
   wait or a device-accessing statement in the program.

4. A queue-delay segment corresponds to a delay while waiting to
   open a bracket.

5. A communication-delay segment corresponds to a delay while waiting for inter-processor communication to take place.

6. A selector-segment corresponds to an unresolved selector-segment
   generated by the front end part of the schedulability analyser.
   A selector-segment is considered to be unresolved when it has at
   least two clause subtrees such that it is impossible to determine
   (until the analysis described in the next Section takes place) which
   subtree will take longer to execute.

We now demonstrate how front end segment trees are converted using
the example of Figures 3.2, 3.3 and 3.4 of Section 3.1.1. Figure 3.5
has the corresponding converted subtree, now a part of a process tree.
The simple segment S_1 maps to an interruptible segment N_1. The call
to B is resolved and N_2, the tree of B, is substituted. We now form
two branches. Since one branch of the subtree involves a kernel call,
both branches are kept. The segment S_3 is combined with the first
interruptible segment of each branch. Thus, S_3 and S_4 together form N_3,
an interruptible segment corresponding to the failed jump case, and S_3
also becomes a part of the first interruptible segment of the right branch.
The way $Kernel.Signal$ operates is as follows: interrupts are turned
off, queues are updated, and interrupts are restored. The interruptible
segment N_4 thus comprises S_3, S_5 and the interrupt disabling code of
the signal. The queue-updating code of $Kernel.Signal$ forms a non-
interruptible segment N_5. The return from $Kernel.Signal$ is combined
with S_7 to form an interruptible segment N_6. Each leaf of the tree of B
is extended with the two branches we just formed.

Once the segment tree conversion is complete, the parameters of the
model we are about to describe are ready to be derived.

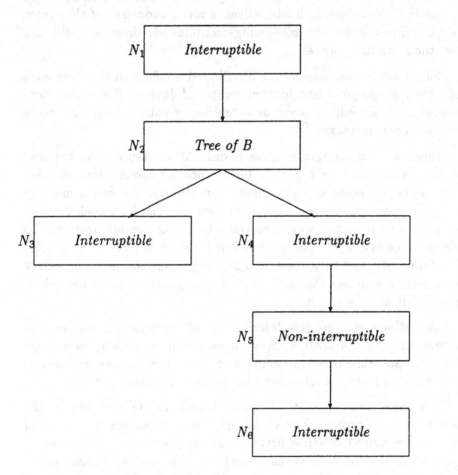

Figure 3.5: The corresponding converted subtree of segments.

3.2.3   A Real Time Model

For the purposes of this book, let us refer to CPUs as *CPUs*, and to other hardware devices or units as well as software resources (such as a monitor) as *resources*. Let us also say that a scheduling discipline **A** is *feasible* if the following holds. Given a set of processes, if they meet their deadlines under any scheduling discipline **B**, then they will also meet their deadlines under **A**.

The model we use assumes a distributed configuration where each node has a single processor, local memory and devices. Processors communicate via a medium, such as a mailbox memory, which supports inter-processor messages.

Processes do not migrate across nodes. All intra-processor communication takes place via brackets. Inter-processor communication takes place in the following way (the mailbox protocol). To send a message to a process on another processor, a process deposits it, asynchronously and in a time-bounded way, into the medium of communication. To receive a message, a process retrieves one (or none, if none are available) asynchronously and in a time-bounded way from the medium. Only one process can access the medium of communications at a time. Thus, queueing delays are possible.

The mailbox protocol just described is not the only possible protocol for real time communication. Any protocol will do, as long as no part of it takes an arbitrarily long amount of time. The mailbox protocol is used in the prototype evaluation system described later.

Each node has a copy of the language kernel. Each (hardware or software) resource is protected by a bracket[4]. Ready processes are scheduled pre-emptive earliest-deadline-first (i.e., at any point in time, the process with the earliest deadline is scheduled), while bracket and communication queueing is first-come-first-served . Various code sections, corresponding to regular, bracket, kernel and other executable statements,

---

[4]Traditionally, *hardware* resource queueing has been measured, but with the increased complexity of system software, software resource queueing has become important. In real time languages, our schedulability analysis is aimed at, all software and hardware resource access is protected by (and serialised through) native inter-process synchronisation primitives.

may be scheduled pre-emptively or non-pre-emptively. One viable way of supporting, in hardware and software, real time execution of these sections is presented in Chapters 4 and 5.

The choice of the scheduling disciplines is summarised in the following argument. No process scheduling is feasible in the presence of shared resources [129]. Earliest-deadline-first ready process scheduling performs, in the sense of meeting deadlines, as well as other disciplines do [161, 166]. Earliest-deadline-first is the simplest deadline-driven scheduling discipline to implement. First-come-first-served is the simplest bracket and communication queue scheduling discipline to implement. Both earliest-deadline-first and first-come-first-served disallow indefinite queue waiting. Thus, they are good choices for our model.

3.2.3.1   A High Level Model Description

For each process, we compute the longest amount of time it may take to execute. This time, referred to as the *guaranteed response time*, is computed as a sum of components. Each component corresponds to either the longest duration a particular class of process requests takes to execute, or to the longest duration the process is delayed due to a particular class of delays. If the process's frame is specified, then its guaranteed response time must not exceed the frame, and the process will not be activated more often than once per frame.

It is conceivable that the frequency of the occurrence of the physical tasks may fluctuate slightly with time. Moreover, fault tolerance considerations may demand that the software be prepared to control some of the physical tasks more often than their normal physical characteristics dictate. Finally, the physical task occurrence frequencies may simply be unavailable early in the software development phase. Thus, it is useful to know what the minimum guaranteed achievable frame is for each process. To derive these frames, an initial set of frames is guessed, and the model is solved iteratively, substituting tighter and tighter frames until a guaranteed response time exceeds its corresponding current frame.

The following system of equations describes the high level of our model, for each of the processors. The composition of each equation is somewhat similar to that in [113] and [166]. However, the terms QD_i,

CD_i, and SD_i are new, and, as we are about to show, a radically different approach is used to derive these terms, and to solve the equations.

$$GT_i = I_i + N_i + QD_i + ID_i + ND_i + CD_i + SD_i \leq F_i \qquad (3.1)$$

for $i \in \{1, \ldots, \#P\}$, where
$\#P$ is the number of processes on this processor,
I_i is the total CPU requirement for executing interruptible sections of process P_i,
N_i is the total CPU requirement for executing non-interruptible sections of P_i,
QD_i is the worst-case amount of time P_i spends in bracket queues,
ID_i is the worst-case amount of time P_i spends waiting due to other processes executing their interruptible parts,
ND_i is the worst-case amount of time P_i spends waiting due to other processes executing their non-interruptible parts,
CD_i is the worst-case amount of time P_i spends waiting due to inter-processor communication delays,
SD_i is the worst-case amount of time P_i spends delayed in wait and device-accessing statements,
GT_i is the guaranteed response time of P_i,
F_i is the specified frame of P_i.

I_i and N_i are easily derived by adding up interruptible and non-interruptible segments of the process P_i, respectively. To derive good upper bounds on QD_i, ID_i, ND_i, SD_i and CD_i, more work than simply adding up various process segment times is necessary. We now survey the state-of-the-art in real time modeling, in an attempt to find an existing method suitable in our case. The reader may wish to skip the survey and go to Section 3.2.3.3.

3.2.3.2   A Survey of Real Time Modeling

Given a real time computer program, it is very important to verify that it meets its critical timing constraints. *Process level real time program modeling* (or *real time modeling* for short) aids greatly in this verification. In this Section we introduce real time models, explain how they are constructed and analysed, and survey some of the significant results in the area.

A general real time model consists of a set of processes, CPUs, non-CPU resources, communication links, and clocks. Each process is associated with a *CPU requirement* and *non-CPU resource requirements*, which are constants expressed in some time units. These requirements may be broken into segments ordered in a sequence. Processes can communicate with each other. *Communication restrictions* may be specified for each process individually, as well as for an entire set of processes.

Each process is assigned a *maximum response time*, expressed in the same time units as the CPU and resource requirements. Once a process becomes active, it must complete before its maximum response time expires. Thus, once a process becomes active, it will have a completion *deadline*, computed to be the sum of the current time and the maximum response time. Each process is also associated with another time constant called a *frame*, sometimes also referred to as a *minimal period*, and always equal to or longer than the maximum response time. No process can be activated more often than once every frame.

A *real time kernel* schedules processes and allocates resources. The kernel is itself using the CPUs and resources, and thus introduces *overhead* which is sometimes included in the model[5]. The choice of the CPU dispatching policy is usually specified in the model. The policy used is typically either a pre-emptive or non-pre-emptive version of:

1. *earliest-deadline-first*, i.e., the earlier the process's deadline, the higher the process's priority;

2. *least-laxity-first*, i.e., the smaller the laxity of the process, the higher the process's priority; where *laxity* is computed to be the time remaining before the deadline less the remaining CPU and resource requirements;

3. *fixed-priority*

4. fixed-priority, i.e., each process is assigned a fixed priority.

The earliest-deadline-first and least-laxity-first scheduling disciplines are dynamic, and take into account up-to-date process information. This contrasts with the fixed-priority scheduling discipline, which only looks

---

[5]In the architecture defined in Chapter 5 this is not the case, since that architecture provides a separate CPU for the kernel.

at predefined process priorities, and ignores any important up-to-date information that may be available. Thus, the two dynamic disciplines are usually preferred over the static fixed-priority one.

In many real time systems, it is important to be able to pre-empt a lower priority process in favour of a higher priority one. For instance, when a consistency check on some data or results fails, it is often important to transfer control to error recovery processes right away. Thus, pre-emptive scheduling disciplines are usually preferred over non-pre-emptive ones.

Non-CPU resource allocation policies are also often specified for each (set of) non-CPU resource(s). These resources are typically allocated according to one of the above three disciplines or on a first-come-first-served basis.

Given a real time model, it is possible to compute an upper bound on the amount of time each process will take to execute. These time bounds are referred to as the *guaranteed response times*. They are compared with the maximum response times requested by the user, to check whether each process can be guaranteed to always execute within its maximum response time. This process of computing guaranteed response times and verifying maximum response times is called *worst-case schedulability analysis*, or *schedulability analysis* for short.

Traditional forms of performance modeling, such as queueing network analytic models and simulation, might offer some help in real time program performance analysis, but they cannot be sufficient. The problem with them is that they only provide an analyst with statistical performance indicators. Real time programs, however, do not have the luxury of having to meet only *most* of the deadlines *most* of the time, but must meet *every* deadline *every* time. Thus, schedulability analysis must be used to analyse real time programs.

Since the early Seventies, there have been a number of important research results in real time modeling. We now survey some of the prominent ones.

Ullman 1973

Ullman [180] proves that finding a feasible non-pre-emptive schedule for the following two problem classes is NP-complete:

1. - at least two CPUs

    - no resources

    - constant maximum response times

    - infinite frames (i.e., processes execute at most once)

    - constant CPU requirements

    - no interprocess communication (IPC)

    - no overhead

2. - at least two CPUs

    - no resources

    - constant maximum response times

    - infinite frames

    - CPU requirements of 1 or 2 time units only

    - arbitrary IPC

    - no overhead

Garey and Johnson 1975

Garey and Johnson [67] establish the NP-completeness of finding a feasible non-pre-emptive schedule of another two problem classes:

1. - at least two CPUs

    - at least one resource

    - constant maximum response times

    - infinite frames

    - CPU requirements of 1 time unit only

    - IPC results in a forest of process precedence constraints;

    - no overhead

2. - at least three CPUs

    - at least one resource

    - constant maximum response times

    - infinite frames

- CPU requirements of 1 time unit only
- no IPC
- no overhead

Though Ullman, and Garey and Johnson only consider non-repetitive (i.e., single-shot) processes in their analyses, they need not go any further. This is because non-repetitive processes are a special case of periodic and other repetitive processes. Hence, if feasible non-pre-emptive scheduling in a model with non-repetitive processes is NP-complete, then so is feasible non-pre-emptive scheduling in the same model with repetitive processes.

Thus, no feasible non-pre-emptive scheduling of real time processes in large systems is suitable from the computational efficiency point of view.

Liu and Layland 1973

Liu and Layland [121] analyse the following model:

- a single CPU
- no resources
- constant maximum response times
- frames equal to their corresponding maximum response times
- constant CPU requirements
- no IPC
- no overhead

The authors establish the following results:

- Rate-monotonic priority assignment (i.e., the shorter the process's frame, the higher its priority) is optimal for all pre-emptive fixed-priority scheduling disciplines.
- The necessary and sufficient conditions for meeting every deadline under the pre-emptive rate-monotonic scheduling discipline are established.
- The least upper bound on CPU utilisation under a pre-emptive fixed-priority discipline is about 70% for a feasible schedule.

- The necessary and sufficient conditions for meeting every deadline under the pre-emptive earliest-deadline-first discipline are established.

- Under the earliest-deadline-first scheduling discipline the CPU is never idle until a deadline is missed.

- The least upper bound on CPU utilisation under a pre-emptive earliest-deadline-first discipline is 100% for a feasible schedule.

- The necessary and sufficient conditions for meeting every deadline under a pre-emptive mixed discipline are established[6].

While the above results provide a good foundation for further work, the model that Liu and Layland consider is too simple for most practical real time systems. Most notably, IPC and overhead must be included in the model to make it more realistic.

Teixeira 1978

Teixeira [173] makes two successive extensions to the Liu and Layland model:

1. maximum response times do not have to be equal to their corresponding frames

2. there is IPC

The following are Teixeira's results:

- The sufficient conditions for meeting every deadline under a pre-emptive fixed-priority scheduling discipline *after priorities have been assigned* are established.

- A priority assigning algorithm is derived for pre-emptive fixed-priority scheduling in the context of both extended models.

- The above two results are also established for *non-pre-emptive* fixed-priority scheduling, though in the context of the first extended model only.

---

[6]A mixed scheduling discipline schedules some processes according to their deadlines, and assigns fixed priorities to the rest.

The Teixeira real time model is certainly more realistic than the Liu and Layland model, but it still lacks realism. Most notably, resources and overhead must also be considered.

Sorenson and Hamacher 1974 – 1975

Like Teixeira, Sorenson [161] and Sorenson and Hamacher [162] also start with the Liu and Layland model and successively extend it twice:

1. there are resources, though there is no resource contention

2. maximum response times can be shorter than or equal to their corresponding frames

Sorenson and Hamacher establish the following results:

- The pre-emptive earliest-deadline-first scheduling policy is feasible in the context of the basic model.

- The pre-emptive least-laxity-first scheduling policy is feasible in the context of the first extended model.

- No non-pre-emptive scheduling discipline is feasible in the context of any one of the three models.

- Sufficient conditions for meeting every deadline under the pre-emptive earliest-deadline-first policy are established in the context of all models.

The Sorenson and Hamacher results still lack realism somewhat. The absence of IPC is actually explained by the authors to be due to non-blocking IPC. However, this assumption may not necessarily be realistic, and, moreover, resource contention and overhead must be accounted for.

Henn 1975, Mok and Dertouzos 1978

Henn [77] and Mok and Dertouzos [130] independently make the following two alterations to the Liu and Layland model:

1. frames are now infinite (i.e., non-repetitive processes)

2. there can be more than one CPU

and, using a scheduling game representation, establish the following results:

- Both the pre-emptive earliest-deadline-first and the least-laxity-first scheduling are feasible on a single CPU.

- No pre-emptive scheduling discipline is feasible on $N>2$ processors unless all (a) maximum response times and (b) CPU requirements are known.

- The least-laxity-first (but not the earliest-deadline-first) discipline on $N>2$ CPUs is feasible if both of the above ((a) and (b)) are known.

- If there is a feasible schedule when all processes start at time zero, then there is a feasible schedule if they start at different times.

IPC, non-trivial frames, and overhead must be included in the Mok and Dertouzos model to make it more realistic.

Leinbaugh 1980

Leinbaugh [113] considers the following model:

- a single CPU
- resources and resource contention
- constant maximum response times
- frames equal to their corresponding maximum response times
- processes consist of sequential segments
- each segment has own constant CPU and resource requirements
- some resources require mutual exclusion in their use
- no IPC other than possible implicit semaphore synchronisation between consecutive segments
- timer overhead
- processes are scheduled by the pre-emptive earliest-deadline-first policy
- resources are allocated first-come-first-served
- a segment cannot proceed until all of its resources are allocated

The author presents a complete schedulability analysis scheme to compute the guaranteed response times. Process blockage and slow-down due to CPU and resource contention are accounted for. Timer and some other overhead is also included. The various forms of contention and overhead are computed in a way ignorant of segments' relative positions and inter-segment distances on the time line. The Leinbaugh analysis assumes that every segment of every process delays every segment of every other process every time. The analysis is of polynomial complexity in the number of segments. It runs quickly, but produces overly pessimistic guaranteed response times, as we shall see later in this Section and in Chapter 7.

The Leinbaugh model is fairly realistic, though it does not treat IPC explicitly. Moreover, his schedulability analysis results in a set of very coarse worst-case response time bounds and can be improved.

Stoyenko 1984

Stoyenko [166] derives a recursive generalisation of the earliest-deadline-first scheduling algorithm to be used on a multiprocessor system in the presence of process blockage and contention due to IPC and resources.

The algorithm schedules a ready process which either has the earliest deadline among all processes (including the ones which are blocked), or, recursively, the earliest deadline predecessor (a blocking process with the earliest deadline) of the process with the earliest deadline. Thus, the algorithm makes sure that a process is scheduled so that the time until completion of the earliest deadline process is minimised. The algorithm is thus feasible with respect to deadline meeting when done pre-emptively in the context of the Sorenson and Leinbaugh models enhanced with IPC and resource blockage and contention.

Stoyenko's algorithm addresses the so-called *priority inversion problem*, independently solved in a very similar way by Sha, Rajkumar and Lehoszky [157] . The main problem with the Stoyenko algorithm is that its performance on a multiple CPU system is not understood.

Leinbaugh and Yamini 1982

Leinbaugh and Yamini [114] extend the Leinbaugh model to systems distributed over a small number of fully connected uniprocessor computers. Though the basic philosophy of the static worst-case analysis is preserved, the model has undergone three significant changes:

1. Processes can now consist of segment trees (as opposed to lists) — this is more than a trivial extension because of the possibility of process self-interference.

2. The CPU scheduling discipline is no longer the pre-emptive earliest-deadline-first, but rather pre-emptive fixed-priority. Moreover, different segments of the same process can have different (though fixed) priorities.

3. Maximum response times can be shorter than their corresponding frames.

The schedulability analysis is developed in three stages:

1. Processes can communicate but not self-interfere, and no communication is ever lost.

2. Processes can self-interfere, but still no communication errors.

3. Processes can self-interfere, and there are transient simple communication errors, namely: at most one message loss for each process execution, and each message may be lost at most once.

Having developed their worst-case analysis, the authors indicate that a number of ways remain to improve it:

- Using position information, i.e., once certain process parts are passed, they no longer cause any blockage.

- Using timing information, i.e., use information on how long each process component takes to execute to determine whether it can possibly cause blockage of other processes in consideration.

- Using the particularities of message passing, i.e., not every (part of a) message can block a particular process.

The Leinbaugh and Yamini analysis is very coarse, and it can be improved in any one of the ways that they indicate, or, perhaps, in some other way.

Mok 1984

Mok [129] considers the Leinbaugh-1980 model with two basic alterations:

1. there can be more than one CPU

2. maximum response times can be shorter than their corresponding frames

The following is established:

- The pre-emptive least-laxity-first algorithm is feasible on a single CPU in the absence of mutual exclusion constraints.

- No feasible pre-emptive scheduling policy exists in the presence of mutual exclusion constraints.

- No feasible scheduler exists when there is more than one CPU.

- A way of replacing sporadic processes with "equivalent" periodic ones is described, such that if the periodic processes are schedulable under the pre-emptive least-laxity-first algorithm, then so are the original sporadic ones.

The Mok model is much more realistic than the Mok and Dertouzos model, but the former still excludes IPC and overhead.

Ramamritham and Stankovic 1984 – 1985

Ramamritham and Stankovic [142] present a distributed hard real time model:

- There is one CPU per node.

- There are no resources.

- There are periodic and sporadic processes.

- Periodic processes are assigned to CPUs and guaranteed prior to system start-up to meet their maximum response times.

- Sporadic processes arrive randomly. They have deadlines and CPU requirements, but are not restricted with respect to their arrival rates.

- Upon arrival to a particular node of a sporadic process, it is checked whether the process can in fact be guaranteed at that node. If so, the process stays there; otherwise another node is picked for it through focused addressing (sending it to a node known to have had sufficient surplus computing power in recent

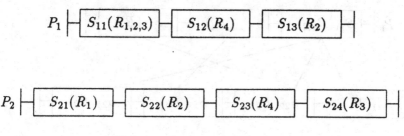

Figure 3.6: A two process system.

past) and bidding (writing/replying to/from nodes which may be able to guarantee the process).

- Guaranteed processes are locally scheduled according to the preemptive earliest-deadline-first discipline.

The authors explain in detail how their distributed scheduling works, and apply it to process sets both with and without IPC.

An extensive computer simulation evaluation of this distributing scheduling scheme is described in [143]. An interesting result is that unless system load approaches 80%, random sporadic process assignment outperforms the combination of focused addressing and bidding.

The Stankovic, Ramamritham et al. model can be extended to incorporate resources and overhead.

Leinbaugh and Yamini 1986

Leinbaugh and Yamini [115] assume the model of Leinbaugh and Yamini [114], and use position information to improve on their worst-case analysis. We demonstrate the improvement technique in the following example. Consider the system of Figure 3.6.

There are two processes, labeled P_1 and P_2, and four resources, labeled R_1, R_2, R_3 and R_4, in the system. P_1 consists of three segments: S_{11}, S_{12} and S_{13}. S_{11} accesses R_1, R_2 and R_3, S_{12} uses R_4, and S_{13} needs R_2. P_2 consists of four segments: S_{21}, S_{22}, S_{23} and S_{24}. S_{21}, S_{22}, S_{23} and S_{24} access R_1, R_2, R_4 and R_3, respectively.

Figure 3.7 indicates all potential ways a single activation of P_1 can block a single activation of P_2. Observe that many of the potential block-

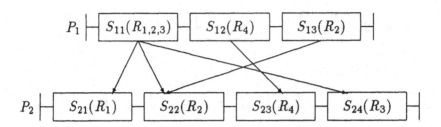

Figure 3.7: All possible ways P_1 can block P_2.

ages are incompatible. Blockages $S_{11} \to S_{21}$, $S_{11} \to S_{22}$ and $S_{11} \to S_{24}$ are mutually incompatible because segment S_{11} can only block once. Blockages $S_{11} \to S_{24}$, $S_{12} \to S_{23}$ and $S_{13} \to S_{22}$ are mutually incompatible because temporally only one blockage can occur. For example, if blockage $S_{12} \to S_{23}$ occurs, then segment S_{12} is run while segment S_{23} is ready. Therefore, (1) segment S_{22} has already been run, and so S_{13} cannot consequently block it, and (2) S_{11} has already been run, and so it cannot subsequently block S_{24}. Blockages $S_{11} \to S_{22}$ and $S_{13} \to S_{22}$ are incompatible because resources are allocated first-come-first-served, and thus if S_{11} blocks S_{22}, then S_{22} will be queued for resource R_2 in front of S_{13}.

To improve upon the Leinbaugh and Yamini [114] assumption that every potential blockage takes place, each set of mutually incompatible blockages is reduced to a single blockage whose cost is the maximum of the costs of all blockages involved. Leinbaugh and Yamini present no algorithm to do the reduction.

The Leinbaugh and Yamini [115] analysis results in more accurate worst-case bounds than the earlier Leinbaugh [113], and Yamini [114] analyses. However, of the three improvements suggested in [114], it only uses the position information improvement. Thus, the method can still be improved upon.

3.2.3.3   Frame Superimposition — Our Solution of the Model

In the last Section we assessed the state-of-the-art in real time modeling. With the exception of one technique [115], all surveyed methods deal with the difficult problems of resource queueing and various forms of contention by means of solutions which make no use of segments' relative positions and inter-segment distances on the time line when estimating delays. These solutions are typically closed-form or of polynomial complexity, and thus work very quickly. However, they result in overly pessimistic worst-case queueing delays, and ultimately in overly pessimistic guaranteed response times.

For example, a well-known solution [113, 114] computes ND_i as:

$$ND_i = \sum_{\substack{j=1 \\ j\neq i}}^{\#P} N_j \left(\left\lceil \frac{F_i}{F_j} \right\rceil + 1 \right)$$

To put it simply, this method assumes that every non-interruptible segment of every process is delayed by every non-interruptible segment of every other process every time: an assumption that is never true.

A technique defined in this book as *frame superimposition* is used to derive all process delays. Since ours is a worst-case analysis, the purpose of the superimposition is to maximise the amount of various types of contention each process can possibly incur. Frame superimposition is a form of run-time simulation. It starts off by fixing a single P_i's frame start at time t_0. The frames of other processes are then positioned in various ways along the time line relative to time t_0. Unlike P_i's frame, the frames of the other processes are not kept fixed. Rather, the algorithm shifts frames exhaustively, for every time unit, for every process, for every combination of frames possible. For every possible combination of frame positions, the amount of contention is recorded temporarily for each type of contention. The total contention, that is the sum of all types of contention, is also recorded temporarily for each possible combination of frame positions. Throughout the course of the superimposition, the maximum amount of contention for each type of contention as well as the maximum total contention are updated. These maximum amounts are substituted for the contention bounds at the end of the superimposition.

Frame superimposition uses relative positions of segments and distances between segments on the time line. Frame superimposition knows the correspondence between CPU rates and clock cycles. Thus, it may "execute" only a part of a segment or more than one segment in a single unit of time.

Frame superimposition can be refined in the following way to make use of the process activation information. The simulation starts when the first process is activated, and proceeds activating processes when necessary. To predict the activation times of a periodic process is trivial: the timing information is explicitly specified in the process definition. Not so easy is to predict the time of an **atEvent** process activation. If the relevant activation bracket is closed via an interrupt, then all possible process activations, provided any consecutive two are at least a frame apart, must be tried. If the activation bracket is closed by another process, then the intervals defined by the earliest and latest times the bracket may be closed must be computed. All possible activation times within these intervals are then tried. Again, any two consecutive activations must be at least a frame apart. The simulation ends after $2LCM_{i=1}^{N}\{F_i\} + \max_{i=1}^{N}\{F_i\} + \max_{i=1}^{N}\{IAT_i\}$ time unit steps (these many steps are sufficient to ensure that all possible combinations of segment interactions are considered [116, 117]), where

$$IAT_i = \begin{cases} atTime & \text{i.e., the initial activation time of } P_i \text{ if } atTime \\ & \text{is defined} \\ 0 & \text{otherwise} \end{cases}$$

These many steps are taken to insure that all possible process mix combinations are tried.

Having described the frame superimposition informally, we now present a more precise, formal description. Let T_i be the segment tree of P_i for $1 \leq i \leq N$. Let $L_{ik} = < S_{ik}^{<1>}, S_{ik}^{<2>}, \ldots, S_{ik}^{<n_{ik}>} >$ be a segment list of P_i, such that
L_{ik} is a subtree of T_i,
$S_{ik}^{<j>}$ is a segment of P_i, for $1 \leq j \leq n_{ik}$,
$S_{ik}^{<1>}$ is the root of T_i,
$S_{ik}^{<n_{ik}>}$ is a leaf of T_i, and
$1 \leq k \leq \Lambda(T_i)$, where $\Lambda(T_i)$ is the number of such unique lists L_{ik} within T_i.

Let $AL_i = \{L_{ik} such that 1 \leq k \leq \Lambda(T_i)\}$ for $1 \leq i \leq N$. The following events are undertaken once for each unique n-tuple $(L_{1k_1}, L_{2k_2}, \ldots, L_{nk_n})$

in $prod_{i=1}^{n} AL_i$. Let $FSL = 2LCM_{i=1}^{N}\{F_i\} + \max_{i=1}^{N}\{F_i\} + \max_{i=1}^{N}\{IAT_i\}$ be the length, that is, the number of real time units, of the time interval the frame superimposition will be run for. Let $RATI_i = (REAT_i, RLAT_i)$ be the relative activation time interval of P_i, where $REAT_i$ and $RLAT_i$ are, respectively, the earliest and the latest relative activation times of P_i. If P_i is activated periodically, then $REAT_i = 0$ and $RLAT_i = F_i$. If P_i is activated by an external interrupt, then $REAT_i = 0$ and $RLAT_i = FSL$. If P_i is activated by an activation bracket close from another process, then we do not need to compute its $RATI_i$, for the reasons that will become clear shortly.

Having determined a $RATI_i$ for each periodic or externally-activated process, we simulate process executions for each possible combination of process activation sequences. PAS_i, an activation sequence of P_i, is a sequence of activation times of $P_i(t_i^{<1>}, t_i^{<2>}, \ldots, t_i^{<k_{x_i}>})$, where
$t_i^{<1>} = IAT_i$,
$FSL - F_i \le t_i^{<k_{x_i}>} \le FSL$, and
$F_i + REAT_i \le t_i^{<j+1>} - t_i^{<j>} \le RLAT_i$, for $1 \le j \le k_{x_i} - 1$.
Therefore, a periodic process is activated exactly once per its frame, and an externally-activated process is activated no more often than once per its frame.

Having determined the only possible activation sequence for each periodic process and a possible activation sequence for each externally-activated process, we now have a totally deterministic schedule to simulate. This we do as follows.

- Set to 0 all global parameters (such as ND_i and I_i) to be maximised.

- Initialise bracket and active queues to empty lists, and the inactive queue to a list of all processes.

- For $T \leftarrow 0$ to FSL do

  - Activate every process P_i to be activated at time T.

  - Set to 0 all P_i's working parameters (such as shadows of ND_i and I_i) to be maximised.

  - Deactivate every process P_i to be deactivated at time T. If a working parameter of P_i exceeds its global counterpart, set the counterpart to the working parameter (such as $GT_i \leftarrow \max_{i=1}^{N}\{GT_i, localGT_i\}$).

- Execute current segments of all active processes for one time unit or until they are blocked or terminate. Update local parameters, queues and lists accordingly.

- If an activation bracket is closed, mark the activated process(es) for activation at the next logical real time tick.

- end For

In addition to maximising parameters during each activation sequence simulation, the overall maxima observed across all possible activation sequence simulations are also recorded. The maxima are then reported to the programmer as overall guaranteed bounds.

We now demonstrate how frame superimposition works by means of a simple example. Consider a system of three processes: P_1, P_2 and P_3. Their frames are equal, $F_1 = F_2 = F_3 = 3$. P_1 is periodic, P_2 is externally-activated and P_3 is activated by P_1. T_1, P_1's segment tree, consists of two segments: the first activates P_3 and takes negligible time to execute, the second is an interruptible segment that takes a single time unit to execute. The segment trees of P_2 and P_3 are identical, and each consists of a single interruptible segment of a single time unit size. $IAT_1 = 0$. The activation sequence of P_1 is $PAS_1 = (0, 3, 6)$, and an activation sequence of P_2 is one of the twenty-eight possible ones:

$PAS_2 \in \{(8),\ (7),\ (6),\ (0,8),\ (1,8),\ (2,8),\ (3,8),\ (4,8),$
$(5,8),\ (0,7),\ (1,7),\ (2,7),\ (3,7),\ (4,7),\ (0,6),\ (1,6),\ (2,6),$
$(3,6), (0,3,8), (0,4,8), (0,5,8), (1,4,8), (1,5,8), (2,5,8), (0,3,7),$
$(0,4,7), (1,4,7), (0,3,6)\}$

The simulation computes GT_i and ID_i, $1 \leq i \leq 3$ for each of these twenty-eight possibilities. For instance, if $PAS_2 = (8)$, then the simulation proceeds as follows:

$T=0$: P_1 is activated. P_1 closes the activation bracket of P_3. P_1 runs 1 time unit. P_1 terminates.

$T=1$: P_1 is deactivated. ID_1 and GT_1 are set to 0 and 1, respectively. P_3 is activated. P_3 runs 1 time unit. P_3 terminates.

$T=2$: P_3 is deactivated. ID_3 and GT_3 are set to 0 and 1, respectively.

$T=3$: P_1 is activated. P_1 closes the activation bracket of P_3. P_1 runs 1 time unit. P_1 terminates.

$T=4$: P_1 is deactivated. ID_1 and GT_1 are set to 0 and 1, respectively. P_3 is activated. P_3 runs 1 time unit. P_3 terminates.

$T=5$: P_3 is deactivated. ID_3 and GT_3 are set to 0 and 1, respectively.

$T=6$: P_1 is activated. P_1 closes the activation bracket of P_3. P_1 runs 1 time unit. P_1 terminates.

$T=7$: P_1 is deactivated. ID_1 and GT_1 are set to 0 and 1, respectively. P_3 is activated. P_3 runs 1 time unit. P_3 terminates.

$T=8$: P_3 is deactivated. ID_3 and GT_3 are set to 0 and 1, respectively. P_2 is activated. P_2 runs 1 time unit. P_2 terminates.

$T=9$: P_2 is deactivated. ID_2 and GT_2 are set to 0 and 1, respectively.

After this particular simulation, we thus get $ID_1 = ID_2 = ID_3 = 0$ and $GT_1 = GT_2 = GT_3 = 1$. After all twenty-eight possible simulations are run, we obtain $ID_1 = ID_2 = ID_3 = 2$ and $GT_1 = GT_2 = GT_3 = 3$. Thus, our simple system of processes is guaranteed to meet its deadlines under all circumstances.

The frame superimposition algorithm has clearly exponential complexity. The following factors contribute to the exponential nature of the algorithm: (1) unresolved selector-segments (resulting from programs with multi-branch case- and if-statements with kernel calls in each clause), (2) externally-triggered events (exceptions, interrupts or activations — these widen possible activation intervals of the processes involved), and (3) both inter- and intra-processor communication. In fact, finding the optimal worst-case bound for resource contention in the presence of deadlines is NP-complete, given that even the most basic deadline scheduling problems are [67, 180]. However, so is compilation in general. Moreover, this part of the analysis operates on segment trees, and there are many instructions, even statements reduced to an aggregate segment. Finally, better delay bounds are derived by our algorithm, than by all but possibly one algorithm discussed in Section 3.2.3.2, as we shall shortly see in an example.

The one technique which may derive bounds comparable in quality to the bounds derived by frame superimposition is the method of Lein-

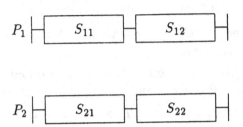

Figure 3.8: A simple two-process system.

baugh and Yamini [115]. The work on this method took place in parallel with our work on frame superimposition. The [115] paper does not define their method algorithmically, and thus it is hard to tell exactly how it would compare to our method. However, because frame superimposition uses both position and timing segment information, while the Leinbaugh and Yamini method uses only position segment information, frame superimposition will not result in bounds more pessimistic than bounds derived by the other method.

The timing complexity of the Leinbaugh and Yamini method is also uncertain. However, it does seem that to derive good worst-case contention bounds the reduction part of the technique has to consider all possible sets of mutually incompatible blockages, as well as the possible intersection subsets of these sets. Then, we assume that the Leinbaugh and Yamini [115] technique runs in exponential time, just as frame superimposition does.

To appreciate the power of frame superimposition, consider the simple two process system of Figure 3.8. F_1 equals F_2. Moreover, the segment trees of P_1 and P_2 are equivalent. There are no resources in the system. Each process consists of two non-interruptible segments. All segments take the same time to execute, say x.

Figure 3.9 demonstrates one possible way of positioning two frames of P_2 against a frame of P_1 so that ND_1 is maximised. Both segments of the first frame of P_2 block the first segment of P_1. A set of any three of the eight possible ways to block P_1 (see Figure 3.10) contains two incompatible blockages, because (1) a segment of P_2 can block at most one segment of P_1, and (2) no segment of P_1 can be blocked by two segments

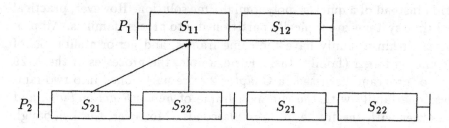

Figure 3.9: One scenario for P_2 to block P_1.

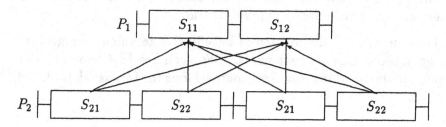

Figure 3.10: All possible ways P_2 can block P_1.

from different activations of P_2. The latter kind of blockage cannot occur for the following reason. Since processes are scheduled earliest-deadline-first and $F_1 = F_2$, once the first activation of P_2 completes, the new deadline of P_2 is passed the deadline of P_1, and consequently P_1 is given control.

Thus actual contention for P_1 cannot exceed $2x$. On the other hand, the contention can certainly be $2x$ (for example, Figure 3.9 has one such scenario). Thus, in our simple example frame superimposition derives the best bound possible, namely $ND_1 = 2x$ (and similarly, $ND_2 = 2x$).

Note that if the aforementioned Leinbaugh and Yamini [113, 114] solution were to be used in our example, we should have to assume that every non-interruptible segment of P_1 is delayed by every non-interruptible segment of P_2. Then we should have obtained $ND_1 = ND_2 = 4x$, an overly pessimistic result.

Observe that if $F_1 = nF_2$, then frame superimposition can result in $ND_1 = nN_2$, and the Leinbaugh method results in $ND_1 = (n + 1)N_2$. Thus, if n is large, then we seem to gain little from using the superimposition instead of a quicker, polynomial-time solution. However, practical real time systems are typically partitioned into process families. All processes within a family have the same frames, and perform subtasks of a common larger (family) task. For example, the processes of the X-29 control program discussed in Chapter 2 were partitioned into two families: one family with the common frame of *humanReactionTime*, and the other with the frame of 25 milliseconds. Moreover, the Leinbaugh [113, 114] and other methods discussed in Section 3.2.3.2 do not take into account such important information as process starting times, **atEvent** process activations and bracket access order. All of these are taken into account by frame superimposition.

Thus, frame superimposition is an effective technique for generating good worst-case delay bounds. We shall see in Chapter 7 that frame superimposition consistently outperforms the Leinbaugh [113, 114] method.

3.2.3.4 Delays

An open-bracket operation starts a bracket segment. Each bracket segment itself is interruptible, but is necessarily in between a queue-delay segment (waiting to enter the bracket) and a non-interruptible segment (updating bracket queues and state variables upon leaving the bracket). The queue delays QD_i's are computed by frame superimposition.

The wait and device-accessing delays SD_i's are computed as follows. Around each close-bracket operation we build intervals defined by the earliest and the latest possible close-bracket times. The relevant SD_i's are then set to the minimum of the maximum amount of time before a close-bracket occurrence, and the delay specified in the **noLongerThan** clause of the open-bracket operation. When external devices are involved, we cannot predict whether or not or when a timeout is going to occur. Thus, we have to define timeout intervals around each **noLongerThan**-delay segment.

The non-interruptible delays ND_i's and communication delays CD_i's are also computed by frame superimposition. In fact, all delays are computed at once and *the sum* of QD_i, SD_i, ND_i and CD_i is maximised. We maximise the sum because it is a part of GT_i, and GT_i is the entity whose upper bound we are ultimately interested in.

Frame superimposition spans across all processors, since while QD_i, SD_i and ND_i are caused by *intra*-processor contention, CD_i is the result of *inter*-processor contention.

3.2.3.5 Interruptible Slow-downs

The slow-down delay ID_i is caused by other processes executing their interruptible segments while P_i is ready.

If P_i is in a bracket, then, it cannot be pre-empted by another process trying to use the same bracket[7]. We thus compute ID_i as

$$ID_i = \sum_{k=0}^{\#B} ID_{ik} \tag{3.2}$$

where ID_{ik} is the kth bracket's contribution to ID_i. Brackets $1, 2, \ldots, \#B$ are real brackets, while bracket 0 corresponds to the non-bracket interruptible segments[8].

The quantity ID_{ik} can be computed in two ways: by frame superimposition, or as

$$ID_{ik} = s_{ik} WID_{ik} \tag{3.3}$$

for $k \in \{0, \ldots, \#B\}$, where
WID_{ik} is the worst-case interruptible interference for the kth bracket, computed as

$$WID_{ik} = \begin{cases} k \neq 0 & \sum_{\substack{j=1 \\ j \neq i}}^{\#P} \sum_{\substack{t=0 \\ t \neq k}}^{\#B} I_{jt} \\ k = 0 & \sum_{\substack{j=1 \\ j \neq i}}^{\#P} \sum_{t=0}^{\#B} I_{jt} \end{cases} \tag{3.4}$$

and s_{ik} is the slow-down rate for the kth bracket, which is further constrained by equations (3.5) and (3.6).

$$0 \leq s_{ik} \leq 1 \tag{3.5}$$

---

[7]Though it can certainly be pre-empted in general. Recall that bracket code is pre-emptible.

[8]We refer to these segments as "bracket segments" to keep our notation unified.

$$\sum_{i=1}^{\#P}(1 - s_{ik}) \leq 1 \qquad (3.6)$$

3.2.3.6   Overall Solution Algorithm

If we are only interested in verifying a given set of frames, then we only have to solve the set of systems of equations (3.1) through (3.6) once. Recall that the sum of QD_i, ID_i, ND_i, SD_i and CD_i is maximised, and not the individual parameters. It is possible for different combinations of values of individual parameters, across all processes, to add up to the same largest sum for each process. Naturally, the individual sums do not have to be maximised for all processes in the same pass of frame superimposition. In principle, it is possible to construct a set of processes for which there is an exponential (in the sum of the number of unresolved selector-segments) number of possible parameter combinations, though this was certainly not the case with the realistic programs we used to evaluate this method.

There can be different combinations of individual parameters resulting in the same largest sum. However, these largest sums are unique for their respective processes (frame superimposition is, after all, deterministic, and there can be but one maximum over any finite set of numbers). Therefore, since the other parameters (I_i and N_i) are computed exactly once and thus have unique values, a single set of guaranteed response times GT_i always results. A solution to (3.1) may or may not exist, depending on whether every derived GT_i is less than or equal to its F_i. However, if a solution does exist, then it is unique, in the sense that any other response time, not in the set of GT_i's, is either overly pessimistic (too large) or not guaranteed (too small).

If we want to determine the tightest set of frames we can guarantee, then we solve the following fixed-point iteration.

$$GT_i^{<x+1>} \leq F_i^{<x>} \qquad (3.7)$$

where
x is the iteration count,
$F_i^{<0>}$, is given or guessed,

$GT_i^{<x>}$ is obtained by solving (3.1) through (3.6), and

$$GT_i^{<x>} \leq F_i^{<x+1>} < F_i^{<x>}. \tag{3.8}$$

Our set of systems of equations is underdetermined. To make it determined, we can make a number of constructive assumptions.

In some systems, processes naturally group into families. Each family is responsible for performing synchronised, related tasks. Often, system engineers would define frame ratios for each process family. As a result, we should then add the following equation to our system.

$$\frac{F_i^{<x>}}{F_j^{<x>}} = \frac{F_i^{<0>}}{F_j^{<0>}} \tag{3.9}$$

for $i, j \in \{1, \ldots, \#P\}$, for all x.

Unless there is a specific reason to do otherwise and if frame superimposition is not used to compute ID_i's, we can assume that for each process the slow-down rates are the same for all brackets:

$$s_{i0} = s_{i1} =, \ldots, = s_{i\#B} \tag{3.10}$$

for $i \in \{1, \ldots, \#P\}$. In other words, a process has the same slow-down rate throughout its execution.

To derive $F_i^{<x+1>}$, any operation on $F_i^{<x>}$ and $GT_i^{<x>}$ satisfying (3.8) will do.

Once we determine (3.1) through (3.10), we iterate until we cannot reduce F_i's anymore, or alternatively, until we get no more reduction in the sum of F_i's. Should an $F_i^{<x+1>}$ be chosen to be less than $F_i^{<x>} - 1$, and the resulting $GT_i^{<x+1>}$ exceed $F_i^{<x+1>}$, then the iteration should not be stopped, but should be tried again with $F_i^{<x+1>} < F_i^{<x+2>} < F_i^{<x>}$.

Observe that there are no numerical approximations involved in these equations, since all parameters are expressed in terms of natural integers (integral time values, typically in clock ticks or instruction cycles). Furthermore, the iteration is clearly convergent, since integers are not dense, the frames become smaller and the guaranteed response times become larger with every iteration (with the exception for the case when we overshoot, and in that case we iterate no more than the largest (and finite) difference between the last two frames of the same process).

Every iteration solves (3.1) through (3.6) once. Thus, given a set of $F_i^{<x>}$'s, there is either no solution (the frames are too tight) or a unique (in the sense of the guaranteed response times) solution of (3.1) through (3.6), as already indicated. However, one can choose different combinations of values of $F_i^{<x>}$'s for every iteration where there is still room for the frames to become tighter. Thus, the tightest set of frames is not unique. Let $GT_i^{<0>}$ stand for the amount of time it takes P_i to execute in the absence of any other processes. Given a set of $F_i^{<0>}$'s, then there can be no more than

$$\prod_{i=1}^{\#P}(F_i^{<0>} - GT_i^{<0>}) \tag{3.11}$$

different sets of tightest frames. Naturally, this number may be quite large. However, given a set of tightest frames $F_i^{<x>}$'s, for some appropriate x, it is unlikely, if not impossible, that the number of different sets of tightest frames may exceed

$$\prod_{i=1}^{\#P}(F_i^{<x>} - GT_i^{<x>}) \tag{3.12}$$

Having solved for guaranteed response times either a single time or iteratively, we then report the F_i, GT_i and s_i for each process, as well as timing information for every subprogram, call, bracket access, mailbox access, even every statement. The programmer will then study the results, and decide whether the program should be run as it exists, or whether it should be modified.

If the purpose of the analysis was to verify a given set of frames, then, in the case of a positive solution of our set of systems of equations, the programmer need not do any changes to the program to achieve guaranteed schedulability. Similarly, if the purpose is to guarantee as tight a set of frames as possible, and the resulting set of frames and response times is satisfactory, no changes to the program are needed.

If, however, the guaranteed response times or frames obtained are too large, the supplementary timing information[9] will be of help to determine where the processes can be streamlined.

For the purposes of process switches, the analysis here assumes the granularity of time to be the one of the logical real time clock (as opposed to the physical hardware clock ticks). Thus, we assume that the logical clock tick is long enough to update all kernel process queues. For example, if *multiple* processes are to be activated at a time t, *all* these processes will be moved to their ready queue(s) before the time $t + 1$, thus preventing jitter from occurring. If there is more than one possible way of ordering a process queue, the analyser will consider all possible orders, thus making sure the worst-case bounds on processes' queue delays are derived properly. While trying all these possibilities adds to the exponential complexity of the algorithm, we found that the exponential effect is not very significant due to (1) short queue lengths, and (2) queues clearing in a small number of logical ticks.

3.3   Schedulability Analysis of Real-Time Euclid and Extended PEARL

Both Real-Time Euclid and extended PEARL follow closely the assumptions we made in Section 1.4 of Chapter 1. It is thus not surprising that the language-independent schedulability analysis techniques presented in this Chapter apply well to both languages.

One point that needs explaining is how inter-process synchronisation mechanisms of the two languages map to brackets. Extended PEARL's **lock** and **unlock** primitives map directly to, respectively, open-bracket and close-bracket. To express Real-Time Euclid inter-process synchronisation using brackets, we do the following. Every monitor and condition variable maps to a unique bracket, enter-monitor and exit-monitor map to open-bracket and close-bracket, respectively. Broadcasts generate a sequence (as many as there are waiting processes) of (cascaded) close-brackets. A wait closes the bracket of the corresponding monitor and opens the bracket of the condition variable. To ensure that no process enters a monitor in between the close and the open, they are performed in

---

[9]Namely specific subprogram, call, and statement information.

a single non-interruptible segment, and the interrupts are turned back on right after the open. Similarly, a signal closes the bracket of the condition variable and opens the bracket of the corresponding monitor, indivisibly, in a single non-interruptible segment.

Since Real-Time Euclid and extended PEARL are based on the same real time model, the schedulability analysis technique described above in a language-independent way can also be applied to extended PEARL programs, if we can show that no language feature takes arbitrarily long to execute. Thus, the information necessary to build the front end segment trees can be obtained. Every Real-Time Euclid construct has been presented with an explicit explanation of why it is time-bounded. We now provide corresponding explanations for extended PEARL constructs.

Sequential and selector statements of extended PEARL are bounded as discussed in Section 3.1.1. As long as the program flow is strictly sequential, there is no problem, since only the processing times of the corresponding compiler generated instructions need to be summed up. Sequential language elements are assignment statements, in-line and access function evaluations, interrupt masking statements, viz., **enable** and **disable**, branching to and from procedures, and operations invisible to the programmer, which are caused by the block structure. Upper bounds on **if** and **case** statements are derived by adding the time required for the evaluation of the conditional expressions occurring in these statements to the maximum of the execution times of the two or more alternatives provided.

To compute an upper bound on an extended PEARL **repeat**, the construct was augmented with the **maxloop** clause, as presented in Section 2.9.3 in Chapter 2. The clause bounds the number of iterations with a compile-time constant.

In extended PEARL, we confine the usage of **goto** statements to the purpose of leaving loops, blocks, and other constructions, when some code is to be skipped. For the purpose of run-time estimation, these jumps can be simply disregarded.

The span between the times a synchronisation operation requesting resources is reached and finally carried through is generally undetermined. Therefore, we have replaced PEARL's present unstructured synchronisation statements by the new **lock** statement. An execution time bound can be obtained by adding the time required to claim the specified resources, the given waiting time, and the maximum of the execution times for the **outtime** string on the one hand and for the **perform** string (including the release of the synchronisers) on the other.

By combining the aforementioned estimation techniques and applying them recursively, run-time bounds for program modules such as blocks, procedures, and task bodies can be determined. In particular, the method can also be applied to procedures, which are part of a PEARL run-time package. Such procedures are invoked by the six input/output statements and the six tasking statements. Hence, run-time estimations can also be derived for the mentioned statements. From the view-point of run-time determination, temporal suspensions of tasks do not need to be considered, since only the residual run-time required after a task's resumption to reach its final completion matter to the scheduler. The two event simulation statements, namely **trigger** and **induce**, are only useful in the software validation phase, and can thus be excluded from run-time estimations.

In PEARL, exception handlers are realised through **on** statements. To take the run-time of exception handling into account, an exception handler is regarded as a procedure, whose maximum run-time can be estimated. This estimated time is added to the execution times of those parts of the task, which are processed when the exception handler is invoked. Finally, the maximum of all exceptionless paths and of all paths which include calls to the exception handlers is an overall upper bound for the task's execution time. According to [45], however, exception handlers ought to be avoided wherever possible. This can be achieved by incorporating, into the application programs, explicit checks for exceptional conditions, and providing corresponding handling code. This method is also advantageous from the standpoint of run-time determination.

To determine how much time is needed to execute an **expect** block, it is natural to treat the block alternatives, the code preceding the block (initial part), and the code following the block (final part) as (at least three) separate tasks. Following the termination of the initial task, every alternative task is scheduled for activation when the events specified in the corresponding **when** clauses will occur. To handle certain erroneous conditions, such as timeouts, additional clauses may be introduced into the **expect** (thus, defining extra alternative tasks). Recall that since multiple events may be handled in a single awakening of an **expect**, the alternative tasks are not mutually exclusive, and thus cannot be modelled as a single task with the run-time set to the maximum of that of the alternatives'. Following the termination of the **expect**, the final task is activated and made ready. The run-time estimation of the initial and final tasks (parts) and the individual alternative tasks proceeds in the usual fashion.

3.4   Summary

The language-independent schedulability analysis techniques presented in this Chapter use frame superimposition and slow-down rate analysis to compute good worst-case delay bounds. These techniques are considerably more effective than any state-of-the-art techniques known to us and surveyed in this Chapter.

We know only one other technique [115] comparable in quality to ours. The research culminating in this method took place independently of our research (and vice-versa). The algorithm defined in [115] operates similarly to frame superimposition, and derives worst-case delay bounds having taken into account position segment information. Unlike our techniques, neither an algorithmic description of the method nor its evaluation has yet been reported.

Having defined our language-independent schedulability techniques, we have indicated how they apply to both Real-Time Euclid and extended PEARL. In both cases the applications are quite straightforward, thus testifying to the good generality of the techniques. Our experience with applying schedulability analysis techniques in practice is reported in Chapter 7.

Chapter 4

A Real Time Hardware Architecture

The very nature of schedulability analysis requires predictable hardware behaviour. In this Chapter we devise the concept of a hardware platform, on which predictably behaving real time systems can be based. To motivate our design, we start off by analysing analogies from everyday life and anatomy. Then, close attention is devoted to the earliest deadline task scheduling policy, which has many advantageous properties and is hence employed in our system. The policy is extended to include resource constraints and non-pre-emptive scheduling. The implications of the extensions on the architecture are elaborated. Having considered the layered structure of typical real time operating systems, we conclude that a real time computer is best organised in form of a general purpose processor, and a co-processor dedicated to the operating system kernel. This architectural concept is outlined and compared with other non-conventional architectures found in the literature.

We leave many details of the general purpose processor as a topic for a future discussion. However, it has to be made clear how much time each machine instruction takes to execute. Moreover, the hardware must not introduce any unpredictably long delays into the program executions. Hardware faults can delay instruction processing in an unpredictable way. Therefore, hardware reacting fail-safe and supporting

the detection of faults is required, thus allowing to recover within predictable durations and to implement the schemes of predictable graceful
performance degradation as described in Chapter 2. Hence, we think of
a simple and well-defined architecture, such as the VIPER [98], with a
comprehensive, but limited instruction set and without any features such
as pipelining, caches, virtual memory or DMA, which render the predictability of system behaviour impossible. As substitutes for them, to
comply with the predictability requirement, we develop a task-oriented
hierarchical storage administration scheme and methods allowing direct
memory access without cycle stealing. Finally, we show, that the I/O
behaviour of a real time system too can be made fully predictable by
endowing the peripherals and their driving software with explicit timing
facilities.

4.1   Useful Analogies

How should a process control computer system be organised internally?
It would appear that this question was not asked in the early days of
real time data processing. Rather, it was considered advantageous and
appropriate to employ conventional von Neumann computers. The only
adaptation to the real time application area were manifested in including
process peripherals and externally available interrupt lines. All other
real time requirements were met by software, viz. by operating systems,
and by carefully programming the requirements in the application. The
problems introduced in Chapter 1, however, could in general not be
solved in this way.

As it is common in engineering, there are always many possible system designs fulfilling a given set of demands — provided the problem
is solvable with available technology. To demonstrate that this can be
done in the case of real time hardware architectures is one of the objectives of this book. To derive such an appropriate architecture, we now
consider some analogies from other fields, where systems coping with
real time conditions have long been developed and used.

The first example is the system comprised of a manager and his[1]

---

[1] or "her". In this book, wherever we say *his*, we mean "his or her". Similarly,

secretary. The duties of the secretary are the reception of mail and telephone calls, the elimination of unimportant chores, and the minimisation of the interruptions of the manager's work by visitors and callers. Furthermore, she schedules the manager's work by arranging the files in the sequence in which they are to be treated and through the administration of his meeting appointments. Thus, the manager's work becomes less hectic — i.e., the work's "real time conditions" are eased — and more productive, because he can perform his tasks with less frequent interruptions in a more sequential and organised manner.

Similar organisational structures have been developed in various other areas in order to prepare and to schedule the work of either highly qualified and paid persons or of expensive resources. Some examples include the reception room of a physician's office, the reception desk of an automobile repair workshop, and the operations room of a data-processing centre. In these and other offices the tasks to be carried out by both single or multiple — usually specialised — resources or persons are organised, supported, and arranged in an appropriate order.

As final analogy consider the human brain, which consists of the cerebrum, midbrain, diencephalon, cerebellum, and the extended spinal cord. The signals to and from various parts of the body are transmitted via the spinal marrow, which has some similarities with a computer bus. The nerves of the spinal marrow end at the side of the brain in the extended spinal cord, which is closely connected to the midbrain, the diencephalon, and the cerebellum. The last four organs have non-arbitrary and routine reflex functions. Specifically, they control the metabolism, the bodies' position, heat, and water content, and regulate respiration and blood circulation. The organs are an important switching site between the nerves of the body and those of the brain. Furthermore, the immediate reflex centre is located here. In contrast to this, the other information processing functions of higher complexity, such as the evaluation of sensual impressions, the control of arbitrary actions, and all intellectual tasks, are performed by the cerebrum.

By taking pattern from these models, we now define the overall structure of a novel real time computer. The concept is displayed in Figure 4.1. The system consists of two dissimilar processors. One is

---

"she" will stand for "he or she" and so on.

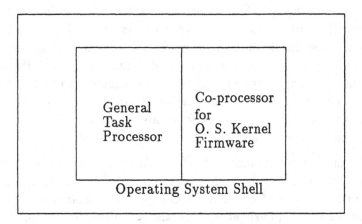

Figure 4.1: The basic architectural concept

a classical von Neumann processor. It executes user tasks and those operating system tasks that interface the user tasks. Specifically, the operating system tasks on this processor are mainly outer supervisor shell services, such as data exchange with peripherals and file management, provided in the form of independent tasks or subroutines called by the user tasks. The operating system kernel is clearly and physically separated from the outer layer tasks. The kernel runs on the second processor. This co-processor thus houses the system functions event, time and task management, communication and synchronisation.

4.2 Properties and Architectural Implications of Comprehensive Deadline-Driven Scheduling

The fundamental requirement, expected of a process control system employed in a hard real time environment, is to carry out all tasks within predefined time frames (assuming this is actually possible). Algorithms generating appropriate schedules for all task sets executable under observation of their given due dates (deadlines) are referred to as *feasible*. Several such algorithms have been identified in the literature [77, 78, 79, 80, 92, 105, 121, 158]. A few of these deal with task sets whose elements can all be started immediately, whereas others operate on task sets for which precedence relations are given. Since (1) precedence relations cannot be specified explicitly using available process control languages and (2) tasks may be activated by external events, the following situation prevails in the majority of today's real time applications. Whenever there is a number of runnable tasks competing for a processor, the tasks are scheduled regardless of whether they are event-driven aperiodic, "single-shot" time-driven or periodic, and regardless of whether they have been activated explicitly, through continuation, or after releasing synchronisers. Rather, all such competing tasks are considered ready and independent.

It has been shown that for scheduling independent tasks on a single processor the earliest-deadline-first algorithm is feasible [121, 161, 77]. Similarly, a modification of the earliest-deadline-first scheme for homogeneous multiprocessors, namely the throwforward algorithm of Johnson, Maddison and Henn is feasible [92, 78, 80]. Furthermore, the least-laxity-first algorithm is feasible for both single and multiprocessor systems [77, 78, 131, 153]. On the other hand, neither of the two scheduling policies supported most frequently in commercially-available programming languages and real time operating systems, namely the first-come-first-served and the fixed-priority algorithm is feasible. Naturally, feasible schedules can be obtained if the user is able to modify task priorities dynamically. This approach, however, is not suitable, because then the entire burden of scheduling is imposed on the application programmer. He would then in turn be prevented from writing software modules independently of each other, and would need to make frequent use of usually unavailable task status information.

Unfortunately, the least-laxity-first algorithm is only of theoretical interest, since it is pre-emptive and requires processor sharing when several tasks have the same laxity. The latter can, for instance, approximately be accomplished by round robin scheduling with a very small time slice. Both properties imply frequent context-switches degrading the system performance by unproductive overhead. Furthermore, the processor sharing may cause synchronisation difficulties with regard to the resources requested by the single tasks.

In contrast to least-laxity-first, the earliest-deadline-first algorithm does not require context-switches unless a new task with an earlier deadline arrives or an executing task terminates. In fact, if the number of pre-emptions enforced by a scheduling procedure is considered as a selection criterion, the earliest-deadline-first algorithm is optimal [77] . Even when tasks arrive dynamically, this policy maintains its properties and then generates optimal pre-emptive schedules [105, 106].

When applied to multiprocessors, the earliest-deadline-first scheme ceases being feasible, however. An extension of the policy that re-establishes feasibility is the throwforward algorithm of [92, 78, 80]. However, the latter algorithm leads to more pre-emptions and is more complex. This fact suggests an argument against using symmetric multiprocessors. To develop the argument further, consider the following example.

Let a set T of six tasks be given at time $t = 0$:
$T=\{T_1=(5,4),\ T_2=(6,3),\ T_3=(7,4),\ T_4=(12,8),\ T_5=(13,8),\ T_6=(15,12)\}$.
Each task is characterised by the tuple (Deadline, Required Execution Time). Let the tasks be processed on a homogeneous 3-processor system. The schedule provided by the throwforward strategy [2] is displayed in Figure 4.2, in the form of a Gantt diagram. The example reveals that the scheduling process requires 5 pre-emptions and corresponding context-switches. The latter may additionally result in repeated program loading, if the different processors do not share memory. The diagram also shows that 2 processors are idle for 6 time units before the task set is completely executed. Since several processors cannot simultaneously work on one task, it is impossible to balance the load and to reduce the task set's overall response time. On the other hand, if the same task set is scheduled earliest-deadline-first on a single processor system 3 times faster than each of three original processors, the Gantt diagram given in Figure 4.3 results. There, each task is uninterruptedly executed after another, and there is no idling. Thus, time-consuming context-switches are avoided and, at any point in time, there needs to be only one program in main storage. Furthermore, the entire task set

---

[2]Note that feasible schedules with fewer pre-emptions may exist. There is, however, no algorithm (yet) to generate such schedules.

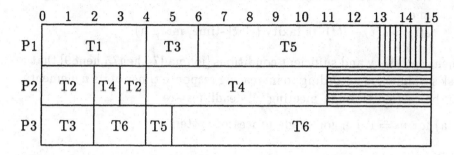

Figure 4.2: Gantt diagram of a feasible schedule for a symmetric 3-processor system

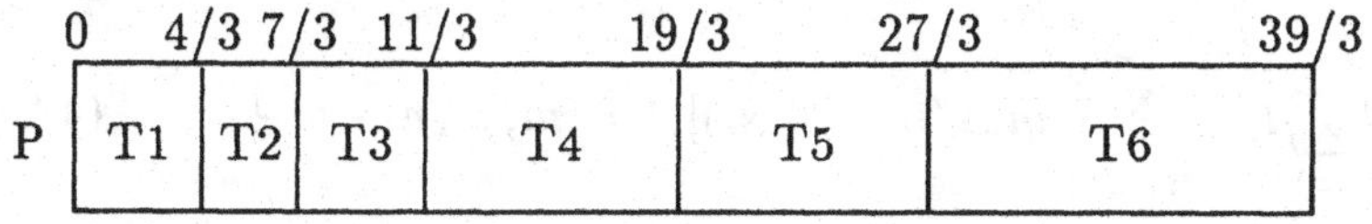

Figure 4.3: Gantt diagram of a feasible schedule for a single processor system

is processed earlier than in the case of the 3-processor system. Since in theoretical considerations the overhead is usually — but unrealistically — neglected, the overall execution time proportion is further shifted in favour of the single processor structure. Hence, the factor for speeding up a single processor system in order to become equivalent to an m-processor as far as performance is concerned will generally be considerably less than m. Moreover, strictly sequential task execution eliminates synchronisation conflicts which may give rise to waiting and processor idling in multiprocessors.

When deadlines and processor requirements of tasks are available a priori, the following necessary and sufficient conditions determine whether a task set given at a certain instant can be executed within its specified deadlines.

For any time $t, 0 \leq t < \infty$, and any task T with deadline $t_z > t$, let

$a(t) = t_z - t$ be its response time,

$l(t)$ the (residual) execution time required before completion, and

$s(t) = a(t) - l(t)$ its laxity (slack-time, margin).

Then, necessary and sufficient conditions [johmad74,hen75,hen89] that a task set, indexed according to increasing response times of its n elements, can be carried through meeting all deadlines are

a) for $m = 1$, i.e. for single processor systems:

$$a_k \geq \sum_{i=1}^{k} l_i, k = 1, ..., n, \tag{4.1}$$

b) and for $m > 1$, i.e. for homogeneous multiprocessor systems:

$$a_k \geq \frac{1}{m}[\sum_{i=1}^{k} l_i + \sum_{i=k+1}^{n} max(0, a_k - s_i)], k = m, ..., n - m + 1, \tag{4.2}$$

$$a_k \geq \frac{1}{n - k + 1}[\sum_{i=1}^{k} l_i + \sum_{i=k+1}^{n} max(0, a_k - s_i) - \sum_{i=n-m+1}^{k-1} a_i], \tag{4.3}$$

$$k = n - m + 2, ..., n,$$

For $k = 1, ..., m - 1$ Equation (4.2) must be valid, except if there are j tasks with $a_k > s_i$ for $k < i \leq n$ and $j + k < m$ then

$$a_k \geq \frac{1}{k + j}[\sum_{i=1}^{k} l_i + \sum_{i=k+1}^{n} max(0, a_k - s_i)] \tag{4.4}$$

must be fulfilled.

Comparing (4.1) with the set (4.2,4.3,4.4) of inequalities, it is quite obvious that the complexity of performing the executability examination is by far higher for the case $m > 1$. The like also holds with regard to the actual processor assignment scheme, since for $m = 1$ the task with the shortest response time is always being executed. In contrast to this, the relations of task laxities to the response times of other tasks already assigned to processors need to be observed, and the algorithm also has to be invoked when a non-running task loses its slack-time. Hence, the procedure must keep track of the time events when the laxities of non-assigned tasks vanish, or when a task's slack-time becomes equal to the response time of another executing task. This feature adds considerably to the already high complexity of the throwforward algorithm.

4.2.1 Implications of Employing Earliest Deadline Scheduling

From the above discussion, it seems that it is best to to structure real time computer systems as single processors. The idea can be extended to distributed systems, by structuring them as sets of interconnected uniprocessors, each of which dedicated to controlling part of an external environment. The earliest-deadline-first scheduling algorithm is to be applied independently from considerations of the overall system load, on each node in a distributed system. The implementation of this scheme is facilitated by the fact that industrial process control systems are already typically designed in the form of co-operating, possibly heterogeneous, single processor systems, even though the processors' operating systems do not yet schedule by deadline.

In the ideal case, the earliest-deadline-first method guarantees one-at-a-time scheduling of tasks, modulo new task arrivals. Unproductive context-switches are thus eliminated. Furthermore, and even more importantly, resource access conflicts and many concurrency problems, such as deadlocks, do not occur, and hence do not need to be handled. Unfortunately, such an ideal case is by its very nature unrealistic. The case establishes, however, the direction in which our architecture should be developed. The objective ought to be to maintain, as much as possible, strictly sequential execution of task sets. The processor(s) need(s) to be relieved of frequent interruptions, caused by external and internal events, in the sequential program flow. These interruptions are counterproductive in the sense that they seldom result in an immediate (re-) activation of a task.

To summarise, earliest-deadline-first task scheduling on a single processor system has the following advantages:

- the concept of task deadlines is problem-oriented,

- the concept of task deadlines allows the formulation of tasks and the extension and modification of existing software without the knowledge of the global task system,
- sporadic, periodic, and precedence-related tasks can be treated by a common scheduling strategy,
- feasibility,
- upon a dynamic arrival of a ready task, the task's response time can be guaranteed (or a future overload can be detected),
- the cost of running the algorithm is almost negligible (its complexity is linear in the number of tasks in the ready queue),
- ease of implementation,
- the cost of checking for feasible executability of a task set is almost negligible (again, linear in the number of tasks in the ready queue), and the check itself is trivial, i.e. the operating system is enabled to supervise the observance of the fundamental timeliness condition,
- facilitation of early overload detection and handling by dynamic load adaptation, thus allowing system performance to degrade gracefully,
- achieves the minimum number of task pre-emptions required to execute a feasible schedule,
- achieves maximum processor utilisation while maintaining feasible executability of a task set,
- is essentially non-pre-emptive, i.e. task pre-emptions may only be caused when dormant tasks are activated or suspended ones resumed,
- the sequence of task executions is determined at the instants of task (re-) activations and remains constant afterwards, i.e. when a new task turns ready, the order among the others remains constant,
- the order of task processing is essentially sequential,
- resource access conflicts and deadlocks are inherently prevented,
- unproductive overhead is inherently minimised,
- the priority inversion problem, which recently has received much attention, does not arise at all, and
- pre-emptable and (partially) non-pre-emptable tasks can be scheduled in a common way.

4.2.2 Sufficient Conditions for Feasible Task Executability under Resource Constraints

The above considerations have revealed that the earliest-deadline-first algorithm is the best one to use in a general multitasking environment, provided that the tasks are pre-emptable at any arbitrary point in time. Unfortunately, this precondition is not very realistic, since it is only fulfilled by pure computing tasks fully independent upon one another. In general, however, tasks have resource requirements and, therefore, execute critical regions to lock peripherals and other resources for exclusive and uninterrupted access. Hence, the elaboration of a task consists of phases of unrestricted pre-emptability alternating with critical regions. While a task may be pre-empted in a critical region, the pre-emption may cause a number of problems and additional overhead, such as the possibility of deadlocks or the necessity for a further context-switch when the pre-empting task tries to gain access to a locked resource. We now propose the following modification of the earliest-deadline-first discipline, to accommodate resource constraints.

Algorithm 1: *Schedule tasks earliest-deadline-first, unless it calls for pre-emption of a task executing in a critical region.*

Note that task precedence relations do not need to be addressed here, since the task set in consideration consists of ready tasks only, i.e. the set consists of tasks whose activation conditions have been fulfilled (and thus their predecessors have already terminated).

We now derive a sufficient condition, that allows to determine a task set's feasible executability at any arbitrary time instance under **Algorithm 1**. Consider a set T of tasks. At any point in time $t \geq 0$, there is the ready task set $\mathcal{F}(t) \subset T$ comprised of all elements of T, whose (re-) activation conditions have been fulfilled and which compete for the allocation of the processor. If all tasks in $\mathcal{F}(t)$ are pre-emptable, then the entire set is executed sequentially and earliest-deadline-first. Therefore, the (partial) non-pre-emptability of certain tasks can only cause a problem if the following three conditions hold together at time t:

1. a further task joins the ready task set $\mathcal{F}(t)$, *and*

2. the new task's response time is shorter than the one of the task

running at time t, i.e. after adding the new task to $\mathcal{F}(t)$, the running one has obtained the index $j \geq 2$ upon sorting the ready task set according to increasing deadlines, *and*

3. the running task T_j is at time t in a non-pre-emptable region of length $r_j(t)$.

Hence, all tasks $T_i, i = 1, ..., j-1$, including the newly arrived one, have to wait for $r_j(t)$ time units, before T_j can be pre-empted. In order to still meet their deadlines despite this delay, it must hold for the laxities $s_i(t), i = 1, ..., j-1$ of $T_i, i = 1, ..., j-1$, that:

$$s_i(t) \geq r_j(t) + \sum_{k=1}^{i-1} l_k(t), i = 1, ..., j-1, \tag{4.5}$$

Naturally, the tasks $T_i, i = 1, ..., j-1$, will complete before their deadlines if their slack-times fulfill the following, less tight, condition:

$$s_i(t) \geq d + \sum_{k=1}^{i-1} l_k(t), i = 1, ..., j-1, \; with \; d \geq r_j(t) \tag{4.6}$$

The quantity d occurring in this inequality can be selected in many ways. Some suitable choices for d, arranged in the order of decreasing sharpness, are:

- (time of termination of the non-pre-emptive region of T_j) - t
- length of the non-pre-emptive region of T_j
- d_j, which is the maximum of the lengths of all non-pre-emptive regions T_j
- $Max \{ d_i \, | \, \forall T \in \mathcal{F}(t) \}$
- $Max \{ d_i \, | \, \forall T \in \mathcal{T} \}$

For practical purposes, the last definition of d will probably offer the best choice, since it is the most general expression fully independent on the actual time and the amount of resource contention.

By rewriting the inequality (4.5) using the definition of laxity, we obtain the following condition which is sufficient for the tasks $T_i, i =$

$1, ..., j - 1$ to meet their deadlines:

$$s_i(t) \geq d + \sum_{k=1}^{i-1} l_k(t) \iff a_i(t) \geq d + \sum_{k=1}^{i} l_k(t), i = 1, ..., j - 1 \quad (4.7)$$

The task T_j, that will be pre-empted after the completion of its non-pre-emptable phase (T_j is in this phase at time t), can only complete by its deadline if

$$a_j(t) \geq \sum_{k=1}^{j} l_k(t) \quad (4.8)$$

holds. Correspondingly, the task T_{j+1}, which is to run after the completion of T_j, can only be feasibly scheduled if

$$a_{j+1}(t) \geq \sum_{k=1}^{j+1} l_k(t) \quad (4.9)$$

This argument extends to all other tasks in $\mathcal{F}(t)$ and leads to the condition

$$a_i(t) \geq \sum_{k=1}^{i} l_k(t), i = j, ..., n = |\mathcal{F}(t)| \quad (4.10)$$

Thus, combining these n inequalities into one set and using the Kronecker symbol, we have proved

Theorem 1: *If at time t a task joins the ready task set $\mathcal{F}(t)$, which is scheduled according to Algorithm 1, and if the exceptional condition mentioned in the algorithm applies at that time t, due to which the currently running task obtains the index $j \geq 2$ upon sorting of $\mathcal{F}(t)$, then all elements of the ready task set will meet their deadlines if the inequalities*

$$a_i(t) \geq d \cdot \sum_{k=1}^{j-1} \delta_{ik} + \sum_{k=1}^{i} l_k(t), i = 1, ..., n = |\mathcal{F}(t)|, \quad (4.11)$$

are fulfilled, wherein the quantity d may be selected as $Max \{ lengths \ of \ all \ periods \ of \ non-pre-emptivity \ | \ \forall T \in \mathcal{F}(t) \}$. In case the exceptional condition does not hold, the arriving task does not pre-empt the running task, and Inequality (4.1) applies to determine feasible executability.

Observe that when there are no critical regions, (4.11) reduces to (4.1). A less general form of (4.11), specific to periodic tasks, will be given in a forthcoming publication [158]. There, the condition is derived from the well-known results of Liu and Layland [121]. Neither theorem version is yet fully realistic, since they both disregard the context-switch times. We shall extend Theorem 1 to accommodate context-switches shortly.

The modified earliest-deadline-first policy offers a practical way to predictably schedule tasks in the presence of resource constraints. The policy maintains most advantageous properties listed in the previous Section. In fact, the only property no longer exhibited is the achievability of maximum processor utilisation. From the point of view of classical computer performance theory, this may be considered a serious drawback. For embedded real time systems, however, it is totally irrelevant whether the processor utilisation is optimal, as costs have to be seen in the framework of the controlled external process and with regard to the latter's safety requirements. Taking the costs of a technical process and the possible damage into account, which a processor overload may cause, the cost of a processor is usually negligible. Moreover, while industrial production cost in general increase with time, the cost of computer hardware decreases. Hence, processor utilisation is not a suitable design criterion for embedded real time systems. Lower processor utilisation is thus the small price to be paid for the simplicity and the other advantageous properties of the scheduling method presented here, which yields high reliability and predictability of system behaviour.

4.2.3   Non-pre-emptive Deadline Scheduling

When the running task may not be pre-empted at all, a newly arrived task with an earlier deadline has to wait until the running task terminates. Since the length of the non-pre-emptive region in a non-pre-emptive task equals to the task's entire execution time, the following **Corollary** of **Theorem 1** states sufficient conditions for feasibly scheduling non-pre-emptive tasks.

Corollary: *If at time t a task joins the ready task set $\mathcal{F}(t)$, which is scheduled according to Algorithm 1, and if the task's deadline is earlier*

*than the one of the executing task $T_j, j \geq 2$, with the ready task set being
indexed according to increasing deadlines, then all tasks in $\mathcal{F}(t)$ will meet
their deadlines if the inequalities*

$$a_i(t) \geq l_j(t) \cdot \sum_{k=1}^{j-1} \delta_{ik} + \sum_{k=1}^{i} l_k(t), i = 1, ..., n = |\mathcal{F}(t)|, \qquad (4.12)$$

*hold. When the deadline of the newly-arrived task is not earlier than
that of the executing task, Inequality (4.1) applies to determine feasible
executability.*

4.2.4 Avoiding Context-Switches Without Violation of Feasibility

In our discussions, we have so far neglected the overhead costs due
to context switching. We shall demonstrate how some of the context
switches can be avoided, and how the cost of the remaining switches can
be taken into account.

Let us assume that the time required to prepare a task's execution
and to load its initial context into the processor registers as well as to
orderly remove the task from the processor after the task has terminated
normally is already included in the maximum execution time specified
for the task. This assumption is realistic, since these context changes
have to be carried out under any circumstances and are not caused by
pre-emptions. Thus, we only have to account for the time required for
a pre-emptive switch. For simplicity of presentation and without loss
of generality, we further assume that this time is the same for all tasks,
and denote it by u, and that to either save or restore a task takes $u/2$.

Again, let the ready task set $\mathcal{F}(t) \subset T$ at time $t \geq 0$ be joined by
new ready tasks. Assume further that $\mathcal{F}(t)$ is always properly indexed
according to increasing deadlines. We now have to distinguish between
the following two cases:

- The deadline(s) of the new task(s) is (are) not earlier than the one
  of the running task. Hence, the simple test of (4.1) applies.

- At least one new task has an earlier deadline than the running
  task $T_j, j \geq 2$. Check the laxities of the tasks $T_i, i = 1, ..., j -$

1, to determine whether the corresponding pre-emption and its associated context-switch can be avoided:

- If the inequalities

$$s_i(t) \geq l_j(t) + \sum_{k=1}^{i-1} l_k(t), i = 1, ..., j - 1 \qquad (4.13)$$

  hold, then the processing of $T_i, i = 1, ..., j - 1$ may be postponed until the termination of T_j and condition (4.12) applies for the check of feasible executability of the ready task set.

- Otherwise, T_j really must be pre-empted and the context-switching time must be accounted for.

The following re-modified form of the earliest-deadline-first task scheduling algorithm not only takes resource constraints into account but also avoids superfluous pre-emptions.

Algorithm 2: *Always assign the ready task with the earliest deadline to the processor unless new tasks arrive, with earlier deadlines than the deadline of the currently running task. If the laxities of the new tasks fulfill the Inequalities (4.13), then continue executing the running task. Otherwise, pre-empt the task as soon as its critical regions permit, and allocate the processor to the task with the earliest deadline.*

Let us examine what occurs when a pre-emption is required. In the course of this we assume, that saving the status of a task as well as restoring it both take the time $u/2$. Extending the inequality (4.7) to account for the context-switch, we obtain the following sufficient condition for the tasks $T_i, i = 1, ..., j - 1$ to meet their deadlines:

$$s_i(t) \geq d + u/2 + \sum_{k=1}^{i-1} l_k(t) \iff a_i(t) \geq d + u/2 + \sum_{k=1}^{i} l_k(t), i = 1, ..., j - 1$$
$$(4.14)$$

Note, that only the status-saving part of the context-switch needs to be considered here, since l_1 already contains the start-up time of T_1. The task T_j, which is pre-empted immediately or as soon as it completes a non-pre-emptable phase, can only observe its deadline provided that

$$a_j(t) \geq u + \sum_{k=1}^{j} l_k(t) \qquad (4.15)$$

holds. In (4.15), the time required to restore the context of T_j after the final termination of T_{j-1} has to be accounted for. Similarly, the total context-switching time u now appears also in the executability condition for all $T_i, i \geq j$. Among these, there are possibly tasks that have been already partially processed and then pre-empted. Let us assume that the residual execution times $l_i, i > j$, of these tasks have each been increased by the amount $u/2$ in the course of their pre-emptions. Combining all the inequalities once again into one set, we have thus established

Theorem 2: *If at time t a task joins the ready task set $\mathcal{F}(t)$, which is scheduled according to Algorithm 2, and if the task T_1 is to pre-empt the task $T_j, j \geq 2$, running at time t, where the ready task set is indexed according to increasing deadlines, then all elements of $\mathcal{F}(t)$ will meet their deadlines if the inequalities*

$$a_i(t) \geq d \cdot \sum_{k=1}^{j-1} \delta_{ik} + \frac{u}{2} \cdot (1 + \sum_{k=j}^{n} \delta_{ik}) + \sum_{k=1}^{i} l_k(t), i = 1, ..., n = |\mathcal{F}(t)|, \quad (4.16)$$

are fulfilled, wherein the quantity d is selected as in Theorem 1. If the running task is not pre-empted, the inequalities (4.12) are sufficient to determine feasible executability.

4.3 The Layered Structure of Real Time Operating Systems

In this Section we want to compare the concept of the co-processor as outlined in the first Section of this Chapter with the general structure of a process control computer operating system as described in [21]. Typical components of the latter are interrupt handling, task management, communication, and synchronisation, as well as time administration, input/output routines, and an operator interface. One distinguishes between the nucleus and the shell of a supervisor, as consisting of operating system processes of the first and second kind, respectively. Processes of the second kind are handled in the same way as user tasks, i.e. under the control of the task management, whereas the former are activated by interrupts.

The co-processor introduced here is dedicated to the execution of the processes of the first kind. Hence, the co-processor is home to event and time management, as well as to task management, communication and synchronisation. In certain application areas it is necessary to perform some user event reactions with the same speed as processes of the first kind. These reactions could then be implemented in the unit's secondary layer in microprogrammed form. Since there is no intrinsic difference between user and system processes of the second kind in real time environments, the functions of the supervisor shell, such as data exchange with peripherals and file management, are provided in the form of tasks or subroutines running on the general processor(s). Thus, the approach proposed here constitutes a *physical* implementation of the layered model for real time operating systems, involving a clear, physical separation between operating system nucleus on one side and operating system shell and application software on the other.

Compared to conventional processor structures, this separation yields a number of improvements. By providing a special device for the handling of all events, unnecessary context-switches are prevented and the normal program flow is only interrupted when required by the scheduling algorithm. Moreover, event-driven tasks are processed not only with respect to their deadlines, but also in a way that disturbs other active tasks as little as possible. Specifically, the tasks are mostly executed in a sequential manner, thus reducing the number of occasions when tasks' readiness is due to deadlock prevention measures. Besides being reduced, the operating system overhead becomes predictable, and an upper bound, independent of the actual workload, can be guaranteed for the time required to react to events. In general, the transfer of kernel functions to specialised hardware contributes to enhancing reliability and efficiency essential in real time applications.

4.4   Outline of the Architecture

With a holistic view we have investigated in the preceding Sections how the hardware of real time computers should be structured. Single processor systems co-operating with devices specialised in carrying through operating system kernels have turned out to be most appropriate. Hence, the concept represents an orthogonal extension [38] of the classical von Neumann architecture, which is predominantly employed for process control applications. The concept can be further described as that of outboard migration of operating system support functions, to be carried out reliably, efficiently, and inconspicuously, into specialised hardware and firmware structures. Such a migration of functions is feasible, as has been shown in [175], since it leaves invariant the execution sequence of a task set imposed by a given synchronisation scheme.

It is the purpose of this Section to outline the structure and the functions of such a co-processor. After compiling the services to be provided by the unit, they are assigned to three different reaction layers. These layers vary with regard to implementation, speed, and complexity. The working methods of the three functional layers are subsequently sketched. The detailed description of the unit's hardware modules and of the algorithms employed is deferred to the following Chapter.

The asymmetric multiprocessor architecture, which we are introducing, can be employed as either a stand-alone device or a node in a distributed system. Each node consists of one co-processor and of one or more general task processors. It is assumed that the latter cannot be interchanged, because process control computers are usually connected to a specific part of a technical process (an external environment). Hence, the functions of the general processors are determined by their respective subprocesses and cannot be migrated. Thus, the tasks on each general processor can be scheduled independently of the tasks on other general processors. The data transmission lines to and from all input/output devices in the system are connected to the task (i.e., general) processors, whereas all interrupt lines are wired to the co-processor.

Real time data processing systems are expected to recognise and to react to occurring events as soon as possible, or even, in the ideal case, instantaneously. In conventional hardware, prompt recognition and reaction are accomplished by interrupting the running task, determining the source of the event, and switching to an appropriate interrupt handling task. The running task is thus pre-empted, even though the task is most likely independent of the interrupt. Furthermore, the interrupt handling task will not necessarily be executed before the pre-empted one, once the interrupt has been identified and acknowledged. Owing to this inherent independence, the possibility to apply parallel processing is given here. In order to preserve data integrity, in the conventional architecture tasks may prohibit their interruptibility during the execution of critical regions. Hence, there is a considerable delay between the occurrence of an event and its recognition, and an upper bound for it cannot be guaranteed. This situation is further impaired, when several events occur (almost) simultaneously, thus resulting in both thrashed pre-emptions of their corresponding handler tasks and in postponement of some of the lower priority reactions.

To address the problems we have just presented, our co-processor should provide a separate, independently working event recognition mechanism capable of commencing a primary reaction to an event within a predefined, guaranteed and short time frame. To achieve this capability, the co-processor is structured into three layers, whose functions are compiled in Table 4.1. In short, the co-processor unit executes the kernel of an operating system developed according to the needs of the extended real time programming language PEARL, presented in Chapter 2.

The unit's basic layer comprises hardware elements required to fulfill the demands for accuracy, predictability, and speed. All time-dependent features rely on an accurate real time clock. In order to keep the quantisation error and the number of time events to be processed as low as possible, a signal is only raised when a time instant is reached for which a certain action is scheduled. To generate this signal, a register is compared with the actual state of the clock. Additional hardware connected to the clock enables the accurate timing of certain operations, and the continuous updating of running tasks' accumulated execution times as well as of their residual times, i.e. the processor times still needed by the tasks before they complete normally. In the software validation phase, external entities entering a program execution need to be simulated. Beside test data (that can be provided through input devices), interrupts have to be generated. The co-processor can be programmed to generate these interrupts, thus enabling the user to obtain exact data on the time behaviour of his software under realistic event-driven conditions. Since the interrupt generator is only needed during the testing and validation phase, it can be designed as a removable hardware extension. Likewise for verification purposes, as well as for the tracking of routine operation malfunctions, the hardware layer of the co-processor houses an elaborate

1. Hardware layer
Accurate real time management based on a high resolution clock
Exact timing of operations (optional)
Separate programmable interrupt generator for software simulation
Event representation by storage element, latch for time of
occurrence, and counter of lost arrivals
Synchroniser representation
Shared variable representation
2. Primary reaction layer
Recognition of events, i.e., interrupts, signals, time events, status
transfers of synchronisers, and value changes of shared variables
Commencement of secondary reactions
Recording of events for error tracking
Management of time schedules and critical instants
3. Secondary reaction layer
Deadline-driven processor scheduling with overload handling
Task oriented hierarchical storage management
Execution of (secondary) event reactions, esp. tasking operations
Synchroniser management
Shared variable management
Acceptance of requests
Initiation of processor activities

Table 4.1: Function Assignment in the Co-processor.

hardware module for each detectable event. Each module consists of a single bit latch to flag the signal, another latch to store the time of the signal occurrence, and a counter to record the number of signal arrivals after the last signal service. The hardware layer of the co-processor also provides dedicated storage space for the implementation of synchronisers and shared variables. Since synchroniser releases and shared variable value changes are handleable events, each such storage unit is connected to an appropriate event module.

The second layer of the co-processor provides primary reactions to relevant events, namely, interrupts from external sources and from the clock comparator, signals, and synchroniser and shared variable state transfers. In order to guarantee an upper bound for each reaction time, the recognition of these events is carried through by continuous cyclic interrogation (polling) of the corresponding storage elements. This method is similar to the one employed by Programmable Logic Controllers (PLC), and was already used in clock-synchronous real time programming [108, 123] to enable timely recognition of external events. Since the recognition time needs to be kept short, the cyclic interrogation has to be carried through with a high frequency. This implies that the complexity of the functions performed by the primary reaction layer needs to be kept low. In the course of the polling, the arrival time latches and counters are interrogated and the data read are saved for future reference. Then, the entire module is reset. A time signal requires more service than other events do. Specifically, time schedules need to be handled by calculating next critical instants and by checking if they have been completely processed. The earliest next critical instant is loaded into the clock's comparison register. Upon the completion of each polling cycle, the secondary reaction layer (to be presented shortly in this Section) of the co-processor is informed of the reactions the layer now needs to execute. The data passed specify the set of schedules actually being fulfilled.

The primary reaction layer does not handle events completely. Rather, the layer is responsible only for fast event recognition and operations related closely to event recognition, and for notifying the secondary reaction layer of the reactions due. Event reactions are not initiated immediately, because each reaction task needs to be submitted to a feasible processor assignment scheme. The primary reaction layer is but moderately complex in organisation, and does not need to be programmable. Thus, the layer can be realised as a rather simple, fully microprogrammed device, with a guaranteed high operation speed. The separation of the operating system kernel functions into a set of simple primary ones, requiring fast reaction, and another set of more complex secondary ones, corresponds to the layer structure of a nucleus as discussed in [21]. Consequently, the two sets of functions are assigned to a fast and simple primary reaction processor and to a more complex secondary reaction processor, respectively.

When a fulfilled schedule is due to be processed, the handling is done in the third and highest co-processor layer — the secondary reaction layer. Here, the associated tasks and other operations are determined, and the subsequent internal operating system event reactions, such as tasking operations, are executed. In the course of task activations and continuations, the deadline-driven scheduling algorithm is called to determine whether the new ready task set can be processed within its critical timing constraints, and to define processor allocations. Should an overload be detected, non-essential tasks are terminated and overload handling ones are activated, as presented in Chapter 2. The task-oriented hierarchical storage administration scheme, as also described there, is carried through as well. Furthermore, the secondary layer of the co-processor manages synchronisers and shared variables. Here, synchronisation requests that cannot be granted immediately are recorded, and the resumption schedules of suspended tasks are handled. Whenever a new value has been written into a shared variable, the secondary layer checks whether the associated relational condition has been fulfilled, initiating the associated operations if so. Finally, the secondary layer processes all communications with the other system components except event recognitions. Parameters describing requests are accepted and inserted into the corresponding internal data structures. As a result of executing requested operations, processor activities may be terminated and others activated.

There are a number of ways in which a general processor and the co-processor may communicate with each other and internally. To prevent excessive overhead, associated with writer/reader synchronisations, it appears most feasible to send operation parameters via first-in-first-out memories from the general processor(s) and from the primary layer to

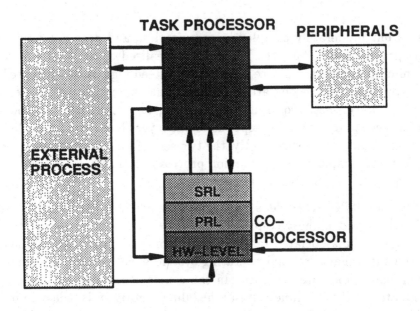

Figure 4.4: General configuration and interconnections

the secondary layer. The data sent from the primary layer need to be processed within a guaranteed amount of time. To store system and internal data (such as the task control blocks) and shared variables, the co-processor provides a common memory area directly accessible by all system components. The shared objects' integrity is protected by associated synchronisers located in the unit, and the access rights are checked by an appropriate hardware mechanism. If the co-processor works in a single processor environment, the common storage could be implemented as a two-port memory or as a block of main storage dedicated to communications. Then the co-processor itself needs a DMA interface. If a multiprocessor (possibly locally distributed) is used, then the common storage should be integrated with the message switching unit. Regardless of the case, the communication with the co-processor must be organised in a way that both achieves high speed, and avoids bottlenecks through simplicity. The diagram given in Figure 4.4 specifies the general set-up of the proposed architecture and all connecting lines used to transfer data, control information, and signals.

4.5   Comparison with other Architectures

We shall now compare our architecture to a number of others, all designed with similar aims. The other architectures are Honeywell series
60 level 64 computer, IBM System /38 and SWARD, Bellmac-32, Mesa,
Intel iAPX-432 and iAPX-86/88, Control Data Corporation 6000, 7600,
and Cyber series, Cray-1, Texas Instruments ASC, Symbol processor,
Bell Laboratories' Signaling and Scheduling Processor, and the supplementary processors for operating system functions described in [174, 176]
and in [150]. The architectures can be divided into two groups: those
that provide operating system support as architectural features and
those that employ separate processors to accommodate the operating
system or essential parts thereof.

An early representative of the former group is Honeywell's series 60
level 64 computer [11]. This machine supports the notion of processes
through special instructions and by context-switching when the processor is assigned to a different process. Furthermore, a semaphore mechanism is available for synchronisation purposes. Specialised for data base
applications, the IBM System /38 [159] manages tasks according to priorities, through hardware features and microcode. Communication and
synchronisation among tasks is accomplished through a queueing mechanism.

Two more recent developments, the Bellmac-32 [23] and the Mesa [93]
processors, also exhibit process-oriented architectures. To organise the
synchronisation of concurrent processes and of shared resources, monitors and condition variables are implemented in the latter. The processor
is dispatched to the ready processes according to priorities. The instruction set contains elements for moving the process state blocks among
various queues maintained in the system and associated with monitors,
condition variables, and the ready state. An interrupt mechanism and
process switching support is also found in the Bellmac-32. Furthermore,
this approach provides hardware support for task rendezvous and assists
in exception handling. The scheduling, however, is carried through by
the software layer (i.e., in the operating system).

IBM's SWARD and Intel's iAPX-432 [132] constitute two further examples that support operating system features architecturally. In the

former, these features are process management, synchronisation, communication, storage administration, and dispatching. Process interaction in the form of the Ada language's rendezvous is realised through port objects. In general, however, the architecture is neither oriented towards a certain language nor towards real time applications, as is obvious by the lack of interrupt facilities. The concept of the iAPX-432 resembles that of the SWARD in many respects. However, the former strongly supports Ada language constructs, such as the selective wait. Furthermore, this design integrates several real time features. Objects can be locked and there are indivisible storage access operations. Communication is accomplished through send/receive queues managed according to the first-in-first-out, priority, or deadline policies. Low-level process scheduling is performed by hardware and firmware. Here the deadline algorithm can be employed, too. The timing facility relying on hardware support for delays is not very accurate. Interrupts are indirectly handled using the message mechanism.

As final representatives of this group we consider Intel's iAPX-86/88 systems [76]. They implement the functions of a real time operating system nucleus in hardware and in a separate Operating System Firmware component, which also contains the interrupt logic and simple timing facilities. For synchronisation purposes the mailbox and semaphore mechanisms are provided. The system supports multitasking applications and schedules tasks by priority. The architectures of the two microcomputers have been specifically developed for embedded systems.

We now turn to the second group of architectures, which have taken the approach of migrating operating system functions to separate processors. An early example of such an architecture is Control Data Corporation's 6000 series of computer systems [159]. A very fast central processor unit is supported by ten independent peripheral processor units (PPU's), mainly dedicated to perform I/O operations. One PPU, however, accommodates the operating system and thus controls the entire configuration. The leading idea for the CDC 6000 approach was to optimise CPU utilisation for arithmetic operations in a multiprogramming batch environment. The succeeding models of the 7600 and Cyber series and other descendants, such as the Cray-1 and Texas Instruments' ASC, have comparable architectures [159].

The Symbol computer [132] is controlled by a system supervisor, and provides no support for real time operations. The architecture essentially defines an interrupt-driven master processor that administers queues and pages, and manages a control table.

A transaction-oriented multi-microprocessor architecture is described in [4]. It supports communication and scheduling with hardware. The microprocessor is to be applied as a network node. Operating system functions, such as scheduling, synchronisation, and interprocess communication, are confined in a separate unit, namely the Signaling and Scheduling Processor (SSP). Furthermore, the SSP handles all internal and external communications, dispatching, and resource assignment. All signaling is carried through by using hardware queues. Larger data sets, however, are exchanged via a shared memory. The architecture enhances system performance by allowing its execution units to work without interference.

Special purpose hardware was applied by Roos [150] to implement the Ada rendezvous with its complex semantics, with predictable and uniformly low overhead at a speed at least two orders of magnitudes higher than software solutions generated by current compilers. Roos' rendezvous support processor co-operates with a conventional CPU in a fashion similar to that of a floating point co-processor.

The approach, which appears to match ours the closest, is Tempelmeier's supplementary processor for operating system functions [174, 176]. The processor is intended to increase the performance of real time computers by migrating most functions of the operating system kernel to a separate processor. Immediate interrupt recognition and reaction, however, is still located in the general processor, which mainly performs user tasks and operating system tasks requested directly by user tasks. It has been shown [175, 177], that this architecture yields a considerable improvement of task response times and interrupt reaction times. The improvement has been achieved by providing parallel processors for user tasks and operating system functions, and by reducing to almost zero the time intervals during which external interrupts need to be disabled (to ensure the integrity of the operating system's data structures). The architecture, which implements the layer model for real time operating systems [21], achieves a simple operating system structure by clearly separating the system from user tasks.

A number of real time systems employ outboard migration to support special application-oriented features, whereas the operating system remains in a classical von Neumann CPU. These so-called real time supersystems aim to achieve high computational performance. Distributed architectures have been considered [10, 172] in order to cope with the computation requirements of such computation-intensive applications as signal and image processing in embedded and satellite- or missile-borne systems. These systems are tailored to yield results within reasonable time-limits under the conditions imposed by the locations of deployment. Hence, the architecture of general purpose process control computers, which support the observation of strict deadlines, is not the scope of this development.

Similarly, special devices, such as that presented in [139], have been built for carrying through certain time-critical algorithms. By implementing these algorithms in firmware, significant speed increases have been achieved. These units are attached as front-end processors to conventional mini- or microcomputers, which are too slow to cope with the desired functions by themselves.

The objective of the Omega/CReStA design [190] is to provide a RISC architecture suitable for real time applications. The design addresses large register set conflicts (a characteristic consideration in RISC architectures), and provides short context-switching times, as required for real time operating mode.

Previous designs have taken a number of approaches to support operating system concepts architecturally. Only a subset of conventional real time features has been migrated, however. No attempt has been made to provide hardware and firmware facilities for the implementation of typical hard real time support features that cannot be realised otherwise. Although architectures have been developed to support some language constructs, such as those of Ada, there has never been an effort to build a complete system according to the requirements of both a process-control language suited for the application engineer and of a corresponding operating system. We now continue with our attempt to define such a system.

4.6   Task-Oriented and Predictable Storage Management

Deadline-driven scheduling orders the elements of ready task sets according to increasing deadlines. Since the tasks are processed in this sequence, it also implies an ordering of the corresponding storage accesses to program code and data by increasing forward distance. This observation suggests that one should base a hierarchical storage administration scheme on task objects, as paging elements. Compared with customary paging schemes, this approach better reflects the software structure, because the task is the basic unit of program flow (and related data) in real time environments. In typical process control applications, storage demands of tasks are relatively small. Without loss of generality, storage demand size can be bounded. Auxiliary tasks may be defined to cope with the rare cases of larger storage needs. To ensure fast and predictable reaction times and short execution times of tasks, it is appropriate to load the entire task segment, comprising code and data, into main storage each time it is needed. While parts of the available storage will temporarily remain unused, this scheme is justified by both the predictability and speed it offers and the still dropping memory prices.

Specifically, the task-oriented hierarchical storage administration proceeds as follows. Main storage is divided into an area for the supervisor, or only resident parts thereof, for shared data structures not subject to paging, and into $K \geq 2$ page frames. The frame size corresponds to the maximum storage allowance for a task. Since the identity of the used frames is irrelevant when changing pages, the assignment problem does not arise.

Let $R_t = \{T_1, ..., T_{n_t}\}$ be the list of tasks ready for execution at a time t. The set has been ordered according to increasing deadlines by the deadline-driven scheduling algorithm. Then, loading the subset $B = \{T_i \mid i = 1, ..., min(K, n_t)\}$ of R_t into main storage represents the solution of the moving-in problem. When a storage-resident task leaves the ready state, its page frame becomes available. Upon termination the frame is simply released. Otherwise the page needs to be written back to mass storage. We shall see later, that such a page might remain in main storage when a refined algorithm is employed. A free frame is occupied by the first task in the ready list not yet loaded into main storage. In accordance with the scheduling algorithm, the task T_1 is always running. Should a task arrive with its deadline earlier than at least one deadline in B, and if the cardinality of B before the arrival of the new element was K, then the last task in B is removed. Since by construction of B the last task possesses the longest forward access distance of all tasks in B, this replacement algorithm is optimal. Only in rare cases does the processor have to wait for the completion of a page replacement process, because typically there are tasks with tighter deadlines to be executed first. The initial loading and replacement methods are look-ahead algorithms, and represent application-oriented implementations of working sets, given in the form of tasks.

Even when $K = 2$, the resulting performance may already be quite reasonable, since T_1 is executed essentially without interruptions, according to earliest-deadline-first scheduling. During its processing time the next task T_2 could be paged in. Ideally, the code of T_2 should be available upon completion of T_1. The actual choice of K depends on several factors:

- the number of I/O channels available for paging,
- the transfer time,
- the average execution time of tasks, and
- the frequency of suspension of the running task due to I/O and synchronisation, when other tasks may be processed while the task is suspended,

For any given hardware configuration and any task system, an appropriate value for the parameter K can be determined by repeated application of schedulability analysis and simulation, aimed at minimising page transfer waiting times.

In the above, only ready tasks are taken into account. However, process control systems frequently have available the information when inactive tasks will be (re-)activated. This information can be utilised in a more sophisticated look-ahead algorithm. Should an activated or resumed task supersede other ready ones, the elements of the subset B need to be changed. Hence, storage is assigned to the first K tasks in a list ordered with regard to ascending deadlines, where the tasks in consideration consist of

- ready tasks,
- buffered task activations [3], and
- the next scheduled activations and continuations of tasks.

In the two former cases, the deadlines are known. For cyclically scheduled (re-)activations, the deadlines can be calculated from the next critical instants specified by the schedules and the relative time conditions assigned to the pertaining tasks. To enable a similar determination of future task (re-)activations also for interrupt driven schedules, the user must supply an average occurrence frequency for each interrupt. We now present a refined look-ahead algorithm for task-oriented hierarchical storage management. We commence by describing the data structures involved.

Let $tcb[i]$ be the task control block of a task, where there are n tasks in the application, and $i = 1, ..., n$. The tcb entries relevant to hierarchical storage management are as follows. The Boolean variable *res* indicates whether a task is permanently held in main storage (as requested by the programmer). The integer *page* indicates the secondary storage page (block) number of the task's segment. If the segment is in main storage, the number of the page frame used is stored in another integer *fra*. If the segment is not in main storage, *fra* contains -1. Furthermore, in any *tcb* there are three items of type **clock**: *tcond*, *tact*, and *tcont*. The parameter *tcond* contains the task's deadline when the task is ready. The two others give the task's time conditions relative to the next — not yet buffered — activation, and to the forthcoming continuation if the task is suspended, respectively. Table 4.2 describes under what circumstances and how the three variables are updated.

In the Table, t stands for the current time and tr for the relative response time contained in the corresponding activation or continuation statement, respectively. Finally, in the case of interrupt-driven

---

[3]Buffering of task activations is defined in the semantics of PEARL. If a task is activated when an earlier activation has not yet been fully processed, the later activation is buffered until the earlier activation completes. There is an upper limit of the number of activations, which may be buffered for a single task.

Event	Assignments
Initial state	$tcond:=tact:=tcont:=\infty$
Activation buffering	buffer $t+tr$ as $tb[*]$
Transfer to ready state	$tcond:=$ first buffered $tb[*]$
Task termination	$tcond:=$ first buffered $tb[*]$ or ∞
Annihilation of schedules	$tact:=tcont:=\infty$
Task suspension	$tcond:=\infty$
Task continuation	$tcond:=t+tr$, $tcont:=\infty$
Setting up and fulfillment of activation schedules:	
– start of cyclic schedule	$tact:=$ start time $+$ tr
– prolongation of cyc. sch.	$tact:=t +$ interval $+$ tr
– exhaustion of cyc. sch.	$tact:=\infty$
– interrupt driven schedule	$tact:=t + int +$ delay $+$ tr
Setting up and fulfillment of continuation schedules:	
– temporal schedule	$tcont:=$ start time $+$ tr
– interrupt driven schedule	$tcont:=t + int +$ delay $+$ tr

Table 4.2: Updating of the Various Task Deadlines.

schedules, *int* represents the average time interval between the interrupt occurrences, calculated as

$$[\sum_i (mean\ time\ between\ occurrences\ of\ i^{th}\ interrupt)^{-1}]^{-1}$$

where the summation includes the mean times of all relevant interrupts, mentioned in a schedule. Upon setting up such a schedule, only $\frac{1}{2} \cdot int$ is to be entered into the corresponding expressions.

Given the data structures, the hierarchical storage management scheme operates according to the following procedure.

vsadmin: **procedure** (*foc* (1:*k*) **bit**);

```
/*
    parameter description:
      k: # pageframes
      foc(1:k): page frame is occupied (initial '0'b)
    variables description:
      r: # resident blocks
      l: ready task with the next deadline
      a: tcb(l).tcond
      z: deadline task tcb(i)
      fi(i): array of tcb indices
      fz(i): deadline of task tcb(i)
*/
```

i,j,l,r,s **fixed**;
fi (1:*n*) **fixed**;
a, z **clock**;
fz (1:*n*) **clock**;

l:=*r*:=*s*:=0; *a*:=*infinity*;
for *i* **from** 1 **by** 1 **to** *n* **do**
  if *tcb*(*i*).*res*
  then
    r:=*r*+1
  else

```
    if tcb(i).tcond lt a
    then
        a:=tcb(i).tcond;  l:=i;
    fin;
    z:=min(tcb(i).tcond,tcb(i).tact,tcb(i).tcont);
    j:=s;  s:=s+1;
    while j gt 0 and z lt fz(j) do
        fi(j+1):=fi(j);  fz(j+1):=fz(j);  j:=j-1;
    end;
    fi(j+1):=i;  fz(j+1):=z;
  fin;
end;


j:=min(s,k-r);  s:=s+1;  r:=1;
if l gt 0 and j lt s
then
    /* the ready task with the next deadline is joined
        with the subset of ready tasks loaded in memory */
    i:=1;  while i lt j and fi(i) ne l do i:=i+1 end;
    if i ge j then fi(j):=l fin;
fin;
for i from 1 by 1 to j do
    if tcb(fi(i)).fra=-1
    then
        while r le k and foc(r) do r:=r+1 end;
        if r le k then
            foc(r):='1'b;
            tcb(fi(i)).fra:=r
        else
            s:=s-1;
            while tcb(fi(s)).fra=-1 do s:=s-1 end;
            /* write task segment back to mass storage */
            save(tcb(fi(s)).fra,tcb(fi(s)).page);
            tcb(fi(i)).fra:=tcb(fi(s)).fra;
            tcb(fi(s)).fra:=-1
        fin;
        /* load task segment from mass storage into page frame */
```

$$load(tcb(fi(i)).fra,tcb(fi(i)).page);$$
   fin;
end;

Certain features of high level process control programming languages, such as PEARL, can be used to provide directives for the storage management. System data and shared objects with **global** scope should be placed together with the supervisor, in the non-paged storage area. The task attribute **resident** triggers the setting of the variable *res* in the corresponding *tcb*. If this attribute is available in a language, the compiler must ensure that the number of simultaneously resident tasks will not exceed a certain fraction of K. The **module** concept can be used in conjunction with permanent residency, to keep shared variables, procedures and frequently-used small tasks in one page. The only feature of the hierarchical storage administration scheme proposed here, that is not supported by a construct in any available high level language, is the indication of average occurrence intervals for interrupts. However, this feature, similar to Real-Time Euclid's **frame** construct, can be easily supported by augmenting the interrupt declaration syntax with the optional attribute **interval**, which was introduced in Section 2.9.10.

4.7 Direct Memory Access Without Cycle Stealing

Peripheral devices engaged in direct memory access (DMA) indirectly and unpredictably slow down other activities in the system by stealing memory cycles from the CPU. Thus, the presence of direct memory access devices makes schedulability analysis very difficult if at all feasible, forcing the user to rely on at best overly coarse (sometimes, by orders of magnitude) run-time task bound estimations. More specifically, predicting the slow-down effect of DMA operations on instruction execution is quite different from predicting the effect of their associated secondary storage access delays. When an instruction is delayed by a secondary storage operation, then the task actually slowed down or blocked is the one embodying the instruction. When DMA cycle stealing occurs, however, the running tasks are delayed, which are independent from the task responsible for the DMA — the latter task itself is already suspended. On the other hand, DMA is a valuable mechanism for speeding up sequential I/O transfers of large data blocks and for relieving the processor from routine work and is, thus, an indispensable feature. Therefore, it turns out to be necessary to search for DMA methods that do not employ memory cycle stealing.

Besides the above mentioned ones, there are still further reasons for trying to prevent cycle stealing operations. Especially important for process control applications are fast system reactions to randomly occurring external events. Generally, these events pre-empt normal program flow, but not the active DMA operations. Thus, reaction times cannot be guaranteed and it is almost impossible to predict the system behaviour.

We shall commence the treatment of DMA methods that do not employ cycle stealing in the following section with the review of the Fairchild F8 microprocessor's [61] DMA facility. Since the facility grants memory accesses to peripheral devices only during the instruction execution phases without bus activities, in an F8 system DMA is fully transparent to the processor.

Subsequently, DMA procedures will be introduced which require that the main storage consists of several independent modules. While the processor reads its instructions from one of such modules and exchanges data with other ones, peripheral devices may communicate with further storage modules, temporarily not accessed by the CPU. The data transfers take place via parallel busses or via parts of a single bus that can be subdivided dynamically, with the help of bus transceivers.

Finally, we shall consider contemporary dynamic random access memories. This last study will reveal the architectural similarity of DMA and memory refreshing operations. In the course of every memory cycle, an entire row of an IC's internal storage matrix is made available in its sense amplifiers, although just a single bit is brought to the output or altered in the matrix, respectively. Since DMA essentially takes place in conjunction with block transfers, this observation suggests to provide shift registers within DRAM ICs capable of holding an entire row's data. With a single memory cycle resembling a refresh cycle, these shift registers can be either loaded or read out. The data transfer to peripheral devices is carried through using an independent, second memory port. The latter only requires a few additional IC pins, because data are exchanged serially via this port. The described DMA procedure is fully transparent, for the CPU can access the main storage at any time through the other port.

To the end of meeting the needs of both predictable program execution and exchanging large blocks of data with peripheral units, we introduce the following open question in hardware research: How can new mass storage devices and high speed transmission facilities (such as optical fibres) be utilised in order to provide burst transfers between main and peripheral storage, during individual instruction executions?

4.7.1 Synchronous Direct Memory Access

A number of older and relatively simple microprocessor systems are equipped with a synchronous bus, i.e., the operation of the entire system is controlled by and synchronised with a single master clock. Hence, memory may only be accessed at certain points in time during each machine cycle. At these instances, however, storage access requests of peripheral DMA devices can supersede the ones of the processor, unless the DMA controller has to observe appropriate restrictions. One example of a system with such restrictions the Fairchild's F8 microcomputer [61]. Here the CPU indicates those phases of the machine cycles which it does not need for memory accesses. Specifically, in the course of every instruction execution, the bus is always available immediately after fetching an instruction word while decoding it and commencing its elaboration. Moreover, there are further idle time periods contained in various instruction cycles. These slots, when the bus is not occupied, are then either utilised by the system's dynamic memory interface to perform refresh cycles, or are granted to the DMA controller. Since memory refresh takes higher priority than DMA operations, and since the execution times of individual machine instructions differ, the slots available for DMA are not uniformly distributed. This non-uniform distribution raises problems for certain peripherals, such as disks or tapes, that require constant data transmission rates for mechanical reasons. To alleviate the problems, first-in-first-out buffer memories are necessary in the corresponding control units. Apart from this shortcoming, the F8 microcomputer exhibits a DMA facility fully transparent to the CPU and, thus, causing no unpredictable degradation of system performance.

4.7.2 Dynamic Bus Subdivision

The method of avoiding cycle stealing when performing DMA operations, which we shall discuss in this Section, may also be applied in systems possessing an asynchronous bus. It requires as a precondition, that the main storage is partitioned into a number of distinct modules with separate bus interfaces. Then the idea to carry through DMA transfers is the following. Peripheral devices directly communicate with one memory module, respectively, over a certain part of the bus, that is temporarily disconnected from another bus section through which the processor addresses program and data storage modules. To illustrate this procedure we consider Figure 4.5 displaying a quite simple set-up. The data transmission on the system's single bus is managed by a bus controller. On request of the CPU, the latter also sets the states of the various bus transceivers, which partition the bus into several simultaneously usable sections. Since the bus is linear, while a DMA operation is in progress, the processor may not have access to all storage modules which do not take part in the transfer. Hence, this architecture considerably reduces but not removes entirely the requirement for I/O in the cycle stealing mode. The reduction effect is application-specific and can be improved by a suitable arrangement of the different components along the bus and, possibly, also by taking the bus topology into account during software development. In the same way as transfers with peripheral units, data may be exchanged between two memory modules in parallel to CPU operation.

The architecture just presented does not accommodate the frequently-applied technique of double-buffering (also known as buffer-switching). In double-buffering, while the data contained in one of the buffers are being processed by the CPU, those of the other one may be being transmitted to or from an external device. The linear bus we have presented disallows this scheme. To overcome this limitation, we employ a cyclic, subdivisible bus instead, as shown in Figure 4.6. Naturally, for

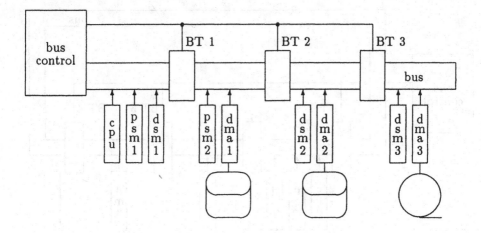

Figure 4.5: Dynamically subdivisible linear bus

electrical reasons, there must be at least one closed bus transceiver in this configuration at any time. The figure gives a simple example with a single peripheral using DMA. Provided that the bus transceivers are appropriately programmed, the CPU can always access its program and data storage in one buffer without losing cycles, also when the other buffer is engaged in a DMA operation.

It is clear that bus contention conflicts may arise when non-adjacent modules need to exchange data. To resolve most such conflicts, the architecture may be extended to provide several parallel busses. The improvement is costly, for both additional bus lines, multiple bus interfaces of each module and additional control units need to be implemented. On the other hand, in co-operation with the dynamical bus subdivision feature a large number of partial busses may be dynamically established allowing the same number of simultaneous transfers with maximum speed and without contention.

The extra hardware requirements imposed by multiple busses may be substantially relaxed by renouncing address busses. Then only store operations of the CPU will need more time, while no time is lost in more frequent read operations of the CPU (since addresses and data have to be transmitted sequentially regardless of the number of busses available). All other forms of internal data transfer, especially to or from

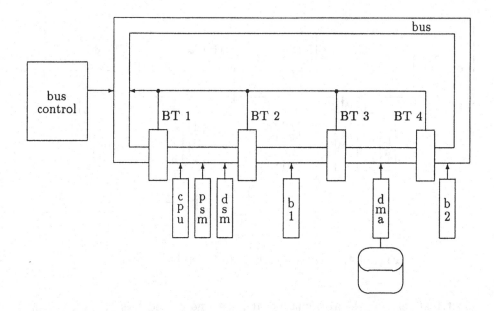

Figure 4.6: Dynamically subdivisible cyclic bus

DMA devices, are generally of sequential nature as well. Hence, address transmissions become superfluous if the storage modules are equipped with a few rudimentary address generation functions and support block moves. These functions, viz., receiving start addresses, block lengths, and further parameters, as well as updating of address and block counts, are therefore to be migrated from the DMA controllers to the memory modules. Then the former only have to initiate data transfers.

Memory modularisation as discussed here, however, contrasts the current tendency towards integration. According to the present state-of-the-art, the entire main storage of a computer can be realised on a single printed circuit board or even on a single chip, i.e., in a single module with a single bus interface. Soon the ultimate objective of this development will be reached, viz., the integration within a single chip of a complete address space together with a processor. Hence, the methods for preventing cycle stealing as described in the previous and following Sections have more potential for the future, than the methods discussed in this Section.

4.7.3 Integration of a DMA Facility into Dynamic RAM Chips

In this Section we shall propose extensions of dynamic random access memory chips, to integrate a second, serial port dedicated to DMA operations. Before the extensions can be outlined, let us first review some facts about contemporary dynamic random access memory (DRAM) design.

DRAM storage cells are arranged in the form of a matrix. To read or write a cell, the entire corresponding row is first read destructively into sense amplifiers, where the its contents may be altered, and then the row is written back into the matrix. Therefore, row addresses are required earlier than column addresses, thus suggesting address multiplexing, which is the current industry standard. Address multiplexing makes it possible to access DRAM in the so-called page-mode treating a matrix row as a page. The row's address is selected once, and then only column addresses are needed to access individual cells within the page. Thus, page-mode access is faster than normal access.

All rows must be periodically refreshed. For instance, NEC's μPD424100 $4 \cdot 10^6$x1 CMOS DRAM chip needs to be refreshed at least once every 16 msec. During a refresh, each row is destructively read, amplified, and written back. How memory refreshing takes place differs from architecture to architecture. Some common possibilities are as follows.

1. All rows are refreshed in a contiguous sequence of memory cycles, i.e., in one burst. Neither the CPU nor any other device can work during the time required for the refresh. An example is DEC's LSI-11 microcomputer, whose microcode has provisions for performing burst refresh.

2. The refresh controller works in cycle stealing mode, similarly to a DMA device, and generates, in equidistant intervals, memory requests with higher priority than those of the CPU to refresh individual rows. This asynchronous refreshing procedure is mainly employed in minicomputers and larger systems, with an asynchronous bus. To resolve bus contention conflicts, a bus arbiter is necessary.

3. The periodical refresh cycles are synchronised with the operation of the CPU by generating the cycles during those time slots, when the processor does not access memory. Generally, these slots occur immediately after an instruction fetching phase, i.e., while the operation code is being decoded. This transparent method is applied primarily in microcomputer systems, such as the already mentioned F8 and in Zilog's Z80 [191]. The Z80 CPU generates the refresh cycles itself, for as long as it executes instructions. This method may cause problems when DMA operations are in progress.

4. Beginning from approximately the time of the generation of chip designs characterised by Mostek's 64Kx1 MK4164, 2Kx8 MK4816, and 32Kx8 MK4856, DRAM chips have integrated refresh address counters. Hence, in these chips, row addresses no longer need to be specified. Immediately after a read cycle, a refresh cycle may be initiated. Since the read operation's data bit is still provided at the output pin, this method is referred to as *hidden refresh.*

Of the different methods, only the synchronous and transparent refreshing procedure (of (3)) appears applicable for realising DMA without cycle stealing. To avoid the DMA contention problems found in the Z80 and other microprocessors, the architecture should provide undisturbed CPU instruction execution and unrestricted access to relevant storage. Combined with hidden refresh, the entire refresh operation may be speeded up by signaling instruction word read cycles to the DRAM chips, which in turn will carry out refresh cycles immediately upon completion of the corresponding read requests.

The page-mode of presently available DRAM ICs is well-suited for fast block transfers. However, page-mode transfers disturb the bus activities of the CPU and, moreover, the necessary specification of sequential column addresses is essentially superfluous. To achieve CPU-transparent DMA, we therefore equip DRAM chips with a second, serially operated port. Its data are provided internally in a shift register with the length of a memory row. Typically, storage matrices are not square but rather have a 4:1 ratio of their side lengths. For practical reasons, the rows and hence the shift register shall have the larger dimension.

Indeed, the periodic refresh operations could be utilised both to load, into the shift register, storage rows being refreshed, and to write the register's contents back into the appropriate row. This, however, is not feasible for predictable real time performance, since the time of the actual transfer is uncertain. Thus, in the case of the aforementioned NEC DRAM chip, there is a worst case delay of 16 msec, before further accesses to the same data are possible.

For the above reasons, the exchange of data between memory rows and the shift register is better carried out under control of two external signals as follows. While the serial port's control line

sercont

is held in the logical true state, a normal refresh cycle is performed specifying the address of the row to be accessed. In accordance with the status of the read/write signal

serwr

the shift register is then either loaded with or copied into the indicated row.

The actual serial memory port has two external connections, namely, the data input/output pin

serd

and the clock input

sercl

The port is presented in Figure 4.7. Initially, i.e., when **sercl** is logically false, the Q-outputs of the two J-K flip-flops I and II, that work in the toggle mode, are both zero. Hence, the tri-state output buffer is switched to the high impedance state, and the **serd** signal is not amplified as well. With the first positive going edge of the clock **sercl**, the Q-output of I turns to the logical state of one, thus causing the

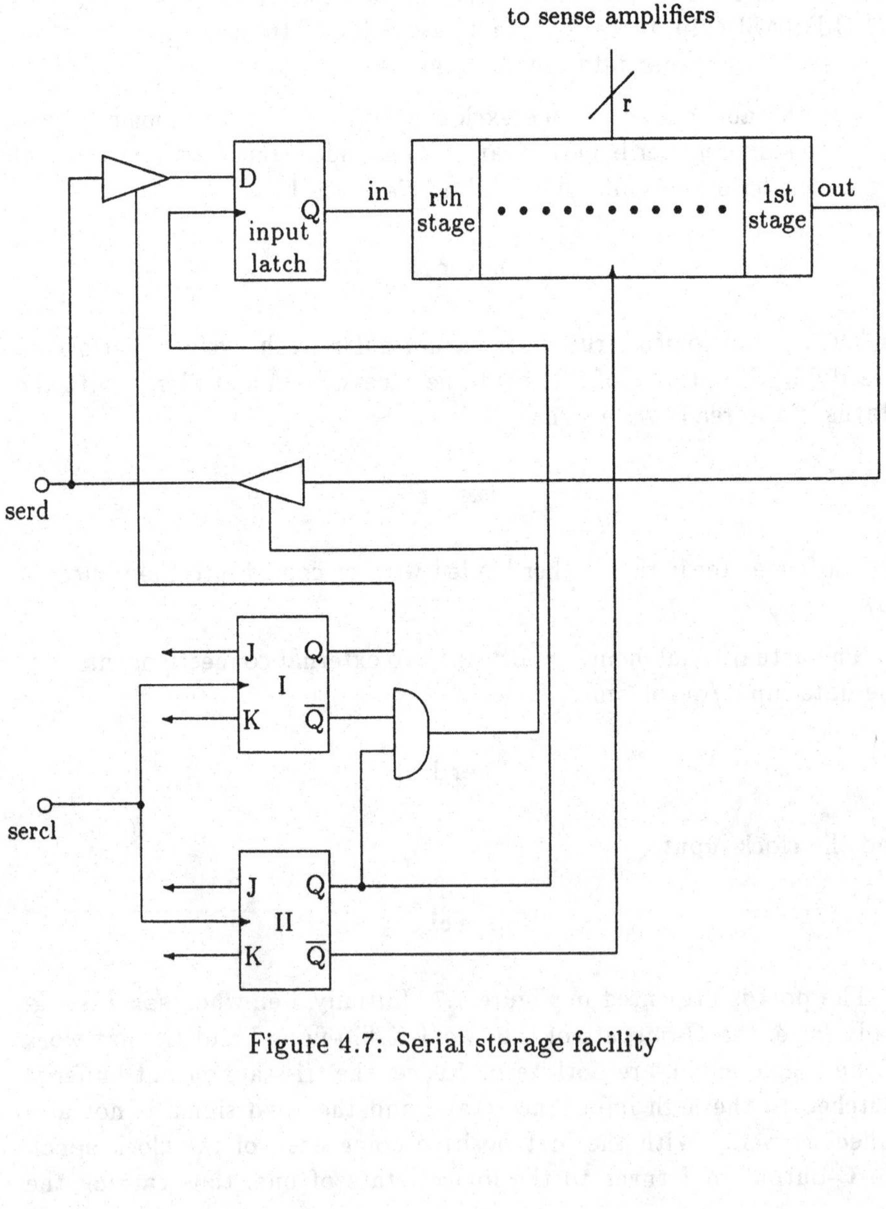

Figure 4.7: Serial storage facility

amplification of the signal **serd** entering the input latch's D-connection. The subsequent falling edge of **sercl** switches on the flip-flop II. This transition of the flip-flop's Q-output triggers the input latch to accept the signal present at the **serd** pin. The next rising edge of **sercl** resets the Q-output of the flip-flop I, thus turning the input buffer off. Simultaneously, the output of the and-gate assumes the value of logical one, making the output of the shift register's first stage available on the line **serd**. Finally, the following negative going edge of **sercl** resets the flip-flop II. Thereby the output buffer is switched off again and the logical zero-to-one transition of the II flip-flop's Q-output shifts the data in the register from the stage i to the stage $i-1$, $i = 2, ..., r$, and from the input latch into the stage r. As is also the case when using the random access ports of memory chips, certain time conditions must be observed to assure data stability when communicating with our serial port. When but a part of a memory row is to be written, our design allows to read and write the shift register within two subsequent cycles of the clock **sercl**. Then, the initial and final sequences of the row remaining unaltered are simply re-read.

We conclude this Section by discussing the application of the serial memory port. The storage chips' serial ports are connected to a second bus, dedicated to DMA operations, that transfers data in blocks. Whereas at any time the CPU bus is under control of the processor and at its disposal, the other one is driven by the DMA controller. Generally, the CPU bus should have the width of the system's word, while the DMA bus should be "byte-wide" to conform to the attached peripheral devices. The number of the latter bus' address lines can also be considerably fewer than that of the CPU bus, because but blocks or pages (as opposed to single words or bytes) need to be addressed. Individual bytes within a page are accessed serially with the help of the clock **sercl**. Thus, even main storage internal block transfers can be performed over the DMA bus, without involvement of the CPU.

Our second, serial memory port is thus used, essentially, to transfer data between main and mass storage within the framework of hierarchical storage management. Thus, it will benefit the architecture to define the sizes of a page, a disk sector, and a memory row in the DRAM ICs to be equal. Here, the former two sizes are measured in bytes, while the row size is measured in bits. According to the serial port's structure, the removal of a page not needed any longer and the loading of another one into the just freed page frame can take place in a single operation, thus resulting in a considerable acceleration. Therefore, memories organised in the form of shift registers are best suited as mass storage devices. In order to utilise the above mentioned direct page exchange mechanism, the external part of the hierarchical storage must be administered chaotically, i.e., a page to be removed is not written back to its original location in the address space, but to the place of the page which is just being loaded. If the address space is selected sufficiently large, all file transfers to disk storage may also be subordinated to the hierarchical storage concept. Consequently, logical disk I/O operations disappear and become page transfers.

4.8   Precisely Timed Peripherals

To keep up with the external process, the acquisition and evaluation of process data, as well as appropriate reactions, must be carried through on time and, due to the nature of the environment, in parallel. Typically, however, and especially when a uniprocessor is used, simultaneous manipulation of parallel processes can be at best approximated. In a macroscopic view, simultaneous execution is only provided if the time constants of the external processes and the corresponding computing times differ sufficiently. Furthermore, it is difficult to guarantee punctuality of a real time system, because the response times depend on the actual workload of the computer, and may differ from one external request to the next. The difficulty of predicting the workload accurately is further exacerbated by the presence of operating system overhead, fluctuating with the workload. Thus, the duration between the arrival of external signals or data, and the output of corresponding control information by the computer, is generally unpredictable at the time a certain control loop program is written.

In control theory it is often assumed that the pure time delay between the measurement of the controlled variable and the resulting control action is negligible. *This assumption is erroneous!* Even a small delay can have a marked destabilising influence on the control loop [125] and can cause the loop to lack robustness with respect to parameter variations or disturbance inputs [56]. It is common practise in digital control to close one or more feedback loops through a computer, which generates the control laws. In order to share its services among several control loops and, generally, among various other tasks, the computer intermittently turns unavailable to handle the requests of an individual control loop immediately. Such irregularities in computer service result in the deterioration of control quality and may even render control systems unstable. It is rather surprising, that no attempt has been made yet to solve this problem by designing a suitable computer architecture, which would be quite natural. Instead, the deficiencies of contemporary computers are obviously regarded as unalterable facts and system theoretical methods are applied (as in [145]) to determine, under which conditions the deterioration of control quality can still be tolerated. Finally, in various multivariable control applications it is necessary to acquire the state variables simultaneously and also to send out the control signals together at one time.

In this Section, we show that the above stated problems can be solved most easily, by endowing real time computers with input/output facilities working fully in parallel and making use of exact time specifications. Thus, even a computer with only a single processor will appear, to the outside world, as a device that provides a dedicated processor for each control loop to be serviced. Considering a process control computer as a black box, our design will fulfill the requirement of simultaneity when the new peripherals are used. In case that also the timeliness condition is met, a process control computer is equivalent to any other physical system which works in parallel, because there is no device that does not show some kind of a delay.

To achieve our objective, the times for every data exchange with the external process are pre-determined. Moreover, the peripheral units need to be equipped with additional hardware to carry through time related functions. Like device addresses, the instants of external data exchanges are part of the control information sent to input/output controllers by the driver software.

The advantage of this design is the predictability it provides. The application programmer selects an appropriate delay, between an input of measurements and the output of the corresponding control information, and then takes this delay into consideration in his program, possibly even compensating for the delay with a suitable algorithm. For the control engineer, a predictable and precisely realised time delay is much more important than high speed of the applied computer. Many methods for measurement and control are based on equidistantly spaced data points. By employing precisely timed peripherals, biased results, caused by random errors in the timing of data transfers, can be prevented.

4.8.1 Required Functions and their Invocation in PEARL

The following features are needed to support precisely timed operations when invoked from a high level real time language, such as PEARL. Firstly, the exact time instants, when the data are actually transmitted between the intermediate storage registers of the computer's peripheral controllers and the external process, need to be specified for program initiated I/O operations. Furthermore, the computer system must adhere to these time specifications, and any deviation from them is to be treated as an exception.

Secondly, for externally triggered input operations, the time instant, when an entered data item was received by the computer's input controller, needs to be made available to the application program in addition to the data item itself. This feature is required, because the application program has no other means of ascertaining the time accurately. An attempt to read the system clock when data are available may result in a highly inaccurate answer, since there is a non-trivial, varying delay between the data available interrupt and the corresponding execution of the input operation.

The language support for the two functions is realised as straightforward extensions of the **basic** type low level transfer statements of PEARL (used to communicate with external peripherals). The two statements, extended by a timing clause (the clock-expression),

> **take** variable **from** source **at** clock-expression;
> **send** expression **to** sink **at** clock-expression;

support precisely timed program initiated I/O. For an externally triggered input operation, the exact time stamp of data arrival is made available to the user task by an alternative **take** statement:

take variable **from** source **received** clock-variable;

4.8.2   Implementation of Hardware Support

Presently available process input/output interfaces are equipped with registers for the intermediate storage of the data to be transmitted, in order to adapt the parallel outside world, i.e. technical processes, to the computers' serial way of operation. When externally initiated inputs arrive, the processors are notified of the availability of data in the storage registers by interrupt signals. The time of data arrival, however, is usually not recorded. Whereas several data items can enter a computer system simultaneously, this feature is not provided on the output side. The reasons for this are the computer's serial operation and the fact that the two data transfers, one between the processor and the device controller, and the other between the device controller and the peripheral, are not uncoupled in time.

In order to implement hardware support for our accurately timed, fully parallel process input/output facility, peripheral interfaces need a few functional extensions. These extensions can easily be implemented with available technology. First, in each input/output attachment, real time must be made available. To avoid high internal cabling expenses, clock counters based on the system's clock frequency are integrated into each controller. The counters are reset and started by the system reset signal. In many cases, it is sufficient to implement such a counter with relatively few bits, and make the counter restart after every overflow.

Once the clock counters are provided, the arrival times of externally triggered data inputs can be latched by the handshake impulses (as depicted in Figure 4.8). Whenever an input event occurs, a processor interrupt is generated, signaling data availability. Provisions are made, in the circuitry, that further handshake impulses have no effect, until this interrupt is serviced. The handshake impulses are, however, counted in the counter HSC, in order to enable the operating system to detect data losses and bottle-necks. In the course of servicing the interrupt, the processor reads out the intermediate storage register, the clock latch,

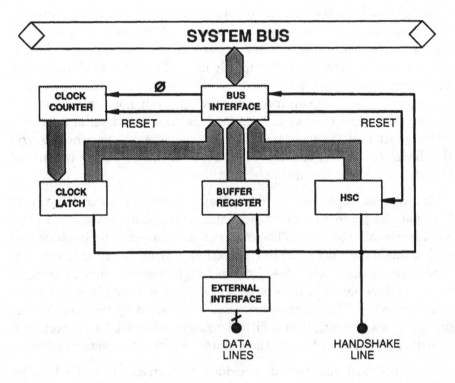

Figure 4.8: An externally-triggered input device with accurate time recording

and the HSC. The HSC is then reset, and both the data item and the time stamp are processed by a corresponding control algorithm.

To handle the other kind of precisely timed input/output operations, namely, internally initiated ones, the peripheral devices need to be further equipped with hold registers for the time instants, and with comparators to link these hold registers and the real time clocks (as shown in Figure 4.9). Upon a data transfer request, the time when the request is to take place is brought into the pertaining unit's hold register. From then on, the unit is marked busy. For an output request, the data item to be transmitted is also specified. Thus, it becomes possible, that several devices perform data transfers with an external process at the same point in time, i.e. in parallel, although they are sequentially handled by the computer. When a comparator detects equality between the value in its hold register and the output of its real time clock, either input data are latched into the unit's data hold register, or the contents of the data hold register are brought to the unit's external output. Besides initiating the actual data transfer, the comparator signal is also utilised as a handshaking impulse, as a data ready interrupt signal, and to reset reset the busy status, thus acting as a hardware semaphore.

In some cases, the time sequence of operations in an independently working peripheral unit can be more complex, in order to meet our requirements. For instance, the operation of a multiplexed analogue input unit can be organised according to the principle of pipelining (see Figure 4.10). The unit already selects the address of its analogue input multiplexer, well in advance of the point in time specified for the actual input. Consequently, the device driver must supply to the unit time instants that are decreased by a device dependent period. After a delay (which is equal to this period), the current input signal is latched into a sample/hold circuitry. Then, a processor interrupt is raised signaling that the unit is ready to accept the next input request, to be comprised of an input line address and a desired input time. In parallel to this, the analogue-to-digital conversion has commenced, after the completion of which the computer is notified by a second interrupt.

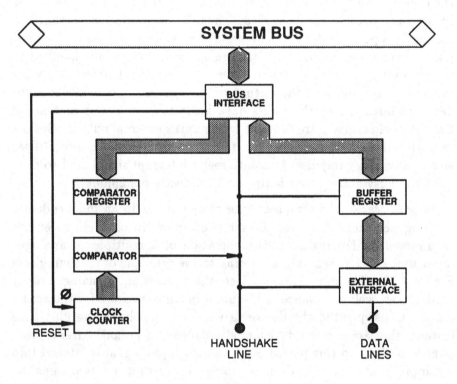

Figure 4.9: A precisely-timed I/O device

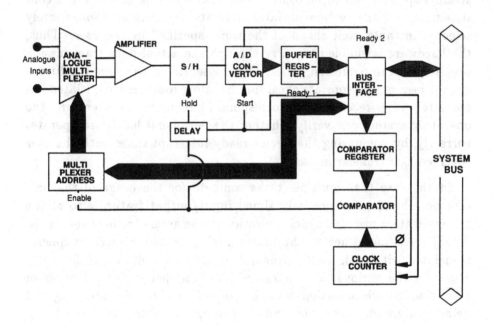

Figure 4.10: A precisely-timed multi-channel analogue input unit

4.8.3   Operating System Support

To support precisely timed peripherals at the operating system level
(i.e., in the peripheral device drivers) is fairly straightforward. Essentially, the device drivers should transmit precise time specifications in
the same way as they handle data and control information. To enable
the transmission, all that is necessary is to convert the time specification
between the external PEARL representation and the internal representation used by the peripheral attachment units.

Moreover, the operating system should check whether time constraints specified for input/output operations can be met and are consistent. If so, the system initiates the data transfers at appropriately
selected instants, well ahead of the times specified by the user. Thus,
the hardware is enabled to carry through the actual data transmission
precisely at the requested times. Otherwise, i.e., if the time conditions
cannot be met, appropriate exception handling routines are initiated immediately after receiving the corresponding requests. Furthermore, the
operating system can verify whether the peripheral hardware operates
correctly, by comparing the device ready interrupt times with the user
specified I/O transfer instants.

In the case that multiple tasks compete for the usage of the process peripherals, the precisely timed input/output feature also allows
for application oriented synchronisation of the access to these resources.
Semaphores, and other synchronisation schemes, are replaced by queues
associated with each such peripheral, in which the data transfer operations of the various user tasks are listed in their temporal order of
execution. Synchronisation with the help of time has the advantages of
being easily understandable, and of yielding maximum resource utilisation with a minimum of access conflicts.

4.8.4   Clock Synchronisation in a Distributed System

The hardware and software mechanisms introduced in this Section rely
heavily on the availability of accurate time readings. Thus, to enable
correct use of these mechanisms in a distributed system, the individual
clocks in the system need to be the synchronised. Clock synchronisation

in distributed environments is a serious problem that has been addressed by many authors (such as, by Kopetz and Ochsenreiter [103]). Their method is rather complicated and requires a special VLSI chip to keep the operating system overhead and synchronisation traffic low. We now present a considerably simpler concept. While our method is not applicable to an arbitrarily interconnected distributed system, it does work for the topology most widely — in fact, almost exclusively — used in industrial environments. Our scheme allows, like the one given in [103], continuous synchronisation. It does not require, however, any additional cabling nor any additional synchronisation traffic.

Our clock synchronisation facility is depicted in Figure 4.11. All nodes are connected to a linear bus. Such busses, sometimes called "data highways", are typically implemented as coaxial cables or optic fibres, and the data transmission is carried out serially. The busses may physically extend over large areas, such as refineries or chemical plants. To increase fault tolerance of data exchange, busses can be closed to rings, without a significant increase in the cost of the transmission device. Our facility thus uses the ring approach.

We assume that the ring traffic is organised by a centrally located control unit, and that a synchronous communication protocol is used. The bit or byte transmission frames of the communication protocol are synchronised with the global clock of the entire distributed system, which has been integrated into the ring's control unit. To avoid additional cabling for clock synchronisation, the control unit alternates the direction in which it transmits subsequent frames on the ring. The time distance between any two frames, however, is an installation constant and is derived from the global time. Let l be the overall length of the ring, d the shorter ring distance between an arbitrary node A and the control unit, and c the velocity of light for the ring's medium. Then, the sum of the transmission delays between the controller and the node A for two subsequent frames is

$$t_1 + t_2 = \frac{d}{c} + \frac{l-d}{c} = \frac{l}{c} = constant,$$

which is an installation parameter, equal for all nodes in the system. The synchronisation of the nodes' local clocks with the global one is thus very simple. All the ring controller needs to do, is to send out,

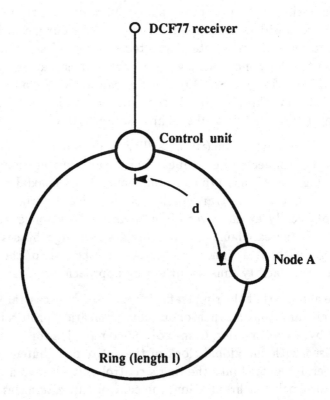

Figure 4.11: Clock synchronisation in ring-based distributed systems

once in a while, a reading of the actual time. Then, given the length of these messages and the transmission delay of the ring, the local clocks can be appropriately adjusted.

Finally, we should like to point out how our approach facilitates the implementation of fault tolerance with respect to the correct operation of the local clocks. The arrival of communication frames is supervised with local watchdog timers. Thus, malfunctions of the global clock, the ring controller, and interruptions of the communication over the ring are immediately detectable. For the latter fault, we distinguish between two cases: the ring is broken at one point, and the ring is interrupted at several points, making any communication impossible. To cope with the first of these two cases, the control unit switches to a bus mode of operating the broken ring. The clock synchronisation scheme described here may no longer be used, but a slightly less accurate procedure can be employed. If the specific transmission delay between the controller and a node is not known, a good estimate can be applied for purposes of clock synchronisation. When the communication fails completely, the local clocks, which were last synchronised before the failure, will continue their operation. The clock's deviations from the actual time will be small, but will increase slightly the longer the interruption lasts. Thus, the performance of the timers and clocks in a ring based distributed system degrades gracefully in reaction to malfunctions of the ring controller and interruptions of the ring itself.

4.9   Summary

The objective of this Chapter was twofold, viz. to devise in great lines the hardware platform allowing to implement predictably behaving real time systems, and to design appropriate alternatives for a number of commonly used features causing unpredictability. To motivate the over-all concept of our architecture, we analysed analogies from everyday life and anatomy. Then, we examined the earliest-deadline-first task scheduling algorithm, because it exhibits a number of useful properties which have consequences for a suitable architecture. In addition, new results were obtained with regard to resource constrained and non-pre-emptive deadline-driven task scheduling and the elimination of unnec-

essary context-switches. These considerations and the layered structure
of real time operating systems suggested that a real time computer is
best organised in form of a master-slave double processor system: a
conventional general purpose computer working under control of a co-
processor dedicated to the operating system kernel. We gave a short
description of this concept and compared it with other non-conventional
architectures found in the literature. Finally, we focussed on three architectural features and demonstrated constructively, that they can be
implemented with a completely predictable behaviour. Thus, we developed a task-oriented hierarchical storage management scheme, methods allowing direct memory access without cycle stealing, and precisely
timed peripherals.

Chapter 5

An Operating System Kernel and its Dedicated Processor

In the previous Chapter, we have presented the concept of a co-processor for the kernel, i.e., the time-critical part, of a real time operating system especially tailored for the extended real time programming language PEARL. The co-processor acts as system controller, and operates in conjunction with one or more conventional processors in hard real time environments. It is composed of three layers, which perform the functions as given in Table 4.1. Some of these functions constitute the operating system processor's user interface, as they are invoked by application programs. In this Chapter we describe in detail the hardware modules of the proposed co-processor, and the software kernel algorithms executed in two separate subprocessors as primary and secondary event reactions.

5.1   Hardware Organisation

The individual hardware components of the co-processor are grouped along a common internal dataway (i.e., a bus). The access to it and further on to the various storage elements is synchronised by a bus controller that uses a time-bounded request grant protocol. The controller co-ordinates the bus activities of the primary and secondary reaction processors, as well as those of the external general task processing unit(s) and a peripheral for storing protocol data. The controller also checks individual access rights. Since a bus controller is a widely-used hardware component, it does not require further discussion here.

To prevent excessive overhead due to writer/reader synchronisations, additional data communication channels are provided for the transmission of operation parameters from the primary layer and the attached task processor(s) to the secondary layer in the form of first-in-first-out memories.

In the sequel, we now specify the different functional units arranged along the dataway.

5.1.1   Time-Dependent Elements

All time-related features, as shown in Figure 5.1, are based on a global clock with a separate current source to maintain correct real time should the system power supply break down. As is customary, the time base for this clock may be a high precision quartz oscillator. A better choice, however, would be the official standard time, which is being radio broadcast on long waves in various countries. In Germany, for example, the time is broadcast by the DCF 77 radio service [22]. Hence, the clock must be equipped with a special, single-frequency radio receiver. At its output, the clock provides three different rectangular pulse trains with frequencies f, f', and f'', the first of which normally triggers the counters for time and date. The counters are divided into individually addressable units that yield day, hour, minute, second, and an appropriate subdivision thereof, selected to keep the quantisation error negligibly small. Opposite to the clock counters stands a correspondingly structured register. The outputs of both units are connected to a comparator generating a time signal upon equality. The signal is fed into a storage module that will be detailed later, in the context of recognition devices for events. The algorithms performed as reaction to this signal are the subject of the next Section.

The purpose of a second combination of registers and a comparator

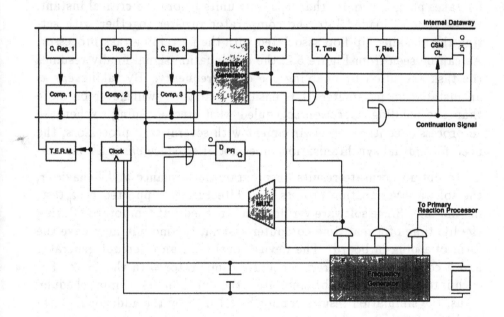

Figure 5.1: Time-related hardware components

is to produce continuation signals to be transmitted to the task processor(s), where they start the execution of operations at precisely given points in time. The continuation signal results from gating the comparator output with the one of a 1-bit storage location that can be set and cleared via the bus. The comparator pulse automatically loads the register with a bit pattern equivalent of the maximum value (infinity). The pulse also resets the enable flip-flop when propagating through the gate. Before a processor requests the exact timing of an operation, it performs all necessary preparations and then transfers the corresponding task into a waiting state by disabling its system clock. This state transfer takes place not more than *eps* time units before the critical instant, whose time is loaded into the comparator register together with setting the masking flip-flop associated with the pertaining task processor. As can be seen from Figure 5.2, the continuation signal finally resumes the task execution by enabling the clock frequency. By taking *eps* as an installation parameter, it is ensured that there will never be more than one pending operation scheduled with precise timing. When the co-processor controls an environment with several task processors, the need for mutual synchronisations does not arise, since *eps* is a constant.

To obtain accurate results on program performance and behaviour, the software verification process is architecturally supported by a testing module. Since software verification is needed but temporarily during the life-time of a real time computer system, the module may have the form of a plug-in board. The device consists of an interrupt generator and a combination of a register and a comparator with the clock. For each interrupt source to be simulated, the unit handles a time schedule. Thus, the simulation results cannot be falsified by the additional workload that would be imposed on the co-processor if it had to take care of these schedules, as well. Upon the comparator's signal, the unit raises the corresponding interrupts via the internal dataway. Then the register is loaded with the next critical instant. The interrupt generator's working method does not need to be described here any further, since it is quite similar to the primary reaction to time events, that will be discussed later. However, two functions that modify the system clock during the test phase must be mentioned. If required by the simulation program, the clock can be stopped by disabling the frequency generator's three output lines. Furthermore, the unit controls the multiplexer,

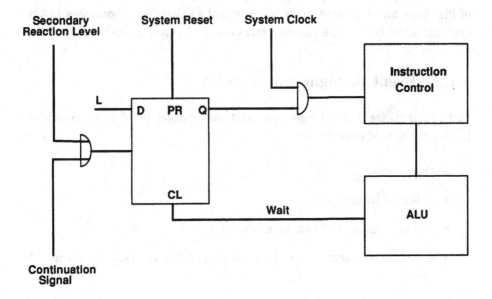

Figure 5.2: Exact timing feature in a general processor

which feeds either the frequency f or the frequency f' into the clock. Normally, f is put through. However, if no task is being executed during a simulation run, the clock may be triggered by the considerably higher frequency f', in order to reduce the corresponding time requirements. Any of the three comparator signals automatically restores the original multiplexer setting. The interrupt generation unit detects an idle state of the task processor(s) by interrogating the processor state flip-flop(s). Their contents gate the frequency f which counts the running tasks' accumulated execution times up and the residual times, required before the tasks' final terminations, down. These counters are necessary as hardware support for the implementation of feasible scheduling disciplines, viz. the earliest-deadline-first algorithm for uniprocessors and the throwforward algorithm [92, 80] for multiprocessors. As many sets of flip-flops and counters must be provided as there are processors in the system, since this is the maximum number of running tasks.

5.1.2   Event Recognition Modules

In the hardware defined here, recognition modules need to be provided for four types of events:

- the time signal,

- external interrupts,

- status transfers of synchronisers, and

- supervised shared variables assume specified relations to given values.

The general structure of an event recognition module is displayed in Figure 5.3.

A signal generated by one of the different sources, whose internal composition will be discussed later, sets the event storage flip-flop and triggers the counter of event occurrences. Furthermore, the current time is latched when the output of the flip-flop turns high. Until the flip-flop and the counter have been serviced and cleared, subsequent incoming signals only increment the value held in the counter. Thus, the number

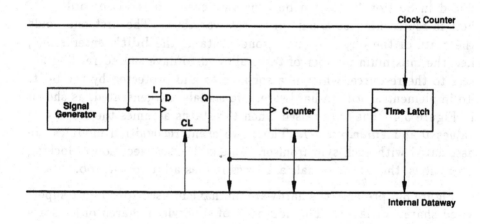

Figure 5.3: An event recognition module

of missed signals can be detected. This feature is mainly used in the application validation phase, to detect performance bottle-necks.

The source of the time signal is the first comparator, applied to a register and the real time clock, as shown in Figure 5.1. Hence, its output is simply connected with a latch and a counter.

Interrupts may be raised externally by physical devices, or internally for simulation purposes (such as by the PEARL statement **trigger**). Since the latter can be accomplished via the internal dataway, a logical disjunction (or-composition) of the dataway with an externally connected signal line serves as the interrupt signal source.

Accessible to all system components, the co-processor provides a common storage area for shared variables and for synchronisation objects of type **bolt**. This type was chosen at the implementation level, because other synchronisation mechanisms, including the **lock** construct introduced in Section 2.9.1, can be expressed easily in terms of **bolt**s. A bolt is represented as a pair of integer variables. The first one holds the state of the object. The second contains the **bolt**'s enter range, i.e., the maximum number of tasks allowed to have shared reading access to the resource, which is associated to and protected by the **bolt**. To implement a **bolt** in hardware, two signals are generated, as shown in Figure 5.4. They are raised when the status assumes the respective values 0 and *enter_range-1*. Thus, two event recognition modules are associated with each synchroniser. To enable fast execution of locking operations, the status signals are accessible as a bit vector, too.

Figure 5.5 presents the hardware mechanism used to support supervised shared variables. The addresses of supervised shared objects are stored in dedicated address registers. All write access data addresses sent to the common storage area are observed by sensing the *Read/Write* and *Address/Data* bus lines. Should an address match with a supervised one, this event is signaled to the associated recognition module. Consequent event handling is done in the primary reaction layer.

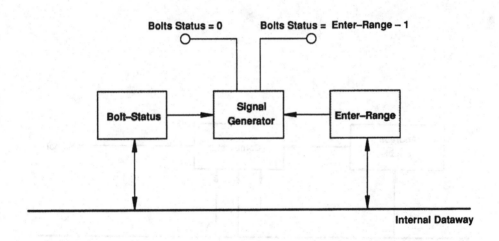

Figure 5.4: Hardware implementation of a **bolt** synchroniser

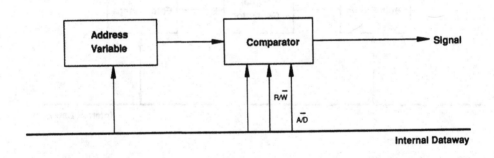

Figure 5.5: Hardware that supports supervised shared objects

5.2   Primary Event Reaction

Before the algorithms of the primary reaction layer can be presented, general time management needs to be discussed. We shall now describe a general representation of time schedules, and the data structures and the procedures, which will be formulated in the process control language PEARL.

5.2.1   Representation of Time Schedules

Since the hardware introduced in this and the previous Chapter supports precise and reliable time management, the distinction between the PEARL language elements **all** and **every** and between **until** and **during** may be dropped. Hence, all time schedules in PEARL can be converted to a common representation, namely

> **at** {clock-expression | [interrupt-expression] +
>   duration-expression1}
> **every** duration-expression2 **during** duration-expression3

where [...] stands for the point in time when the specified interrupt occurs. The duration-expressions must yield non-negative values. This language construct is also representable by the following 3-tuple:

> $T(n) = (t(n), dt, rt(n))$, $n \geq 0$, where
> $t(n + 1) := t(n) + dt$, $rt(n + 1) := rt(n) - dt$, $n \geq 0$,
> $t(0) = clock - expression$ | $[interrupt - expression] +$
> $duration - expression1$
> $dt = duration - expression2$, and $rt(0) = duration - expression3$.

At time $t = t(n)$, $n \geq 1$, the two calculations in the above equation are carried out in parallel. The schedule is worked off if $rt(n + 1) < 0$ holds. Otherwise, $t(n + 1)$ is handled as a future critical instant.

5.2.2   Algorithms and Data Structures of the Time Management

Let $n > 0$ be a configuration parameter. The just introduced time schedule 3-tuples are stored in the one-dimensional data structure $T = \{(t(i), dt(i), rt(i)) \mid i = 0, ..., n\}$. When $T(i)$ does not contain a valid schedule, $dt(i)$ is set to 0. The set of critical moments, for which operations have been scheduled, is given in an unordered form by $\{t(i) \mid dt(i) \neq 0 \text{ and } i = 0, ..., n\}$. The four one-bit-arrays p, q, g, and e of length $n + 1$ are used to describe $T(i)$ as follows:

$$p(i) = \begin{cases} 1, & T(i) \text{ will be due at the next time signal and } t(i) \text{ is already} \\ & \text{the next but one critical instant of } T(i), \\ 0, & \text{otherwise} \end{cases}$$

$$q(i) = \begin{cases} 1, & T(i) \text{ will be due at the next but one time signal,} \\ 0, & \text{otherwise} \end{cases}$$

$$g(i) = \begin{cases} 1, & T(i) \text{ is associated with a precisely timed operation,} \\ 0, & \text{otherwise} \end{cases}$$

and

$$e(i) = \begin{cases} 1, & T(i) \text{ is exhausted (past due, worked off)}, \\ 0, & \text{otherwise} \end{cases}$$

Finally, let $zk1$ and $zk2$ be the next and the next but one, respectively, critical points in time, found by searching all schedules. The value of the variable $zk1$ is for any time $t < zk1$ equal to the value held in vr, the clock's first comparator register.

When the time $zk1$ is reached, i.e., with recognising the time signal, the following procedure is be performed. First, the comparison register of the clock is updated. The information in p is saved in a vector r, which is used by the event processing algorithm (given below) to initiate the operations currently due. The schedules no longer due after $zk1$ are marked as exhausted. Then, the schedules are re-evaluated that will be due at the next critical moment, to yield new next but one instants. The new contents of the vector q and the minimum of all valid $t(i)$, $i = 0, ..., n$, are determined, to enable immediate redefinition of vr after the occurrence of the next time signal. Thus, the delay between

the comparator signal and the reloading of the corresponding register is
minimised.

```
update: procedure;
          vr:=zk1:=zk2; r:=p; e:=(n+1)'0'b;
          for i from 0 by 1 to n repeat;
            if p(i) and rt(i) lt 0 then
              dt(i):=0; e(i):='1'b;
            fin;
          end;
          p:=q;
          for i from 0 by 1 to n repeat;
            if p(i) then
              t(i):=t(i)+dt(i); rt(i):=rt(i)-dt(i);
            fin;
          end;
          call minimum;
        end;
```

with

```
minimum: procedure;
          zk2:=infinity; q:=(n+1)'0'b;
          for i from 0 by 1 to n repeat;
            if rt(i) ge 0 and dt(i) gt 0 then
              if t(i) le zk2 then
                if t(i) lt zk2 then
                  zk2:=t(i); q:=(n+1)'0'b;
                fin;
                q(i):='1'b;
              fin;
            fin;
          end;
        end;
```

where **inf** is an appropriately selected large constant ("infinity") and "(repeat) bit-literal" is a loop that sets an array of bits. The complexity of the above procedures is of the order $O(n+1)$. It is possible to speed the procedures up by performing the operations of the loops in *update* in parallel on n+1 array components. In order that the routines work properly, several variables need to be initialised as follows:

```
init: procedure;
          for i from 0 by 1 to n repeat;
          dt(i):=0; p(i):=q(i):=g(i):=e(i):='0' b;
          end;
          vr:=zk1:=zk2:=infinity;
      end;
```

To delete a time schedule $T(i)$, $0 \leq i \leq n$, only three assignment operations are necessary:

```
delete: procedure(i fixed);
            dt(i):=0; p(i):=q(i):='0' b;
        end;
```

A side-effect of this extremely simple $O(1)$ solution is that time signals may be generated while no element of p or q has been actually set.

Before the secondary reaction layer requests the primary one to insert a new schedule $S=(ts,dts,rts,ex)$ into T, the former layer checks the validity of the schedule's parameters and determines the index i of an unoccupied array element where the components of S will be stored. Then, depending on the value of ts, the variables vr, $zk1$, $zk2$, p, and q, may be updated.

```
insert: procedure(ts clock, (dts,rts) duration, ex bit, in fixed);
            t(in):=ts; dt(in):=dts; rt(in):=rts; g(in):=ex;
            if ts lt zk1 then
                vr:=zk1:=ts;
                for i from 0 by 1 to n repeat;
                if p(i) then
                    t(i):=t(i)−dt(i); rt(i):=rt(i)+dt(i);
```

```
            fin;
        end;
        p:=(n+1)'0'b; p(in):='1'b;
        t(in):=ts+dts; rt(in):=rts-dts;
        call minimum;
    else
        if ts eq zk1 then
            p(in):='1'b; t(in):=ts+dts; rt(in):=rts-dts;
            call minimum;
        else
            if ts lt zk2 then
                zk2:=ts; q:=(n+1)'0'b; q(in):='1'b;
            else
                if ts eq zk2 then q(in):='1'b; fin;
            fin;
        fin;
    fin;
end;
```

If the loop in the above instruction sequence can be parallelised, to determine, for instance, which components of p have the value '1'B, the *insert* routine's complexity can be reduced from $O(n+1)$ to $O(1)$. Since the **then** clauses are partly identical, it is possible to compress code, thus conserving storage in a microprogrammed implementation. When the schedules are inserted or deleted, their relevant times and pertaining parameters are written into a protocol file.

5.2.3 Algorithms and Data Structures of the Event Management

As we have pointed out previously, the set of events the unit reacts to consists of

- the time signal z,

- the external interrupts $u(i)$, $i=1,...,cardinality(U)$, as enabled by the corresponding masking bits $m(i)$,

- the synchronisation events $s(i)$, $i=1,...,cardinality(S)$, and

- the assumption of certain relations between supervised, shared variables and given values $v(i)$, $i=1,...,cardinality(V)$.

Hence, the event set is defined as $E = \{z\} \cup U \cup S \cup V$, where $m=cardinality(E)=1+cardinality(U)+cardinality(S)+cardinality(V)$. At any point in time there is a set of scheduled activities $A = \{a(i) \mid i = 0, 1, ...\}$. Since a time schedule may exist for each $a \in A$, the maximum possible number of the activities to be handled equals the dimension $n+1$ of T (described in the last section). The elements of A can be

- tasking and synchronisation operations in the sense of PEARL,

- prologues of program units reacting to **on** exceptions,

- beginnings of alternatives in **expect** statements,

- prologues of routines handling the exceptions of temporal surveillance features,

- calls to the processor scheduler, and

- prologues of handling routines, to be executed when supervised, shared variables have assumed specified value relations.

The following relation exists between the two sets E and A:

$R \subset E \times A :$ eRa iff the activity a must be executed upon the occurrence of an event e, $e \in E$ and $a \in A$.

For $e = z$, only those elements of $R \subset \{(z,a(i)) \mid i = 0,...,n\}$ may be considered for which $r(i)='1'B$, $i=0,...,n$, holds. The relation R is implemented as a two-dimensional array *rel* of bits. A primary reaction is activated by every clock pulse, arriving with the frequency f'', where f'' is an appropriate fraction of the basic system clock rate f. Hence, the recognition time of an event never exceeds $\frac{1}{f''}$. To detect all events that have occurred, the m event recognition modules are polled in a loop. First in the loop, the corresponding time latches and counters are read out. These data are recorded in the protocol file together with the event identifications. Then, the event storage flip-flops and the occurrence counters are reset:

protocol: **procedure**(*i* **fixed**);

        write *i*, *tl*(*i*), *cr*(*i*) **to** *protocol_buffer*;

        ff(*i*):='0'*b*; *cr*(*i*):=0;

    end;

For the time signal the procedure *update* is executed. The procedure generates the vectors *r* and *e*, that indicate the schedules currently due and worked off, respectively. To recognise the time dependent activities now due, the component-wise logical conjunction of *r* and the first row of the relation R is carried out. The vector *g* is masked with the result, to mark the activities requiring precise timing. An interrupt is considered only if the associated masking bit is set, which is also recorded in the protocol file. The masking data do not require special flip-flops for storage. Instead, they can be held in the unit's working storage area. The primary interrupt handling concludes with the logical disjunction of *r* and the row of R associated with the event just considered. The determination of the activities that are to be subsequently carried out in the secondary reaction processor is now complete. Synchronisation and supervised, shared variable events are treated in an analogous manner. In the latter case, however, one extra step is required, namely the comparison of the new value that has just been stored into the supervised variable with the specified quantity. This is done by calling the procedure *compare*, whose parameters are an index and the arrays *ad*, *rl*, and *v*, which represent the shared variables' addresses, the arithmetic or logical relations, and the comparison values, respectively. Should *compare* conclude that the shared variable has indeed assumed the expected value (or fulfilled the expected relation), a message is written into the protocol file and *r* is appropriately updated. Linked to the first shared variable are time schedules' insertion and deletion operations. These operations are handled as described in the next Section. Upon the completion of a polling cycle, the vector *r* identifying the elements of A to be performed is sent, along with the current time, to the secondary layer processor. The task *primary_reaction* has the overall complexity of the order $O(n+m+1)$.

when *f"* **activate** *primary_reaction*;

where

```
primary reaction: task;
    r:=(n+1)'0' b;  t:=clock;
    /* time signal */
    if ff(1) then
       call protocol(1); call update;
       write r,e to protocol_buffer;
       r:=r and rel(1,0:n); gm:=g and r;
    fin;

    /* external interrupts */
    for i from 2 by 1 to upb u + 1 repeat;
       if ff(i) then
          call protocol(i);
          if mk(i) then
             write mk(i) to protocol_buffer;
             r:=r or rel(i,0:n);
          fin;
       fin;
    end;

    /* synchronisation events */
    for i from upb u + 2 by 1 to upb u + upb s + 1 repeat;
       if ff(i) then
          call protocol(i); r:=r or rel(i,0:n);
       fin;
    end;

    /* shared variables */
    i:=upb u + upb s + 2;
    if ff(i) then
       call protocol(i);
       /* cont ad(1) related to insert and delete */
       if cont ad(1) eq 1 then
          call insert(ts,dts,rts,ex,in);
          write ts,dts,rts,ex,in to protocol_buffer;
       else
          if in ge 0 then
```

```
            call delete(in);
            write in to protocol_buffer;
        else
            for in from 0 by 1 to n repeat;
              if dv(in) then
                  call delete(in);
                  write in to protocol_buffer;
              fin;
            end;
        fin;
    fin;
    cont ad(1):=0;
  fin;
  for i from upb u + upb s + 3 by 1 to
  upb u + upb s + upb v + 1 repeat;
    if ff(i) then
        call protocol(i); k:=i − upb u − upb s − 1;
        if compare(k,ad,rl,v) then
            write ad(k),v(k) to protocol_buffer;
            r:=r or rel(i,0:n);
        fin;
    fin;
  end;

  /* push data into input fifo
      of the secondary level processor. */
  write t,r,e,gm to secondary_level;
 end;


and


compare: procedure(k fixed, (ad,rl,v) ( ) fixed identical)
              returns (bit);
              case rl(k)
                  alt b:=cont ad(k) eq v(k);
                  alt b:=cont ad(k) ne v(k); ...
                  /* and other appropriate comparisons */ ...
```

> **out** $b := {}^{\prime}0{}^{\prime}\,b;$
> **fin**;
> **returns** $(b);$
> **end**;

5.2.4   Implementation of Other Features

To enable internal event communication, PEARL provides objects of type **signal**. In the hardware we have presented, there is no special support for **signal**s, since they are easily implemented with supervised, shared variables. Specifically, a signal is associated with a shared object of type **bit**. Then, to raise or to **induce** a signal, one only needs to set the corresponding variable, and the signal reaction is scheduled as an activity to be commenced when the variable assumes the value $'1'B$.

As the program given in the last Section shows, the insertion and deletion of time schedules into the internal data structure is also linked to a supervised, shared variable, that assumes special values. When the variable has been set by the secondary layer processor to 1 or 2, for insertion or deletion, respectively, the corresponding parameters are fetched from their locations in the common memory in the next event polling cycle. The requested operation is then performed (possibly several times, in case of a delete) and the shared variable is finally reset to zero.

In certain applications, it may be necessary to know in the user program, which particular events have given rise to an activity. Information on the just occurred events can be provided by copying the stati of the flip-flops *ff* into a bit vector during execution of the task *primary reaction*, and by sending the information consequently to the secondary layer.

The verification of reliable software performance, especially with regard to the critical timing constraints, is an aspect of fundamental importance for real time data processing. The enabling of the verification is the reason why all data necessary to reconstruct the occurrence of events and the associated operations are recorded by the above stated procedures. The recorded information is essential not only during the implementation and acceptance test phase of an application, but also when analysing later software malfunctions. Physically, to make the information available to the secondary reaction layer, it is written into a buffer in the common memory. As has been already mentioned, there is a dedicated device that formats the data into readable form and sends the data to a mass storage medium, when the buffer is filled to a given threshold. A further duty of this device could be the selection of specified subsets of all protocol data, when the entire information is not needed any more.

5.3   Secondary Event Reaction

In this Section we first describe the functions of the secondary reaction layer processor, as required by extended PEARL. Then, we present the layer's main control programs, that accept operation parameters and initiate requested services. After that, the entries of task control blocks managed by the unit, and the various associated functions, are discussed in detail. The functions are stated in the form of PEARL routines that involve low level features only, thus suggesting a microprogrammed implementation.

5.3.1   Functions

In PEARL, as well as in other real time programming languages, concurrent processing is typically realised by the task concept. To support tasks, the operating system kernel and the corresponding co-processor need to provide the following functions:

- the initialisation of a control block for a task, upon the elaboration of the task's declaration,

- the scheduling and execution of the tasking operations **activate**, **terminate**, the normal termination of a task, **prevent, suspend, continue**, and **resume**,

- the buffering of task activations,

- the scheduling and execution of task resumptions associated with synchronisation operations and **expect** statements,

- the prevention of **expect** schedules, and finally

- the scheduling and initiation of **on** reactions, i.e., exception handlers.

Since there is generally more than one ready task, the processor dispatching must be organised. For this purpose, the feasible earliest-deadline-first algorithm is called in the course of the above mentioned operations. This processor assignment scheme handles also overload situations as early as possible and calls for its part the hierarchical storage management. The latter employs a look-ahead algorithm as described in Section 4.6. The algorithm allocates page frames for the code and data of complete tasks, and uses information provided by the earliest-deadline-first dispatcher and extracted from the schedules of task (re-)activations. All these operating system features are controlled by the language elements introduced into PEARL in Section 2.9. The support includes the precise timing of tasking operations, which requires additional functionality from the secondary layer processor, to be described shortly. The assumption of certain value relations by shared variables is a class of events occurring in schedules. The primary reaction layer uses special hardware modules (described earlier) to perform the necessary surveillance of the shared variables. Providing parameters to this feature and controlling it is a further function to be carried through by the co-processor's highest level.

The secondary layer also has functions that facilitate the execution of high level language constructs. Specifically, they comprise the interpretation and processing of operation parameters, the validation of time schedules, and the assignment and pre-emption of the task processor. Schedule management is the most complex of these functions, owing to their relation to activities to be performed when corresponding events occur. This holds especially in the case of time driven schedules whose initial times depend on interrupts ("two-stage schedules"),

5.3.2   Control Programs

We begin our presentation of the procedures executed by the co-processor's secondary reaction layer (SRL) by introducing relevant data structures, and two routines which accept service request parameters and initiate the requests' elaboration.

As we have already stated, in order to prevent excessive overhead due to synchronisations of producer and consumer tasks, operation parameters are transmitted from the attached task processor(s) and the unit's primary reaction layer (PRL) to the SRL via two first-in-first-out memories. To guarantee the system's high speed of event reactions, the reception of PRL data takes precedence over other functions. The data specify the activities associated with the just occurred events. The activities are represented by one or more parameter sets for the individual SRL functions stored in the array b. The various objects involved — which have been partially already introduced and discussed in Section 5.2 — and their interdependence are displayed in Figure 5.6. The parameters are first stored in a temporary buffer for further treatment. Each parameter set consists of a function identifier word followed by the actual function parameters. The total size of the parameter set is determined by calling the procedure *parno*, that takes a function identifier as its parameter.

We now state the control programs in an implementation oriented form. To avoid context-switches associated with processing the data arriving from the two first-in-first-out memories, the SRL is equipped with two register sets: one associated with the PRL and the other with the task processor(s). If the set associated with the PRL is active, then the data-available interrupt of the corresponding first-in-first-out memory is disabled. The interrupt is enabled upon switching to the other register set. The main task cyclically calls the hierarchical storage administration procedure *vsadmin*, which has been described in Section 4.6. The parameter of the administration procedure is the Boolean array *foc*, whose entries indicate whether the corresponding page frames are occupied. Initially, the elements of *foc* are cleared. The procedure call *protocol* appearing at various locations in the sequel stands for the writing of appropriate data into the log file.

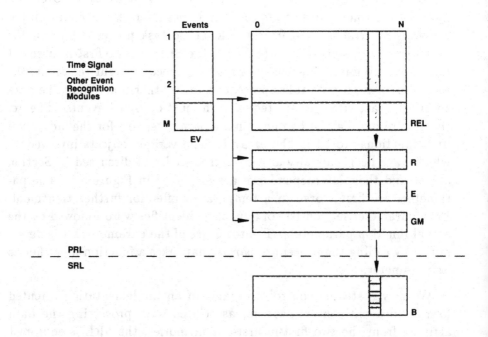

Figure 5.6: Interdependence of the objects maintained by the co-processor

```
module(srl_control_programs);
  problem;
  /*
      variables description:
        b: parameter set
        parno: # datawords required by routine
  */

    prl_service: task priority 1;
        disable prl_fifo data_available_interrupt;
        switch_context(register_set_1);
        while prl_fifo data_available repeat;
          read t,r,e,gm from prl_fifo;
          call protocol;
          for i from 0 by 1 to n repeat;
            if r(i) then
                j:=1;
                while b(j,i) ne nil repeat;
                  execute(b(j,i));
                  j:=j+parno(b(j,i));
                end;
            fin;
          end;
        end;
        switch_context(register_set_2);
        /* thus the infinite loop in the other task is continued. */
        enable prl_fifo data_available_interrupt;
      end;

task priority 2;
        when prl_fifo data_available_interrupt activate prl_service;
        enable prl_fifo data_available_interrupt;
wait: while processor_fifo empty repeat;
          call vsadmin(foc);
        end;
        /* tb: temporary buffer */
        read tb(1) from processor_fifo;
```

```
    j:=parno(tb(1));
    for i from 2 by 1 to j repeat;
        read tb(i) from processor_fifo;
    end;
    execute(tb(1));
    call protocol;
    goto wait;
end;
modend;
```

5.3.3   Task Control Blocks

To implement task control blocks, an array $tcb[1 : cb]$, $cb \geq 1$, is allocated in the common storage. Each array element represents an individual task control block, and consists of the records as presented in Table 5.1.

In the Table's initial value column, the abbreviations d and l stand for appropriate data to be extracted from the task declarations or to be provided by the linkage editor, ∞ is an appropriate, very large constant, and *zero* stands for a vector of an appropriate number of '0'B entries. Three installation parameters are specified as array bounds, viz., mba, $creg$, and cs. They denote the maximum number of permitted buffered task activations, the number of the task processor's internal registers, and the number of synchroniser hardware implementations, respectively. The elements of the bit arrays of lengths $n + 1$ correspond to the ones in the vectors r, e, and gm.

The meaning of the individual tcb entries will become clear in detail from the context in which they are applied as described in the next Section. There, the virtual tcb field *active* is interrogated. It is defined as an abbreviation for the expression

$$ready \textbf{ or } run \textbf{ or } susp \textbf{ or } sync$$

of real tcb fields.

Entry	Data Type	Initial Value	Meaning
tid	character(8)	d	Task identifier
res	bit	d	'1'B, if task declared with resident attribute
keep	bit	d	'1'B, if task declared with keep attribute
trsp	duration	d	Task's response time
trun	duration	d	Task's maximum run time
onm	(1:m) bit	d	Mask of signals occurring in task's on statements
fsa	fixed	0	Continuation address after handling an on-event
sigid	fixed	0	SIGNAL identification for an on-event
aon	fixed	1	Start address of the generic on-event
sta	fixed	1	Task code start address
page	fixed	1	Page number of task code in mass storage
frame	fixed	-1	Page frame number of task, if resident; -1 otherwise
reg	(0:creg-1) fixed	0	Processor register status
bolt	(1:cs) bit	zero	'1'B, if bolt seized by task
tl	duration	0	Maximum residual run time
rt	duration	0	Accumulated run time
tcrit	clock	∞	Time of next precisely-timed operation; ∞ if none
int	duration	∞	Average activation interval of interrupt-driven schedules
tcond	clock	∞	Deadline if task is ready; ∞ otherwise
tact	clock	∞	Time condition for next not yet buffered activation
tcont	clock	∞	Time condition for a forthcoming activation
ba	fixed	0	Number of buffered activations; $0 \leq ba \leq mba$
ring1	fixed	mba-1	1.) Index for administration of circular buffer
ring2	fixed	mba-1	2.) of buffered activations
ta	(0:mba-1) clock	∞	Deadlines of buffered activations
opt	fixed	0	Parameter for synchronisation resume
exp	(0:n) bit	zero	Parameter for expect statement processing
ready	bit	0	'1'B, if task is ready
run	bit	0	'1'B, if task is running
susp	bit	0	'1'B, if task suspended explicitly or by expect
sync	bit	0	'1'B, if task suspended for synchronisation
em	(0:n) bit	zero	Mask of task's expect schedules contained in rel
acs	(0:n) bit	zero	Mask of task's activate schedules contained in rel
tes	(0:n) bit	zero	Mask of task's terminate schedules contained in rel
prs	(0:n) bit	zero	Mask of task's prevent schedules contained in rel
sus	(0:n) bit	zero	Mask of task's suspend schedules contained in rel
cos	(0:n) bit	zero	Mask of task's continue schedules contained in rel, also used for resume schedules
tos	fixed	0	Column index in rel of timeout schedule
sys	fixed	0	Column index in rel of synchronisation resume schedule

Table 5.1: Task Control Block Layout.

5.3.4   Kernel Algorithms

We now describe the routines called by the control programs to perform the SRL functions compiled earlier. For ease of presentation, the routines are formulated as PEARL procedures. By coding the procedure names as one word quantities, however, and appending the appropriate procedure parameters, the data sets describing the requested services are formed. We already know them as contents of the arrays b and tb from Section 5.3.2.

The following two procedures initialise and terminate the surveillance of shared variables. For the meaning of the mentioned arrays we refer to the procedure *compare* in Section 5.2.2.

```
initsurv: procedure((a,op,w) fixed);
          /*
                  parameter description:
                  a : address of shared variable,
                  op: relational operator specification,
                  w : value
          */
              i:=1;
              while ad(i) ne nil and ad(i) ne a repeat;
              i:=i+1;
              end;
              ad(i):=a;  rl(i):=op;  v(i):=w;
              call protocol;
          end;
```

and

```
termsurv: procedure(a fixed);
              i:=1;
              while ad(i) ne a repeat;  i:=i+1;  end;
              ad(i):=nil;
              call protocol;
          end;
```

We next consider the routines that put the first task of the ready list, i.e., the most urgent one, into the running state or perform the reverse operation, respectively. To execute a task, the processor needs to be pre-empted. The following routine thus first waits until the non-interruption bit is reset. As presented earlier, the bit is set by a task that needs to execute a critical region without interruption. The *tcb* index of the task, to which the processor is currently assigned, is stored in the variable *ass*. If the processor is idle, its state as well as the value of *ass* are zero. The further objects occurring in the following processor withdrawal procedure were introduced in Sections 2.9.7 and 5.1.1. Here and in the sequel, the parameter *i* always specifies the *tcb* index of the task, to which the function is applied.

```
preempt: procedure(i fixed);
         /*
                 variable description:
                     ass: tcb index of task currently assigned to processor
         */
             if ass eq i then
                 while non_interruption_bit repeat; end;
                 processor state:='0'b;
                 tcb(i).rt:=t_time; tcb(i).tl:=t_res;
                 /* save registers */
                 for j from 0 by 1 to creg-1 repeat;
                     tcb(i).reg(j):=processor_register(j);
                 end;
                 tcb(i).run:='0'b; ass:=0; call protocol;
             fin;
         end;
```

The array *ti* contains the *tcb* indexes of the tasks ready for execution and ordered according to increasing deadlines. The actual number of the ready list's elements is available as *ct*. Accordingly, the processor assignment routine reads as follows.

```
procadm: procedure;
         /*
```

```
                variables description:
                    ti(1:ct): ready list, tcb indices of tasks
                                ordered according increasing deadlines
                    t_time, t_res: cp. Section 2.9.7
        */
            if ass ne ti(1) then
                if ass ne 0 then call preempt(ass); fin;
                ass:=ti(1); tcb(ass).run:='1'b;
                    if tcb(ass).frame eq −1 then
                        call vsadmin(foc);
                    fin;
                for j from 0 by 1 to creg−1 repeat;
                    processor_register(j):=tcb(ass).reg(j);
                end;
                t_time:=tcb(ass).rt; t_res:=tcb(ass).tl;
                if tcb(ass).tcrit ne infinity then
                    /* preparations for task (re-) start
                        at precisely given time */
                    comparison_register_2:=tcb(ass).tcrit;
                    tcb(ass).tcrit:=infinity;
                    continuation_signal_mask:='1'b;
                fin;
                processor_state:='1'b;
                call protocol;
            fin;
        end;
```

When a task is ready for execution, the following procedure is invoked. It first inserts the task's *tcb* index into the ready list. Then, the routine *schedule* is called to ascertain whether the actual ready task set can be executed and still meet all its deadlines. If need be, an overload situation is handled by terminating all tasks that have not been declared with the **keep** attribute and by preventing any further (re-)activations. All interrupts are disabled by resetting the mask *mk* and the overload signal is set. To handle the overload further, special tasks may be scheduled, depending on the application.

```
toexec: procedure(i fixed);
            tcb(i).ready:='1'b;
            tcb(i).tcond:=tcb(i).ta(tcb(i).ring1);
            k:=ct; ct:=ct+1;
            /* insert task i in array ti */
            while tcb(i).ta(tcb(i).ring1) lt
            tcb(ti(k)).ta(tcb(ti(k)).ring1) and k gt 0 repeat;
               ti(k+1):=ti(k); k:=k-1;
            end;
            ti(k+1):=i;
            call schedule;
            call protocol;
        end;
```

where

```
schedule: procedure;
            /*
                  variables description:
                     zg: deadlines can be met
                     s: max residual runtime of all tasks
                         upto k in array ti
            */
               if ass ne 0 then tcb(ass).tl:=t_res; fin;
               s:=0; zg:='0'b; t:=clock;
               for k from 1 by 1 to ct repeat;
                  s:=s+tcb(ti(k)).tl;
                  if tcb(ti(k)).ta(tcb(ti(k)).ring1)-t lt s then
                     goto out;
                  fin;
               end;
               zg:='1'b;
        out: if zg then call procadm;
             else
                  for k from 1 by 1 to ct repeat;
                     if not tcb(ti(k)).keep then
                        call execprev(ti(k)) /* prevent task ti(k) */;
```

```
              call  execterm(ti(k)) /* terminate task ti(k)*/;
         fin;
       end;
      mk:=zero;
      /* raising signal associated with an overload situation */;
      sv(2):='1'b
     fin;
     call protocol;
   end;
```

The inverse operation of removing a task from the ready list is performed by

```
backexec: procedure(i fixed);
          if tcb(i).ready then
             if tcb(i).run then call preempt(i); fin;
             tcb(i).ready:='0'b; l:=0;
             /* remove task i from array ti */
             for k from 1 by 1 to ct repeat;
                if i ne ti(k) then l:=l+1; ti(l):=ti(k); fin;
             end;
             ct:=l; ti(l+1):=0;
             call procadm;
             call protocol;
          fin;
        end;
```

The next procedure described here prepares the schedules of tasking operations and inserts the corresponding data into the appropriate data structures. First, an existing (old) schedule is deleted before a new one for the same task and the same operation is to be inserted. Should a resume operation be requested, the pertaining task is immediately suspended and a continuation is scheduled. This applies to the **resume** tasking statement as well as to the future task reactivations, associated with **expect** and synchronisation operations. The parameters of the operations to be performed when their schedules are due are received from the task processor via a first-in-first-out memory. The validity of the parameters is checked, and then they are stored in the array *b*. New values for the *tcb* entries, as required by the storage administration scheme, are determined. In the course of this, the array *ivl* is used stating for each interrupt the average time between its occurrences. Finally, appropriate schedule pointers are stored in the task's *tcb*.

A special schedule is common to all tasks. It links the signals to an **on** reaction, as is described later. The schedule always resides in *rel(1:m,0)*.

To simplify the formulation of the following procedure, the *tcb* entries *acs(.)*, *tes(.)*, *prs(.)*, *sus(.)*, and *cos(.)* are addressed as *sch(1:5,.)*.

```
schtop: procedure((i,s) fixed);
   /*
        parameter description:
        i: tcb index,
        s: operation selector:
                                1=activate,
                                2=terminate,
                                3=prevent,
                                4=suspend,
                                5=continue,
                                6=resume,
                                7=expect-resume,
                                8=synchronisation-resume,
                            10=on
   */
     if s eq 10 then
        b(1,0):=s; b(2,0):=nil;
        read rel(1:m,0) from processor_fifo; goto return;
     fin;

     l:=if s ne 6 then s else 5 fin;
     if l le 5 then
        if tcb(i).sch(l,0:n) ne zero then
           hv:=zero;
           for j from 0 by 1 to n repeat;
```

```
    if tcb(i).sch(l,j) then
        hv(j):=rel(1,j);  rel(1:m,j):=zero;  b(1,j):=nil;
      fin;
    end;
    if hv ne zero then in:=-1; dv:=hv; sv(1):=2; fin;
    tcb(i).sch(l,0:n):=zero;
  fin;
  if l eq 1 then tcb(i).tact:=tcb(i).int:=infinity; fin;
  if l eq 5 then tcb(i).tcont:=infinity; fin;
fin;

if s ge 6 and s le 8 then
  call execsusp(i) /* suspend task i */;
  if s eq 6 then s:=5; fin;
  if s eq 8 then
    tcb(i).susp:='0'b; tcb(i).sync:='1'b;
  fin;
fin;
k:=1; hv:=zero; tvs:=infinity; dti:=0;
while k le n and b(1,k) ne nil repeat; k:=k+1; end;
if k gt n then goto return; fin;
/* no more space for schedule storage */;
read rel(1:m,k) from processor_fifo;
kk:=1; hv(k):=ei:='1'b; tcomp:=0;
if not rel(1,k) then
  tcomp:=clock
else
  read ts from processor_fifo
  /* this variable and dt0 use the same storage location. */;
  read dts from processor_fifo;
  read rts from processor_fifo;
  read q from processor_fifo; ex:=q and '01'b;
  if (q and '10'b) eq '00'b then
    if ts le clock or dts le 0 or rts lt 0 then
      hv(k):=ei:='0'b; rel(1:m,k):=zero;
    else
      tcomp:=ts; in:=k; sv(1):=1;
```

```
      fin;
   else
      if dt0 lt 0 or dts le 0 or rts lt 0 then
         hv(k):=ei:='0'b; rel(1:m,k):=zero;
      fin;
      /* parameter preparation for the second stage
         of a two-stage schedule */
      rel(1,k):='0'b; b(1,k):=11; b(2,k):=dt0;
      b(3,k):=dts; b(4,k):=rts; b(5,k):=ex; b(6,k):=k;
      tcomp:=dt0+clock; kk:=7;
   fin;
fin;
b(kk,k):=if s eq 8 and rel(1,k) then 9 else s fin;
kk:=kk+1; b(kk,k):=i;

if s eq 1 or s eq 5 then
   /* input of further parameters for
      activation and continuation operations */
   kk:=kk+1; read b(kk,k) from processor_fifo;
   tcomp:=tcomp+b(kk,k);
   if s eq 1 then
      for ll from 1 by 1 to 4 repeat;
         kk:=kk+1; read b(kk,k) from processor_fifo;
      end;
   fin;
   if ei then
      if rel(2:m,k) ne zero then
         dta:=0;
         for ll from 1 by 1 to cinterrupt repeat;
            if rel(ll+interrupt_displacement,k) then
               dta:=dta+1/ivl(ll);
            fin;
         end;
         if s eq 1 then dti:=dti+dta; fin;
         tcomp:=tcomp+0.5/dta;
      fin;
         tvs:=min(tvs,tcomp);
```

```
      fin;
   fin;
   kk:=if ei then kk+1 else 1 fin;  b(kk,k):=nil;
   if s le 5 then
      tcb(i).sch(s,0:n):=hv;
      if s eq 1 then
         tcb(i).tact:=tvs;
         if dti ne 0 then tcb(i).int:=1/dti; fin;
      fin;
      if s eq 5 then tcb(i).tcont:=tvs; fin;
   else
      if s eq 7 then
         tcb(i).em:=hv;
      else
         j:=1; while not hv(j) repeat; j:=j+1; end;
         tcb(i).sys:=j; j:=j+1;
         while not hv(j) repeat; j:=j+1; end;
         tcb(i).tos:=j;
      fin;
   fin;
return: call protocol;
end;
```

The routine reacting upon the fulfillment of two-stage schedules reads as follows. It initiates the execution of the scheduled operation when a corresponding event has occurred. In case an interrupt was detected, the associated cyclic time schedule, i.e., the schedule's second stage, is newly set up.

```
secstage: procedure((dt0,dts,rts) duration,ex bit,k fixed);
   if ev(1) then
      execute(b(7,k)); /* with parameters b(j,k), j=8,... */
   fin;
   if ev and '01...1'b ne zero then
      in:=k;  sv(1):=1;  rel(1,k):='1'b;  ts:=clock+dt0;
      if b(7,k) eq 1 then
         tcb(b(8,k)).tact:=ts+b(9,k);
```

```
      fin;
      if  b(7,k) eq 5 then
         tcb(b(8,k)).tcont:=ts+b(9,k);
      fin;
      /* wait one prl cycle. */; in:=k; sv(1):=2;
      if dt0 eq 0 then
         execute(b(7,k)); /* with parameters b(j,k), j=8,... */
      fin;
   fin;
   call protocol;
end;
```

The following procedures undertake the operations, whose parameters and schedule links are processed by the last two routines.

The first routine implements the SRL reaction to signals, and performs the preparations required by the application program to branch to an appropriate on handler. Then, the task processor is restarted. The index of the program counter in the processor's register set is denoted as *pc*.

```
execon: procedure;
            if ass ne 0 then
               hv:=ev and  tcb(ass).onm;
               if hv ne zero then
                  tcb(ass).fsa:=processor_register(pc);
                  processor_register(pc):=tcb(ass).aon;
                  j:=1;
                  while not  hv(j+signal_displacement) repeat;
                     j:=j+1;
                  end;
                  tcb(ass).sigid:=j;
                  processor_continuation_signal:='1'b;
               fin;
               call protocol;
            fin;
         end;
```

The following procedure removes all schedules set up by àn **expect** statement.

prevexp: **procedure(*i* fixed)**;
        $hv:=tcb(i).em$ **and** $rel(1,0{:}n)$;
        for *j* **from 1 by 1 to** *n* **repeat**;
          if $tcb(i).em(j)$ **then**
            $tcb(i).em(j):=\text{'0'}b$; $rel(1{:}m,j):=zero$;
            $b(1,j):=$**nil**;
          fin;
        end;
        if hv **ne** *zero* **then** $in:=-1$; $dv:=hv$; $sv(1):=2$; **fin**;
        call *protocol*;
      end;

When an event specified in an **expect** statement's alternative occurs, the following procedure resumes the execution of the task containing the **expect**.

resexp: **procedure(*i* fixed)**;
        $hv:=tcb(i).em$ **and** e;
        if hv **ne** *zero* **then** $in:=-1$; $dv:=hv$; $sv(1):=2$; **fin**;
        $hv:=tcb(i).em$ **and** r; $tcb(i).exp:=tcb(i).exp$ **or** hv;
        if $tcb(i).susp$ **and not** $tcb(i).ready$ **and**
        not $tcb(i).run$ **and not** $tcb(i).sync$ **then**
          $tcb(i).susp:=\text{'0'}b$; **call** $toexec(i)$;
        fin;
        call *protocol*;
      end;

When a task or an activation operation is suspended for synchronisation, two reactions may be scheduled: one to check whether the required resources can now be claimed and the other to handle the timeout associated with the blockage. For the former, the bit vector *boltevent*, which comprises the status outputs of the synchroniser hardware implementations, is examined in appropriate positions.

```
testsync: procedure(i fixed);
              if rel(1:m,tcb(i).sys) and boltevent exor
              rel(1:m,tcb(i).sys) eq zero then
                 tcb(i).opt:=tcb(i).opt+1;
                 call protocol; call ressync(i);
              fin;
           end;
```

and

```
timeout: procedure(i fixed);
              tcb(i).opt:=tcb(i).opt+2;
              call protocol; call ressync(i);
           end;
```

where

```
ressync: procedure(i fixed);
              tcb(i).sync:='0'b; in:=tcb(i).tos; sv(1):=2;
              rel(1:m,tcb(i).sys):=rel(1:m,tcb(i).tos):=zero;
              b(1,tcb(i).sys):=b(1,tcb(i).tos):=nil;
              tcb(i).sys:=tcb(i).tos:=0;
              if not tcb(i).susp then
                if tcb(i).opt le 2 then
                   call toexec(i);
                fin;
              fin;
              call protocol;
           end;
```

The last set of routines we consider processes the actual tasking operations. We commence with schedule prevention. In accordance with the semantics of PEARL, any schedule for tasking operations associated with a certain task and eventual future buffered activations of the task are deleted.

```
execprev:  procedure(i fixed);
               tcb(i).ba:=0;  tcb(i).tact:=tcb(i).tcont:=infinity;
               hv:=tcb(i).acs or  tcb(i).tes or  tcb(i).prs or
                   tcb(i).sus or  tcb(i).cos;
               for j from 1 by 1 to  n repeat;
                 if  hv(j) then
                     hv(j):=rel(1,j);  rel(1:m,j):=zero;  b(1,j):=nil;
                 fin;
               end;
               if  hv ne  zero then in:=−1;  dv:=hv;  sv(1):=2; fin;
               tcb(i).acs:=tcb(i).tes:=tcb(i).prs:=
               tcb(i).sus:=tcb(i).cos:=zero;
               call protocol;
            end;
```

In order to simplify the forthcoming procedures, we introduce the following subroutine for the annihilation of exhausted time schedules.

```
annexsch:  procedure(bc() bit  identical);
              /*
                   parameter description:
                       bc(0:n): bit array
              */
                 hv:=bc and  e;
                 if  hv ne  zero then
                     in:=−1;  dv:=hv;  sv(1):=2;
                     for j from 1 by 1 to  n repeat;
                       if  hv(j) then
                           rel(1,j):='0' b;
                           if  rel(1:m,j) eq  zero then
                               b(1,j):=nil;  bc(j):='0' b;
                           fin;
                       fin;
                     end;
                 fin;
                 call protocol;
              end;
```

Employing the above routine, the procedure performing task suspension can be easily formulated:

```
execsusp: procedure(i fixed);
            if tcb(i).active then
               call backexec(i);
               tcb(i).susp:='1'b; tcb(i).tcond:=infinity;
               call annexsch(tcb(i).sus); call protocol;
            fin;
         end;
```

The inverse tasking operation, viz. continuation, is carried through by the next procedure. In this and in the activation procedure, presented next, the parameters for the operation's precise timing are set, if so requested. The actual operation takes place *eps* time units after the corresponding premature time event.

```
execcont: procedure(i fixed, tc duration);
          /*
               parameter description:
                 i : tcb index,
                 tc: response time
          */
             if tcb(i).susp and tcb(i).em eq zero then
                tcb(i).susp:='0'b; tcb(i).tcont:=infinity;
                tcb(i).ta(tcb(i).ring1):=tcb(i).tcond:=clock+tc;
                av:=tcb(i).cos and gm; call annexsch(tcb(i).cos);
                if not tcb(i).sync then
                   if av ne zero then
                      tcb(i).tcrit:=clock+eps;
                      tcb(i).ta(tcb(i).ring1):=tcb(i).tcrit+tcb(i).tl;
                   fin;
                   call toexec(i);
                fin;
                call protocol;
             fin;
          end;
```

When a task is to be activated, the request and the corresponding parameters are first buffered. If there are no former task activations to be processed, the task execution is prepared and initiated.

```
execact: procedure(i fixed, tc duration, usg fixed,
                      tor duration, toa clock, ii fixed);
            /*
                parameter description:
                  i : tcb index of task,
                  tc : response time,
            */
              if tcb(i).ba lt mba then
                tcb(i).ba:=tcb(i).ba+1;
                tcb(i).ring2:=tcb(i).ring2+1 rem mba;
                tcb(i).ta(tcb(i).ring2):=tvs:=clock+tc;
                av:=tcb(i).acs and gm; tcb(i).tact:=infinity;
                for j from 1 by 1 to n repeat;
                  if tcb(i).acs(j) and not e(j) then
                    tcb(i).tact:=min(tcb(i).tact, tvs+
                        if rel(1,j) then dt(j) else tcb(i).int fin);
                  fin;
                end;
                call annexsch(tcb(i).acs);
              fin;
              call protocol;
            end;
```

When a task reaches its normal end, the task requests the execution of the following SRL procedure. It removes the task from the ready list and makes the next buffered activation (if any) ready.

```
execend: procedure(i fixed);
            call backexec(i); tcb(i).tcond:=infinity;
            if j gt 0 then
              bolt_status(j):=0; tcb(i).bolt(j):='0' b;
            fin;
            tcb(i).ring1:=tcb(i).ring1+1 rem mba;
```

```
            tcb(i).ba:=tcb(i).ba−1;
            if tcb(i).ba gt 0 then
               av:=zero;
            fin;
            call protocol;
         end;
```

Furthermore, all eventual synchronisation, timeout, and **expect** schedules are deleted, and all synchronisers seized by the task are released in the course of the **terminate** tasking operation:

```
execterm: procedure(i fixed);
            if tcb(i).active then
               call backexec(i); call annexsch(tcb(i).tes);
               tcb(i).susp:=tcb(i).sync:='0'b;
               tcb(i).tcond:=infinity;
               if tcb(i).sys ne 0 then
                  rel(1:m,tcb(i).sys):=zero;
                  b(1,tcb(i).sys):=nil; tcb(i).sys:=0;
               fin;
               if tcb(i).tos ne 0 then
                  in:=tcb(i).tos; sv(1):=2;
                  rel(1:m,tcb(i).tos):=zero;
                  b(1,tcb(i).tos):=nil; tcb(i).tos:=0;
               fin;
               call prevexp(i);
               for j from 1 by 1 to cs repeat;
                  if tcb(i).bolt(j) then
                     tcb(i).bolt(j):='0'b;
                     if bolt_status(j) eq −1 then
                        bolt_status(j):=0;
                     else
                        bolt_status(j):=bolt_status(j)−1;
                     fin;
                  fin;
               end;
               tcb(i).ring1:=tcb(i).ring1+1 rem mba;
```

```
tcb(i).ba:=tcb(i).ba−1;
if tcb(i).ba gt 0 then
    av:=zero;
fin;
call protocol;
fin;
end;
```

5.4   Summary

In this Chapter, we have presented a real time operating system kernel and its dedicated, three-layered co-processor. The first (basic) co-
processor layer is comprised of hardware elements that support the time
dependent features and the recognition of events.

The hardware modules of the basic layer are controlled by the next
higher layer, we refer to as the primary event reaction processor. This
layer guarantees predefined time frames for event recognition and servicing, and operates similarly to a programmable logic controller. We
have presented the data structures and algorithms for time and event
management as performed by the layer. Essentially, the layer's activities
are limited to recording and initiating of event reactions.

Once recognised, recorded and initiated, the events are handled by
the last and highest layer, called the secondary event reaction processor.
The functions of this layer are to carry out specified event handling
routines, which form the core of the real time operating system kernel,
and to control the execution of the users' tasks in the general processor,
presented in the previous Chapter.

Chapter 6

Implementation

In this Chapter we report on the implementation status of our work. While Real-Time Euclid has been implemented, and empirical Real-Time Euclid evaluation data exist (see Chapter 7), no implementation of extended PEARL has yet taken place. Therefore, only a qualitative evaluation is possible of extended PEARL. Moreover, the predictable real time hardware and system software, as presented in Chapters 4 and 5, so far exist in their design stage only. We expect that in a few years extended PEARL will be standardised in the European Community and then be fully implemented. Then, the hardware and software will be implemented together, at which point a substantial, quantitative evaluation may take place. Some new compilers for the present version of PEARL already include various features of extended PEARL.

6.1 Real-Time Euclid

Real-Time Euclid has been implemented and evaluated as a result of a number of co-ordinated projects, one Doctoral, one Master's and five Bachelor's, using the facilities of the Computer Systems Research Institute and administered by the Department of Computer Science and the Computer Group of the Department of Electrical Engineering, at the University of Toronto. The second author of this book has acted as principal designer and project leader. Other project members have included Eugene Kligerman, Chris Ngan, Gerry Parnis, Scott Thurlow, Greg Nimich and Victor Anderson.

6.1.1 Compiler

We have designed and built a Real-Time Euclid compiler [101, 166, 169, 100, 137]. Due to our limited resources and time, we had to omit exception handling and floating-point arithmetic from the compiler. Moreover, at the time we were interested in strictly worst-case schedulability analysis, and thus exception handlers did not contribute anything new to the analysis of Real-Time Euclid programs (already containing interrupt handling and conditional flow of control).

Based on a production Concurrent Euclid compiler[1], the compiler has four passes: scanner/parser, semantic analyser, allocator and coder. The assembly code generated is for the NS16000/32000 microprocessor family.

The control-data flow rules for each pass of the compiler are defined in S/SL (*S*yntax/*S*emantic *L*anguage) [43]. The rule drivers are written in Sequential Euclid (the sequential part of Concurrent Euclid).

The compiler is about 30K lines of Sequential Euclid code long, including S/SL rule table generation code (generated in the form of Euclid arrays by about 20K or $\frac{2}{3}$ of all code), and is thus quite small. It generates both straightforward code with run-time checking and optimised code. The optimised assembly code is as compact and fast as the standard C compiler under a 4.2 Berkeley UNIX System[2].

6.1.1.1 Kernel

To support Real-Time Euclid programs at run-time, we have designed and built a two-layer Real-Time Euclid kernel. The upper layer, referred to as *the Time Manager*, keeps track of time in real time units. The Time Manager maintains the status of each process, next activation times,

---

[1] Our compiler is about 30% different from the Concurrent Euclid compiler.
[2] UNIX is a trademark of AT&T Bell Laboratories.

frames and other timing information. A Concurrent Euclid module of about 1K lines of code, the Time Manager also handles timer interrupts.

The lower kernel layer, referred to as *the Basic Kernel*, is responsible for initialising the hardware, transferring timer interrupts to the Time Manager, handling device interrupts, maintaining various process queues, and basic earliest-deadline-first scheduling. It is written in assembly language and consists of about 4K lines of code.

6.1.1.2 Schedulability Analyser

A prototype schedulability analyser, as described in Chapter 3, has been implemented [170]. The front end of the schedulability analyser is embedded in the coder pass of the compiler. While assembly code is generated, this part of the schedulability analyser extracts timing information, and builds lists and segment trees. The front end is written in Sequential Euclid, like the rest of the coder, and is about 4K lines long.

The back end of the schedulability analyser acts along the lines of Section 3.2. All delays, including ID_{ij}'s, are computed using frame superimposition. It is assumed that process frames (F_i's) are given. The analyser verifies the suitability of the frames by solving the equations of Sections 3.2.3.1 and 3.2.3.3 once[3] for guaranteed response times. This part of the schedulability analyser is written in the language Turing [83], and is about 5K lines long.

Real-Time Euclid's synchronisation primitives (monitors, condition variables, waits, signals and broadcasts) have been mapped to brackets as described in Section 3.3 of Chapter 3. To ensure that all resource synchronisation is done via brackets, all software and hardware resource access must use monitors. This means, we insist that the programmer builds a monitor around every resource. To ensure that resource queueing is first-come-first-served, priority condition variables are not used.

An important problem in real time modeling is that of incorporating overhead into the models. We do so as follows. The amount of time it takes to process a timer interrupt, increment the time count, and return from the interrupt is bounded. This timer interrupt bound is then used

---

[3]That is, the fixed-point iteration is performed for a single iteration only.

to reduce the CPU rate for each CPU. Process activation code is bounded and a chain of segments (interruptible segment, non-interruptible segment, interruptible segment) is generated to correspond to this code. A copy of the chain is then prefixed to each process segment tree. Similarly, overhead chains corresponding to deactivation, monitor access, waits, signals, broadcasts and time-outs are also inserted appropriately into the trees.

The schedulability analyser has been thoroughly tested. First, the raw execution times of various NS32016 instructions were benchmarked, in different execution contexts. Second, the analyser was tested on toy problems, such as single process systems, straight-line code, reducible conditional control flow systems and the like. Third, the analyser was tested on small programs, involving communication and resource-sharing. In all cases analyser predictions were compared with hand-derived predictions. At all stages of testing, the analyser was tested at both inter- and intra-module levels. Only when there were no more errors observed in the analyser execution, was the analyser tried on the applications of Section 7.1.1 of Chapter 7.

6.1.1.3 Hardware

The hardware configuration used in the evaluation of this work is shown on Figure 6.1. This distributed configuration consists of three computer nodes and an independent megabyte mailbox memory board, interconnected by a Multibus. Each node has a NS32016 CPU, a megabyte of local memory, and a terminal. The processors can communicate via the mailbox memory board.

The Real-Time Euclid kernel supports the abstraction of mailbox communication. The mailbox is viewed as a Real-Time Euclid module, possibly containing monitors, but not processes or condition variables. The mailbox variables are mapped onto the independent mailbox memory board, while the code is duplicated for each CPU.

There was no way to suspend a process executing a *wait*. Therefore, *waits/signals* in the mailbox monitors were not supported in the evaluation tests.

Mailbox monitor access is serialised with Dekker's algorithm [50] with interrupts turned off on the CPU attempting to gain monitor access. The reason we used Dekker's algorithm is twofold. First, we decided to treat the configuration as symmetric, and not to choose a particular node to be the mailbox manager. Moreover, although it follows a busy-wait protocol, Dekker's algorithm is fair and guarantees first-come-first-served monitor access. Second, we had no choice but to use a busy-wait solution due to hardware problems. Originally, mailbox memory access was meant to be serialised by a special semaphore board, shown by the dashed-line box in Figure 6.1. The semaphores were to provide low-level support for every monitor access primitive: **EnterMonitor**, **ExitMonitor**, **Wait** and **Signal**. However, during the course of our implementation, it was discovered that the semaphore board was unreliable. Serialisation of mailbox monitors was not always ensured. Moreover, the use of semaphores often led to the locking of the bus. In view of these hardware problems, we had to use a solution which required no semaphore level serialisation. Dekker's algorithm required memory interlock only, something the Multibus itself provides, and thus served our purposes. Due to the small number of processors, this busy-wait supporting mutual exclusion in mailbox monitors solution was feasible, though inefficient. A side-effect of the busy-wait solution was that we could not suspend a process executing a **Wait** in a mailbox monitor, and thus had to exclude applications using mailbox monitor **Wait**s and **Signal**s from the evaluation stage.

In distributed real time systems, it is essential to keep sufficiently accurate track of time. Therefore, it is essential to prevent time values at different nodes from drifting too far apart. When interrupts are turned off it is possible to miss a hardware timer tick. Even if the hardware timer can always interrupt the running process, it may take different amounts of time on different nodes to serve the interrupt before resetting the timer. For these reasons, we keep the time variable in the mailbox, and limit access to it to two procedures: *IncrementCurrentTime* and *GetCurrentTime*. The two subprograms are kept outside of all mailbox monitors regardless of the application. Thus, bus contention (bounded by a constant) is the only contention in accessing the time variable.

One of the nodes is dedicated to just keeping the time. The node's only process has but a single function: to call *IncrementCurrentTime*

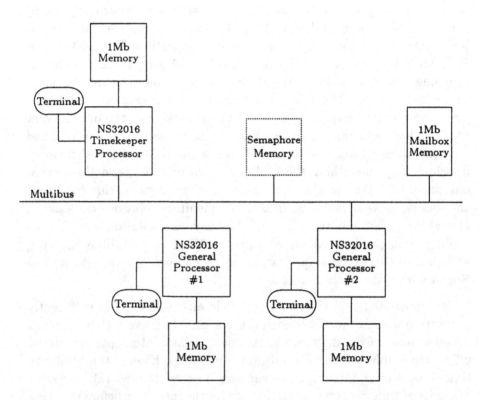

Figure 6.1: The system used in the evaluation.

exactly once every real time unit. This node never misses a tick, and never turns its interrupts off. The other two nodes are used as general purpose nodes. Their Time Managers call *GetCurrentTime* at every local timer interrupt to restore the time. Thus, a local time variable cannot differ from the correct time by more than the number of ticks that fit in the longest local non-interruptible code section at any given time, and is always restored to the correct current value at every timer interrupt occurring after a non-interruptible section.

6.2 Extended PEARL

In this Section we detail the additional steps a compiler for extended PEARL has to take, when preparing programs for execution on the process control computer architecture introduced in the last two Chapters. The steps are comprised of a number of compile-time checks, of the processing of options, and, mainly, of the generation of special code and task control data. Specifically, we describe how the language elements are translated into calling sequences of the operating system co-processor and how direct hardware access of the co-processor's hardware components is generated. For several language constructs it is outlined how they interact with functions of the co-processor and how they are transformed into program sequences involving only low level language features. For these constructs, the corresponding machine code generation is then rather straightforward.

6.2.1 Compiler Functions

Compilation functions needed to support extended PEARL can be triggered by compiler pragmas and directives. The compiler is instructed to flag and/or disallow dynamic language features, to prevent unpredictable storage administration delays. In the test phase of a program, program verification language elements including the **trigger** and **induce** statements, are inserted into the program, to control execution and to examine performance. A pragma is used to select whether these statements are to be regarded as comments, so that they do not need to be removed and can be retained for later use. Alternative syntax check procedures for the **lock** synchronisation statement are invoked by another pragma. The available alternatives are the application of either the resource releasing or of the resource hierarchical deadlock prevention scheme. The latter allows the nesting of **lock** statements, provided the sequence of resource requests complies with a predefined resource hierarchy.

The remaining pragmas address the compiler's code generation pass. One pragma states whether a program module is to be executed on the task processor. If not, different code is generated to run under the test monitor in the co-processor's interrupt generator, to simulate external events. Should the task processor turn idle, the test monitor redefines the system time to the next scheduled instant, in order to speed up the simulation. Another pragma specifies the extent of the event recording desired, and has to be converted by the compiler into parameters for the protocol hardware.

We now consider the compiler functions that are carried out during the processing of declarations and specifications. When a task declaration is elaborated, a corresponding control block is allocated and initialised, unless the maximum number of tasks that can be simultaneously handled has been exceeded. The PEARL language element **interface** is treated the same way as a task. When encountered, interrupts and synchronisers are assigned to the corresponding hardware elements in the co-processor. Accordingly, object names are transformed into hardware addresses. In the course of the compilation, information from the **system** division is utilised, and interrupt array references are reduced to lists of single interrupt references. When shared variables are declared, appropriate storage space is allocated in the common memory. Furthermore, for to synchronise shared variable access, each such variable is associated with an implicitly defined bolt. The application of the **sync** monadic operator to a shared variable is replaced by a reference to its implicit bolt. The system- or user-defined objects of type **signal** are represented as shared one-bit variables. They do not require protection by implicit bolts. The data in the **interval** attributes of interrupt specifications are gathered for later use in the array *ivl*, located in the common memory. The task attributes **keep** and **resident** give rise to corresponding task control block entries. Here the maximum task run-times are recorded as well. These times are either provided by the user or estimated by the compiler, according to the method outlined in Section 3.3. Task loading times are accounted for in the run-times.

In order to subject a program to the hierarchical storage administration scheme described in Section 4.6, the program's object code generated by the compiler must be divided into pages. Tasks and procedures with the **resident** or **reent** attributes, respectively, as well as objects of **global** scope are placed in the pages that remain permanently in storage. However, the maximum number of these pages is subject to a limit.

6.2.2   Run-Time Features

In this Section we discuss the implementation of both the new language constructs introduced in Section 2.9 and of other functions, which require to communicate with the operating system processor.

The co-processor's hardware layer is accessed by the following instructions and functions. To determine values for the monadic operators **now** and **tstate** (that stand for the current time and the stati of tasks, respectively), the clock register and appropriate task control block entries are directly read out, respectively.

The **update** statement is converted into writing a new value into the down counter T.**res** (that determines the executing task's maximum residual run-time). Certain one-bit storage locations in the common memory are used to mask the interrupt lines. The locations are set and reset by the **enable** and **disable** statements. To **trigger** an interrupt, the corresponding interrupt recognition hardware element is written to. The **induce** statement is implemented similarly, viz. by writing a logical 1 into the shared variable associated with the signal to be raised.

To implement the **maxloop** clause of the **repeat** statement, the compiler generates an iteration counter and a counter overflow branch to the pertaining **exceeding** statement sequence.

To schedule an activity for later execution, its corresponding parameters are transmitted to the co-processor, as described later. In the course of preparing these parameters for a time schedule defined with the **exactly** attribute, an associated indicator is set and the installation parameter *eps* is subtracted from the initial time of the schedule. Furthermore, the sum of the (residual) maximum task run-time and *eps* is computed, and installed as time condition that will cause the scheduler to run the task immediately. All other preparations are carried through by the operating system processor within the reaction time span of length *eps* before the hardware actually starts the task execution at the exactly specified instant. No provisions are to be made within the code of the task.

Since the occurrence of an interrupt is unpredictable, the implementation of **when** reactions without delay is impossible, unless the event is expected with the program loaded and the processor in the idle state. However, this possibility is not considered, because it is inefficient and the system cannot perform any other tasks. Nevertheless, if this feature is really needed, the external hardware generating the interrupt must be constructed in such a way that it can already raise a signal some time before the computer service is actually needed. Then the feature can be realised with the help of a two stage schedule having the **exactly** attribute.

We now turn to the implementation of the **expect** statement. Recall the syntax of the statement:

> expect-statement::=**expect** expect-alternative-string **fin**;
> with
> expect-alternative::=**await** event-list **do** statement-string

Suppose an **expect** statement appears in a task, whose control block is stored under the index i in the array *tcb*. The data describing the event lists are transmitted to the co-processor, thus scheduling the future execution of the statement. The single lists or alternatives correspond to the bits set in the array $tcb(i).em(0{:}n)$. For each specified event, the alternatives to be executed are marked in the bit array $tcb(i).exp(0{:}n)$ by the operating system processor. When an event or events occur(s), the task is resumed and all marked alternatives are executed in the sequence they have been listed. Then, the task either re-suspends or branches to new alternatives that have become due since the resumption. Thus, an **expect** statement can be replaced by the following equivalent code sequence.

/* Schedule an EXPECT-Resume operation for the occurrence
  of any event contained in event-list1, event-list2,...;
  this implies the suspension of the task */;

begin: $hv:=tcb(i).exp$; $tcb(i).exp:=zero$;
        /* zero is an appropriately long vector of '0'B */;
        $j:=0$;
        for k **from** 1 **by** 1 **to** n **repeat**;
          if $tcb(i).em(k)$ **then**
            $j:=j+1$;
            if $hv(k)$ **then**
              case j
                alt *statement−string1*;
                alt *statement−string2*;
                  ...
            fin;
          fin;
        fin;
      end;
        if $tcb(i).exp$ **eq** *zero* **then** *suspend*; **fin**;
        goto begin;
end: /* request the OS to prevent the task's expect schedule */;

The **quit** instructions are replaced by branches to the label *end*, where
the operating system processor routine *prevexp* is called that prevents
(cancels) the associated **expect**-resume schedule.

We now consider the **lock** synchronisation mechanism, defined as
follows.

        lock-statement::=
        lock synchronisation-clause-list [**nonpreemptively**]
            [timeout-clause] [exectime-clause]
        perform statement-string
        unlock;
        with
        timeout-clause::=

timeout {**in** duration-expression | **at** clock-expression}
outtime statement-string **fin**
exectime-clause::=**exectimebound** duration-expression
synchronisation-clause::=
    exclusive(shared-object-expression-list) |
    shared(shared-object-expression-list)

Let i again be the tcb index of the control block of the task where a **lock** statement occurs. First, the synchronisation clause list is converted to entries in the array $lv(1{:}cs,1{:}2)$ of bits according to the following procedure

$lv(j,1){:=}'1'B$, if exclusive access to the protected object is requested,
$lv(j,2){:=}'1'B$, if shared access to the protected object is requested,
$lv(j,*){:=}'0'B$, otherwise,

for $j{=}1,...,cs$, where cs designates the number of hardware implemented synchronisers. The synchroniser status outputs are available as the matrix $boltevent$, that has the same structure as lv. The comparison of the two matrices determines whether the synchronisers can be claimed as requested. The indicator nia is set to 1, when the **nonpreemptively** attribute is present, and to 0, otherwise. The indicator is used to program the non-interruption hardware register, which determines whether the running task may be pre-empted (not if the register holds '1'B). The code sequence given below specifies how values are assigned to this bit, when the resource releasing deadlock prevention method is used, i.e. when there may be no nesting of **lock** statements. When the other method, namely the resource hierarchical algorithm, is employed, the sequence of assignments to the bit as shown in form of comments is slightly more complicated and requires the integer variable nni with initial value 0 as a further tcb entry. In the following piece of code that replaces the **lock** statement, the tcb fields opt and $bolt$ are used to control the flow of processing and to mark claimed bolts, respectively. When claiming a synchroniser, appropriate new values are written into the synchroniser's status register. We are not supporting the exectime-clause here, since it is only intended as an additional safety net.

```
non_interruption_bit:='1'b;
if lv and boltevent exor lv eq zero then
   tcb(i).opt:=1;
else
   non_interruption_bit:='0'b;
   /* or: non_interruption_bit:=tcb(i).nni gt 0; */
   /* parameter preparation and transmission to
        the operating system processor for scheduling
        the perform and outtime clauses;
        this implies task suspension */;
fin;
if tcb(i).opt eq 1 then
   non_interruption_bit:='1'b;
   for j from 1 by 1 to cs repeat;
      if lv(j,1) or lv(j,2) then
         tcb(i).bolt(j):='1'b;
         if lv(j,1) then
            bolt_status(j):=-1;
         else
            bolt_status(j):=bolt_status(j)+1;
         fin;
      fin;
   end;
   tcb(i).opt:=0;
   if nia eq 0 then non_interruption_bit:='0'b; fin;
   /* or: tcb(i).nni:=tcb(i).nni+nia;
        non_interruption_bit:=tcb(i).nni gt 0; */;
   /* execution of the perform clause;
        quit statements are replaced by jumps to "unlock" */;
unlock: for j from 1 by 1 to cs repeat;
            if lv(j,1) or lv(j,2) then
               tcb(i).bolt(j):='0'b;
               if lv(j,1) then
                  bolt_status(j):=0;
               else
                  bolt_status(j):=bolt_status(j)-1;
               fin;
```

```
        fin;
      end;
      non_interruption_bit:='0'b;
      /* or: tcb(i).nni:=tcb(i).nni-nia;
           non_interruption_bit:=tcb(i).nni gt 0; */;
else
   tcb(i).opt:=0; /* execution of outtime clause */;
fin;
```

Within the **perform** clause, seized resources can be released already before the end of the **lock** statement is reached, by executing the following **unlock** instruction:

unlock-statement::=**unlock** shared-object-expression-list;

The lists of specified synchronisers are converted to the elements of the array $uv(1:cs,1:2)$. The use of the array is analogous to that of lv. Accordingly, **unlock** is implemented as follows.

```
for j from 1 by 1 to cs repeat;
  if uv(j,1) or uv(j,2) then
    tcb(i).bolt(j):='0'b;
    if uv(j,1) then
      lv(j,1):='0'b; bolt_status(j):=0;
    else
      lv(j,2):='0'b; bolt_status(j):=bolt_status(j)−1;
    fin;
  fin;
end;
```

We now turn to the implementation of **on** event handlers. When a task raises a signal, the co-processor's scheduled reaction is activated via the signal hardware and the task processor ceases to execute instructions. This is necessary in order to prevent further operations on undefined data, such as in the case of a divide check. The operating system processor now loads the current contents of the program address counter as the continuation address, and the identification of the occurred signal, into the task's *tcb* fields *fsa* and *sigid*, respectively. Then, the start address of the general **on** reaction within the application program is written from the *tcb* entry *aon* into the program address register and the task execution is restarted.

As shown in the piece of code given below, the general reaction routine commences with saving the continuation address and the signal identification in the two stacks *cad* and *sid*, to enable the handling of nested **on** requests. The procedures *push*, *pop*, and *top* perform the usual stack operations. A Boolean lock variable is associated with each signal, to prevent the nested treatment of the same signal. Should the reaction to a signal re-raise the same signal, the operating system is called to handle this event. Normally, the **on** reaction proceeds with resetting the occurred signal, invoking the corresponding handling procedure, and returning to the address where the program flow was interrupted. The individual **on** handling procedures are contained within the bodies of the blocks, where they are defined as implicit subroutines. When processing the **on** statements in an application program, the starting addresses of these procedures are loaded into the array *rpa* in accordance with the block's structure and scope.

```
call push(cad,tcb(i).fsa); call push(sid,tcb(i).sigid);
if lock(top(sid)) then
    call pop(cad); call pop(sid); induce system reaction signal;
else
    lock(top(sid)):='1'b; signal(top(sid)):='0'b;
    call cont rpa(top(sid)); lock(top(sid)):='0'b;
    next:=top(cad); call pop(cad); call pop(sid);
    goto cont next;
fin;
```

The last set of functions we consider in this Section are calls for operating system services. As discussed earlier, service call parameters are passed from the task processor to the SRL through a first-in-first-out memory. The first parameter always specifies the desired function and the rest are parameters needed by the function. In the remainder of the

Section, we describe these function specific parameters.

To commence or terminate supervising a shared variable, the address of the variable is provided. For the former, a relational operator and a corresponding comparison value, to be watched for, are specified as well.

The **on** event reaction, which is part of the application tasks, is initiated by an operating system procedure scheduled at the start of the user program for the occurrence of all possible signals. This general routine has no parameters.

The majority of the operating system functions requires only a single parameter, namely the pertaining task control block's index in the array *tcb*. Among these functions are the tasking services **prevent, suspend, terminate**, and the normal task termination, as well as the procedures which resume a task upon occurrence of one of the events mentioned in an **expect** statement's alternative and which prevent the corresponding schedules, respectively. A task must cease its execution by stopping the processor after having requested its normal termination. The functions **continue** and **activate** also take the *tcb* index, but additionally require the task's response time needed to calculate the time condition.

The rest of the functions schedule operating system services for future execution, and require more elaborate parameters. The first two parameters are the *tcb* index and a function selector, with the value 10 for the **on** event reaction, or 1 through 8 signifying the operations **activate, terminate, prevent, suspend, continue, resume, expect**-resume, and synchronisation-resume, respectively. Should an **on** event be scheduled, the third parameter is a bit vector that enables a desired subset of signals. Otherwise, the third parameter is a number that states the number of basic schedules that follow.

Each basic schedule data set starts with a bit vector that marks all desired events. If the time-event-bit is set in this vector, four additional data items describing a time schedule must be provided. The first item is either the schedule's initial value or an offset to be added to the occurrence time of a future interrupt yielding an initial value. The remaining three items are the interval between consecutive time events, the validity duration of the schedule, and two further bits. The first bit indicates that the schedule is two-stage, i.e., one with an interrupt time offset. The second bit indicates that the operation is requested with exact timing. In the case of the tasking statements **continue**, **resume**, and **activate**, each basic schedule is followed by a response time. When scheduling a synchronisation-resume, two basic schedules are needed, requesting two co-processor reactions. The first reaction is to check whether the synchronisation request has been enabled following the release of one or more synchronisers. The second reaction initiates the handling of the timeout condition.

6.3   Summary

We have presented an implementation of Real-Time Euclid and its schedulability analyser, and have proposed an implementation of extended PEARL. The implementation of Real-Time Euclid and its schedulability analyser attests to the fact that implementations of schedulability analysable languages — such as extended PEARL — are feasible. While Real-Time Euclid has never made it out of the laboratory, it is our expectation that the implementation of extended PEARL and a corresponding schedulability analyser, which will be quite similar to the one of Real-Time Euclid, will also be a successful application of our ideas, and will have a significant, positive impact on the development practice of real time systems in industry.

Chapter 7

Evaluation

In this Chapter we quantitatively evaluate Real-Time Euclid and its schedulability analyser. While Real-Time Euclid has been implemented, and empirical Real-Time Euclid evaluation data exist, we expect that corresponding results would not differ too much for the yet unimplemented extended PEARL, due to the comparable structure of the two languages. The second part of this Chapter shortly evaluates the architecture and the operating system kernel we have introduced. Since a prototype of the computer has not been built yet, the evaluation will only be a qualitative one.

7.1 Real-Time Euclid and its Schedulability Analyser

The evaluation of Real-Time Euclid and its schedulability analyser has taken place as follows. Simulated software applications have been designed and implemented using the Real-Time Euclid implementation as described in Chapter 6. The applications have been analysed with the schedulability analyser, and then run on the actual system. The guaranteed response times predicted by the analyser have been contrasted with those actually observed, and all times as well as their corresponding deviation (actual from predicted) margins have been tabulated.

7.1.1   Applications

Two advanced undergraduate students have designed and implemented two programming projects [179, 138]. A third project, undertaken by two other students, was aimed at a considerably more ambitious application, and unfortunately has failed to complete in time to be included in this evaluation. Each successful project involved producing a medium size (between 3K and 5K lines of code) distributed Real-Time Euclid program, targeted at the hardware described in Section 6.1.1.3 of Chapter 6.

Each project has served as a beta-test of Real-Time Euclid and its schedulability analyser. Thus, the students have been exposed to the language through conventional teaching techniques, and then the students have been asked to provide their own simulated process control applications and to implement them in Real-Time Euclid. The students have been allowed to interact with each other as well as with those better familiar with the language for as long as only the functionality of the language had been discussed and not ways of using the language to construct their programs. Thus, the programs resulting in the projects have not been tailored, in any way, to fit the desired results.

We now present these projects. The tabulated evaluation results are presented in Section 7.1.1.3.

7.1.1.1   A Simulated Power Station

For the purposes of this experiment, a simplified model of a power station is used [179]. In this model, the only factors needing monitoring are the boiler temperature, the boiler pressure, and the turbine rotation speed. All these factors are related to the burn rate of the fuel heating the boiler and the current load on the generators. The control system for this power station is loosely based on the control system for the Drax coal fired power station in the United Kingdom [37]. In the Drax station, each boiler/turbine generating unit is supervised by seven "data centres" which monitor the unit and report to a central CPU. The latter is responsible for tracking faults as reported by the data centres. Each data centre consists of a PDP-11/23 while the central CPU consists of a PDP-11/44.

In the simulation, only five data centres are used. Each data centre collects information from five sensors monitoring the boiler temperature, the steam pressure, and the turbine speed. Each data centre is designed to cope with sensor failures and the central CPU is designed to cope with data centre failures. A data centre is responsible for validating the sensor input by comparing the readings with readings from other sensors. The central CPU validates recommendations of the data centres by comparing the recommendations from the data centre with one another. If a sensor fails, it is deactivated. If a data centre fails, it is deactivated. If a certain number of sensors or data centres fails, the central CPU shuts the boiler/turbine and all data centres down.

The simulation software consists of the *DataCenter* module, the *CentralCPU* module, the *Failure* module, the *Simulator* module, the *MailBox* module, and the *Console* module. The *DataCenter* module simulates the five data centres. The *CentralCPU* module simulates the central CPU. The *Failure* module simulates sensor and data centre failures by deactivating communication units in the *MailBox* module. The *Simulator* module simulates the boiler and turbine and sets the values for the sensors to be read by the *DataCenter* module. The *MailBox* module provides communication units that serve two purposes. First, the communication units allow the various modules to communicate with each other regardless of the physical CPU the modules are located on. Second, the existence of the units enables the *Failure* Module to deactivate the units to simulate sensor or data centre failures. The *Console* module provides a means for the *DataCenter* and *CentralCPU* modules to communicate with the human operator by printing output on a console.

Console Module

The *Console* module provides a means for the power station control program to communicate with the human operators of the power station. It exports two routines: *DisplayString* which displays a string using the *PutString* procedure, and *DisplayInt* which displays an integer using the *PutInt* procedure. In a real system, this module would be replaced by a module whose routines would print output on a special printer or monitor.

Mailbox Module

The *MailBox* module provides facilities that allow the other modules to communicate with each other via communication units. A communication unit is a 32-bit memory location accessible from any physical CPU. The value of a communication unit can be set with the procedure *WriteComm* or read with the procedure *ReadComm*. In addition, communication units can be deactivated by the procedures *KillComm* or *LooneyComm* and reactivated with the routine *RepairComm*. *KillComm* deactivates a communication unit by setting a flag which instructs *ReadComm* not to return a value for that communication unit. *LooneyComm* deactivates a communication unit by instructing *ReadComm* to return a random number rather than the value of the communications unit. *RepairComm* repairs a communications unit by clearing the flags set by *KillComm* and *LooneyComm*.

Mutually exclusive access to the communication units is assured by placing all communication units in a single monitor. This solution is not optimal since separate communication units have no relation to one another and, thus, there is no reason why reading or writing to a communications unit should prevent another process from reading or writing to a different communication unit. However, due to the large number of communication units (twentyfive), and the fact that all accesses to the communication units consist of only a few machine instructions, the advantages of allowing higher concurrency by placing each communication unit in its own monitor are far outweighed by the awkwardness of managing a large number of monitors that are carbon copies of each other. Also, the solution to the readers and writers problem cannot be used, since hardware faults (see Section 6.1.1.3 of Chapter 6) prevent the use of conditions in the memory shared by the CPU's on the NS32000 multiprocessor computer, used by the current implementation of the Real-Time Euclid system.

DataCenter Module

The *DataCenter* module contains five periodic processes, and one procedure. Each process simulates a data centre by calling the procedure *DataSim*. The The *DataSim* procedure first polls all sensors for the boiler temperature, the steam pressure and the turbine speed. If a sensor read fails to return a value, a message is printed on the console to inform the operator of the sensor failure. Once all the sensors have been read, the values for each type of sensor are averaged and all the sensor results that are outside a tolerance range from the average are discarded. If the readings for a sensor are discarded, a message is printed on the console informing the operator that a sensor is returning an inconsistent value and the error count for the sensor is incremented.

If the error count for a sensor exceeds a certain value (five), then the sensor is deactivated until repaired. If fewer than three sensors are still active and are returning consistent values, the data centre informs the central CPU that it wishes to shut down the power station. Once all the sensors have been read and validated, the data centre computes a recommended fuel burn rate for the boiler and informs the central CPU of this recommendation.

Central CPU Module

The *CentralCPU* Module contains one periodic process which simulates the central CPU. The process polls each data centre to obtain a shutdown or a fuel burn rate recommendation. If the majority of active data centres recommends a system shutdown, all data centres are deactivated, a message is printed on the console, and the power station is shut down. If a data centre recommends a system shutdown, but the majority of the data centres does not recommend a system shutdown, the error count for the data centre recommending system shutdown is incremented. The burn rate recommendation for all active data centres is averaged and any recommendations outside a tolerance zone of the average are discarded. If the recommendation for a data centre is discarded, the error count for that data centre is incremented. When the error count for any data centre reaches a critical level (five), that data centre is deactivated until repaired. If fewer than three data centres are active and returning consistent values, the central CPU deactivates all data centres, prints a message on the console, and shuts the power station down.

Failure Module

The *Failure* module contains a single periodic process. The process deactivates communication units with *LooneyComm* and repairs communication units with *RepairComm* at random intervals. The *Failure* module schedules the deactivations so that there is one failure every 60 real time units, and schedules repairs so that a deactivated communication unit is repaired after 180 real time units.

Simulator Module

The *Simulator* Module contains a periodic process which reads the fuel burn rate from the *CentralCPU* and sets all the sensors to the appropriate values. Since the status of a communications unit is handled when the communications unit is read rather than when the communications unit is written to, the *Simulator* module need not be concerned with the current status of the sensors as it sets them.

Suitability of Real-Time Euclid

Real-Time Euclid provides many features that simplify the implementation of the power station control system. Identical periodic frames are used for the data centre processes, the central CPU process, and the simulator process, since they are generating and manipulating the same data. The *Failure* module process has a longer periodic frame to reduce the frequency of system failures and repairs. Time-bounded waits are used to insure that data from sensors and from the data centres are obtained within a deadline or emergency measures are taken if the deadline is not met.

7.1.1.2   A Simulated Packet-Level Handshaking in X.25

The purpose of this project is to reproduce the sequence of packet type exchanges that occur between DTE and DCE during the call set-up and disconnect phases of the X.25 protocol [138]. The brand of X.25 modeled is DATAPAC's Standard Network Access Protocol (SNAP) [151, 47]. The Real-Time Euclid programming language is employed successfully to implement the simulation. The multiple-microprocessor run-time environment allows dedicated CPUs to be assigned to both DTE and DCE simulation modules. The Mailbox module construct of Real-Time Euclid facilitates easy inter-processor communication for simulating the inbound and outbound packet channels between the DTE and DCE.

In general, hosts (DTEs) connected to a packet network can activate many virtual circuits and carry on many conversations at once, each de-

Figure 7.1: DTE states for a successful DTE *CallRequest*.

lineated by its logical channel number. In this simulation, it is assumed that the DTE only sets up and maintains one connection at any time. Hence only the packet types of the handshaking between DTE and DCE are simulated. Other aspects, such as logical channels, virtual addresses, and packet formats, are not incorporated in the simulation.

When the DCE receives a request packet from the DTE, it must send the packet out onto the sub-net to the remote DCE and receive a positive response before acknowledging the DCE request. In this simulation, if the delay is too long the DCE assumes a network error has occurred and sends a *NetworkError* packet (not specifically contained in SNAP) to the DTE. Both DTE and DCE assume the transaction has been canceled and change their states appropriately.

Figures 7.1, 7.2, 7.3, and 7.4 illustrate the DTE/DCE state transitions. The states inside the ovals correspond to the states of either the DTE or DCE or both. The edges represent actions taken. Referring to Figures 7.1 and 7.2, assume that both DTE and DCE are in the *Ready* state. To make a connection with a remote host, the DTE sends a *Call-Request* packet to the DCE and goes into the *DTEWaiting* state. Upon receiving the *CallRequest* packet from the DTE, the DCE goes into the *DCEwaiting* state and simulates a remote DCE connection delay. Assuming the delay is not too long, the DCE goes into the *DataTransfer* state and sends a *CallConnected* packet to the DTE. Upon receiving the *CallConnected* packet, the DTE also goes into the *DataTransfer* state.

As previously described, the DCE may return a *NetworkError* packet in response to a request by the DTE. Figures 7.3 and 7.4 illustrate the state diagram for a failing DTE *CallRequest*.

In [47] actions are specified to be taken by the DCE when unexpected packets are received while in various states. The same is not provided

Figure 7.2: DCE states for a successful DTE *CallRequest*.

Figure 7.3: DTE states for a failed DTE *CallRequest*.

for the DTE. For the purposes of the simulation it is assumed that the DTE acts in a manner symmetrically equivalent (in relation to the state diagrams) to the way the DCE acts.

The implementation is comprised of three modules: *DTE*, *DCE*, and *Mailbox*. The simulation of a packet transaction consists of passing integers corresponding to specific packet types between the *DTE* and *DCE* modules via the *Mailbox* module. The *DTE* and *DCE* modules keep track of their own state and co-ordinate the initiation of packet transactions based on requests entered at a terminal connected to their respective processor.

DTE Module

This module contains three processes. The *PollKybd* and *DTEreceiver* processes poll for input to the module. The *DTEsender* process is awakened to send output to the *DCE*. The *DTE* module also contains the Finite State Machine (*FSM*) monitor. This monitor holds the *DTE*

Figure 7.4: DCE states for a failed DTE *CallRequest*.

present and previous (to the latest transaction) state and decides what is to be done when inputs are received. The previous state is kept so that state transitions can be printed as part of the trace of a transaction. Once the *DTEsender* process has awakened and entered the monitor, if a packet is to be sent, the packet type is determined and relayed to the *DTEsender* process. The module receives input from two sources: the terminal and the *InboundChannel* mailbox monitor. The terminal is used by a human operator, and the *InboundChannel* monitor holds packets sent to the *DTE* from the *DCE*.

The *PollKybd* process periodically prompts the terminal for input commands. Once a recognisable command is given, the process enters the *FSM* monitor to see if the command can be executed. For example, if a request for a data packet transmission is made and the *FSM* is not in the *DataTransfer* state, then the command is not executed and a message is printed on the *DTE* terminal. If the command can be executed then the *packetToGo* variable is set to the corresponding packet. The *DTEsender* process is then awakened via a broadcast statement, and a confirmation is printed on the terminal.

The *DTEreceiver* process periodically polls the *InboundChannel* mailbox monitor to see if a packet has been placed there by the *DCE*. If a packet is obtained, the process calls the *FSM* monitor procedure *ReceivePacket*. This procedure decides whether a state change or a packet response or both should take place. The process learns of the *DTE* state before and after receiving the packet, and awakens the *DTEsender* process if a response is required. The *DTEreceiver* then prints a trace of the transaction at the *DTE*'s terminal.

When awakened by a broadcast statement, the *DTEsender* process calls the *FSM* monitor procedure *PacketToSend*. The procedure determines what packet is to be sent, causes a state change (unless the packet is pure data), notes the old and new state of the *FSM*, and prints a trace of the transaction on the *DTE* terminal. The process then enters the *OutboundChannel* mailbox monitor, places the packet there, and sets the *packetInChannel* flag.

DCE Module

This module contains symmetrically equivalent structures and three of its processes execute in a similar manner to those of the *DTE* module. However, the *DCE FSM* expects to see and sends packet types different from those of the *DTE*. The *DCEreceiver* process polls the *Outbound-Channel* mailbox monitor for packets sent by the *DTE*. The *DCEsender* process places packets destined for the *DTE* in the *InboundChannel* mailbox monitor.

The *DCE* also contains a fourth process, *NetworkDelay*. This process simulates the delay of a packet request from the *DTE* traversing the sub-net to the destination *DCE* and back. *NetworkDelay* is awakened whenever the *DCEreceiver* process enters the *DCE FSM* monitor with a request packet from the *DTE*. A delay value is determined from a pseudo-random number generator, and the process is delayed for that long. The process then decides whether the delay time was too long and signals the *DCEreceiver* process waiting for the delay to pass. The *DCEreceiver* process is made aware whether the delay was too long. If so, the *packetToGo* variable is set to the *NetworkError* packet and the *DCE* state goes back to its state prior to receiving the packet from the *DTE*. Upon receiving this error packet from the *DCE*, the *DTE* resets its state to the state it was in prior to sending the request packet. Thus, the complete transaction is effectively nullified in the case of a network error.

Mailbox Module

The *Mailbox* module accommodates packet deliveries between *DTE* and *DCE* modules. It contains two monitors corresponding to packet flow in each direction: *InboundChannel* and *OutboundChannel*. There is no buffering of packets beyond one in either direction. Both monitors provide procedure entries to set and to read the packets in transit.

Suitability of Real-Time Euclid

The periodic process construct is a convenient way of implementing a polling process, with the polling frequency being the process frame length. By knowing how often processes poll in real time, one has a definite upper bound on the frequency with which requests for action can occur. Thus CPU time can be allocated without being concerned by activities executed during request service time, if a good estimate of the maximum duration of a poll is known.

The **broadcast** statement is used in the program whenever a sending process, such as *DTEsender*, needs to pass a packet between processors. This is a useful construct, allowing a designer to have a process started up from any point within the code. This construct accommodates situations where the frequency of execution of a process varies as is the case in this simulation.

7.1.1.3 Schedulability Analyser Evaluation

As reported in Section 7.1.1, Real-Time Euclid was found to be a suitable language to use in real time application writing. We now present the results of the evaluation of Real-Time Euclid's schedulability analyser, based on the simulated real time applications of Section 7.1.1. The static decompositions of the programs are tabulated in Tables 7.1 and 7.2. Table 7.3 summarises the process content of the programs.

In our evaluation, we varied process resource requirements (by inserting idle for-loops into various parts of the programs) while keeping the frames constant. We gathered sets of predicted and actual response times. We measured load in terms of ratios of actual process response times to their corresponding frames. The evaluation took place in the context of four different loads (and thus four different sets of resource requirements): light load of 7% to 20%, medium load of 13% to 50%, heavy load of 35% to 80%, and overload (some processes missed their deadlines) of 42% to 120%.

The predictions were made by our method and the Leinbaugh and Yamini [113, 114] method. We used this method for comparison with our method, because of all methods surveyed in Section 3.2.3.2 of Chapter 3 it is the one second best suitable for the analysis of real time systems like ours. The best existing method is probably the Leinbaugh and Yamini [115] technique. Unfortunately, because no algorithmic description of it is available, it is not clear how to implement it. Moreover, one of the aims of this evaluation is to demonstrate the superiority of frame superimposition over existing closed-form and polynomial techniques. The Leinbaugh and Yamini [115] method is not such a technique.

Tables 7.4 through 7.11 present the results of the evaluation.

Program #	Computation	Control	Synchronisation	Communication
Power Plant	53%	19%	15%	13%
DTE/DCE	54%	15%	18%	13%

Table 7.1: Static Program Decomposition By Function

Program #	Process	Monitor Subprogram	Non-monitor Subprogram	Mailbox
Power Plant	24%	20%	33%	23%
DTE/DCE	26%	16%	28%	30%

Table 7.2: Static Program Decomposition By Construct

Program #	process frames	periodic
Power Plant (cpu1)	15, 15, 15, 15, 15	Yes, Yes, Yes, Yes, Yes
Power Plant (cpu2)	60, 15, 15	Yes, Yes, Yes
DTE/DCE (cpu1)	10, 2, 14	Yes, No, Yes
DTE/DCE (cpu2)	10, 4, 14, 3	Yes, No, Yes, No

Table 7.3: Evaluation Program Processes

Program #	maxRespTimes	predictedRespTimes	difference (%)
Power Plant (cpu1)	all 3	all 3.10	all 3.33
Power Plant (cpu2)	4, 2, 2	4.11, 2.07, 2.04	2.75, 3.50, 2.00
DTE/DCE (cpu1)	1, 0, 1	1.04, 0.23, 1.05	4.00, n/a, 5.00
DTE/DCE (cpu2)	1, 0, 1, 0	1.02, 0.31, 1.04, 0.45	2.00, n/a, 4.00, n/a
average (%)	n/a	n/a	3.33

Table 7.4: Performance of Our Method Under Light Load

Program #	maxRespTimes	predictedRespTimes	difference (%)
Power Plant (cpu1)	all 3	all 3.69	all 23.00
Power Plant (cpu2)	4, 2, 2	5.10, 2.51, 2.49	27.50, 25.50, 24.50
DTE/DCE (cpu1)	1, 0, 1	1.48, 0.93, 1.42	48.00, n/a, 42.00
DTE/DCE (cpu2)	1, 0, 1, 0	1.31, 1.03, 1.30, 1.20	31.00, n/a, 30.00, n/a
average (%)	n/a	n/a	28.63

Table 7.5: Performance of Leinbaugh Method Under Light Load

Program #	maxRespTimes	predictedRespTimes	difference (%)
Power Plant (cpu1)	all 6	all 6.37	all 6.17
Power Plant (cpu2)	8, 4, 4	8.43, 4.24, 4.20	5.38, 6.00, 5.00
DTE/DCE (cpu1)	2, 1, 2	2.12, 1.08, 2.17	6.00, 8.00, 8.50
DTE/DCE (cpu2)	2, 1, 2, 1	2.09, 1.10, 2.17, 1.08	4.5, 10.00, 8.50, 8.00
average (%)	n/a	n/a	6.71

Table 7.6: Performance of Our Method Under Medium Load

Program #	maxRespTimes	predictedRespTimes	difference (%)
Power Plant (cpu1)	all 6	all 8.25	all 37.50
Power Plant (cpu2)	8, 4, 4	11.34, 6.31, 6.28	41.75, 57.75, 57.00
DTE/DCE (cpu1)	2, 1, 2	3.16, 1.58, 3.72	58.00, 58.00, 86.00
DTE/DCE (cpu2)	2, 1, 2, 1	2.85, 1.61, 3.12, 1.58	42.50, 61.00, 56.00, 97.50
average (%)	n/a	n/a	50.90

Table 7.7: Performance of Leinbaugh Method Under Medium Load

Program #	maxRespTimes	predictedRespTimes	difference (%)
Power Plant (cpu1)	all 12	all 13.39	all 11.58
Power Plant (cpu2)	21, 12, 12	22.94, 13.83, 12.96	9.24, 15.25, 8.00
DTE/DCE (cpu1)	7, 1, 10	8.27, 1.26, 11.38	18.14, 26.00, 13.80
DTE/DCE (cpu2)	7, 3, 11, 2	8.12, 3.41, 12.63, 2.40	16.00, 13.67, 14.82, 20.00
average (%)	n/a	n/a	14.19

Table 7.8: Performance of Our Method Under Heavy Load

Program #	maxRespTimes	predictedRespTimes	difference (%)
Power Plant (cpu1)	all 12	all 17.34	all 44.50
Power Plant (cpu2)	21, 12, 12	34.23, 21.76, 21.68	63.00, 81.33, 80.67
DTE/DCE (cpu1)	7, 1, 10	13.45, 1.97, 22.77	92.14, 97.00, 127.70
DTE/DCE (cpu2)	7, 3, 11, 2	13.57, 5.86, 22.34, 3.95	93.86, 95,33, 103.09, 97.50
average (%)	n/a	n/a	76.94

Table 7.9: Performance of Leinbaugh Method Under Heavy Load

Program #	maxRespTimes	predictedRespTimes	difference (%)
Power Plant (cpu1)	all 16	all 21.65	all 35.31
Power Plant (cpu2)	25, 16, 16	31.23, 21.09, 20.60	24.92, 31.81, 28.75
DTE/DCE (cpu1)	9, 3, 12	12.87, 4.14, 15.21	43.00, 38.00, 26.75
DTE/DCE (cpu2)	9, 5, 12, 4	12.97, 6.95, 15.98, 5.09	44.11, 39.00, 33.17, 27.25
average (%)	n/a	n/a	34.22

Table 7.10: Performance of Our Method Under Overload

Program #	maxRespTimes	predictedRespTimes	difference (%)
Power Plant (cpu1)	all 16	all 37.14	all 132.13
Power Plant (cpu2)	25, 16, 16	53.35, 35.11, 34.04	113.40, 119.44, 112.25
DTE/DCE (cpu1)	9, 3, 12	21.86, 7.83, 35.13	142.89, 161.00, 192.75
DTE/DCE (cpu2)	9, 5, 12, 4	22.14, 14.18, 37.64, 10.12	146.00, 183.60, 213.67, 153.00
average (%)	n/a	n/a	146.61

Table 7.11: Performance of Leinbaugh Method Under Overload

As expected, both algorithms predict less accurate bounds in the case
of the DTE/DCE program than they do in the case of the Power Plant
program. This is due to the fact that while the Power Plant program
contains periodic processes only, half of the DTE/DCE processes are
aperiodic (**atEvent**). The times of periodic process activations are easily and accurately predicted by both algorithms. However, only ranges
of the times of aperiodic process activations (as defined by **broadcast**
statements) can be determined by our algorithm, and the Leinbaugh algorithm has no means of doing even that (and thus this latter algorithm
assumes that aperiodic process activations can occur at any time at all).

As we mentioned previously, our frame superimposition algorithm is
exponential in nature. Thus an important question is how much time
our schedulability analysis contributes to the compilation-and-analysis
phase of real time software development. While we do not attempt to
answer this question in general, our experience with the two applications described in this Chapter has been that the analysis increases the
pure compilation time by about 60 – 100%. For example, one of our
programs took 5 minutes to just compile and 10 minutes to compile and
be analysed. Thus we feel that the analysis does not take unacceptably
long to run — though this is just a speculation for the case of very large
programs with complex resource contention patterns.

Despite the relative difficulty our algorithm has with aperiodic processes, it performs well on the absolute scale. The method gives very
accurate (within 2% to 5%) predictions in the light load case, good
(within 4.5% to 10%) predictions in the medium load case, reasonably
accurate (within 8% to 26%) predictions in the heavy load case, and
only marginally inaccurate (within 24.92% to 44.11%) predictions in the
overload case. The performance of the Leinbaugh method is in sharp
contrast with the performance of our method. Under every load, the
Leinbaugh method predicts guaranteed response times that differ quite
considerably from the actual response times. In fact, the Leinbaugh
method even falsely predicts missed deadlines in the case of heavy load
(see, for example, Table 7.9 in which the predicted response times for
the Power Plant (cpu1) processes are all 17.34 > 15 (their frames) >
12 (their observed maximum response times)).[1]

---

[1]Since our method also results in somewhat pessimistic predictions, it is possible

7.2 Qualitative Evaluation of the Co-processor Architecture

In the course of evaluating the computer architecture developed in Chapters 4 and 5 some qualitative considerations will be sufficient, since a quantitative evaluation for a comparable configuration based on analytic modeling has already been carried out by Tempelmeier in [175, 177, 178].

First of all, it needs to be stressed that the evaluation criteria of real time embedded systems are quite different from those of batch or time-sharing computer systems. For the latter, the objective is to increase processing throughput, response times and utilisation. For real time systems, on the other hand, the throughput, the CPU utilisation and other traditional performance criteria are less important. Rather, what the users expect is the dependable and predictable fulfillment of their requirements. Moreover, the cost of a process control computer has to be seen in a larger context. Naturally, the costs of a two-processor system as proposed in this book are higher than those of a conventional von Neumann computer. Since the latter cannot guarantee reaction times, it may be unable to cope appropriately with exceptional and emergency situations of the external, time-critical environment. In comparison to the costs of damage in such an environment, caused by a computer malfunction, such as non-timely execution of a scheduled task or loss of an interrupt, the price of the co-processor is (almost) negligible.

In a conventional real time computer, every interrupt causes considerable overhead. This is especially unproductive, if the context contained in large register files needs to be saved and later reloaded. In most installations, the majority of the interrupts are generated by the interval timer, typically one thousand times per second, thus providing a system clock with a one millisecond resolution. The clock interrupt handling routine updates its time and date variables, and checks — mostly unsuccessfully — whether any time-scheduled activities have become due. It is clear that thus a considerable amount of a computer's available

---

to find a load for any system of processes under which no actual deadline will be missed while the predictions will indicate a missed deadline. However, since our method appears to be quite accurate, the circumstances under which such a false alarm would occur should be quite rare.

processing time is wasted. Our architecture uses simple hardware support to provide the same functions with higher accuracy and based on less wasteful timing checks. By migrating the operating system kernel to a dedicated device, the number of context-switches, which remain to be processed on the task processor, is minimised. Moreover, this small number of interrupts depends only on explicit application requests and system scheduler decisions, and is thus fully deterministic. Finally, as we have stated earlier, earliest-deadline-first scheduling is optimal with respect to the number of pre-emptions it causes.

In his dissertation [153], Schrott points out the problem of prolonged reaction times caused by long phases, during which the operating system (see also [21]) disables the recognition of interrupts. This measure is usually applied to prevent interrupt cascades while executing elementary operating system functions, and to synchronise the access to operating system data structures. Our architecture solves this problem by distributing the intrinsically independent functions of event recognition, task administration, and task execution to separate processor units.

In the early days of real time computing, the fundamental requirements of timeliness and simultaneity were realised by the user himself. Within his application software, he explicitly synchronised the execution schedules of the various tasks with a basic clock cycle. To this end, he usually wrote his own organisation program, a so-called "cyclic executive" [123]. Thus, predictable software behaviour was realised and the observation of the time conditions was guaranteed. Later, this method of cycle synchronised programming was replaced by the more flexible approach of asynchronous multi-programming, which was based on the task concept. Tasks could be activated and run at any time, asynchronously to a basic cycle. The flexibility and conceptual elegance of the method was gained at the expense of renouncing predictability and guaranteed time conditions. Our co-processor architecture has been designed to solve these problems of asynchronous multi-tasking.

The most important measure of the performance of real time systems is the timeliness of the response. The timeliness is heavily influenced by the software organisation, especially that in the operating system. The operating system overhead affects both the task response times and the interrupt reaction times. The former depend on the overall computing speed of a system and on the operating system functions, which are executed together with the user tasks in an interleaved manner. Thus, the overhead becomes part of the task response times. The interrupt reaction times depend on the system's hardware and on software characteristics. As we have already stated, the internal organisation of the operating system may introduce unnecessary overhead, such as context-switches, and unpredictably long delays, such as that before acknowledging an interrupt. We have addressed these problems in the architecture developed here. Specifically, we made use of the inherent mutual independence between running user tasks and operating system shell functions on one hand, and operating system kernel routines and external requests on the other. Based on this independence, the mentioned activities were assigned to different devices, where they can be carried out in parallel, which reduces both task response and interrupt reaction times.

7.3   Summary

We have evaluated Real-Time Euclid and its schedulability analyser. Both the language and the analyser have been used on two realistic real time applications, and results have been quite positive. Real-Time Euclid has been found to be a suitable language for real time applications development. Real-Time Euclid's schedulability analyser, based on our new techniques presented in Chapter 3, has been applied successfully to these applications, and has predicted accurate worst-case guaranteed response times. We have also undertaken a qualitative evaluation of our new architecture. It addresses optimality criteria uniquely characteristic of real time systems, by implementing an array of essential real time functions in hardware and providing a separate processor for the operating system kernel. Our architecture solves the major problems of conventional systems by reducing the semantic gap to the real time application domain.

Chapter 8

Outlook

In this last Chapter, we summarise our contributions and give directions for future research.

8.1 Summary of Contributions

Real time systems are embedded in many mission- and life-critical industrial, scientific and military environments. No matter what the environment is — a nuclear reactor, an amusement park ride or a fighter plane — the embedded real time programs have to monitor and control their external tasks in a timely fashion. Thus it is very important to design and develop real time software in such a way as to facilitate the verification of its critical timing constraints. Since it is expensive and hard to do this verification by testing the programs within the actual environments, it pays off to verify the timing constraints before the programs are actually run.

We believe that the most natural and easiest way to make programmers write verifiable real time software is to make them use a timing-constraint verifiable (i.e., a schedulability analysable) language. We feel that our belief is as justified as the widely held belief that writing general (i.e., not necessarily real time) software in a structured, secure, strongly-typed and modular language makes that software much easier to verify for general correctness. A schedulability analysable language must disallow any constructs that take arbitrarily long to execute. The run-time environment of the language must prevent any arbitrarily long delays from taking place. The language must bound the number of processes that can exist at any given time. Critical timing constraints must be expressed explicitly at the language level. Thus, once the program has been written, it will be possible to determine at compile-time what the timing constraints are and whether or not the program will meet them.

We made a survey of languages either actually used in real time programming or in experimental development. Some languages allow some timing constraints to be expressed explicitly. Others introduce time-outs into various forms of delays. Yet others make provisions for a limited form of schedulability analysis, such as estimating various process resource requirements in the absence of contention. However, none of these languages makes sufficient provisions for schedulability analysis. Thus, it is impossible to take a real time program written in one of these surveyed languages and ascertain at compile-time whether or not the program will meet its timing requirements.

We described Real-Time Euclid — the first programming language with a set of schedulability analysis provisions built-in. Real-Time Euclid programs can always be analysed for guaranteed schedulability. This is achieved through (1) time-bounding loop and suspension constructs, (2) disallowing recursion and dynamic storage allocation, and (3) specifying timing information explicitly for each process. Apart from being schedulability analysable, Real-Time Euclid addresses other important language design requirements. The language is well-structured, modular and strongly typed. It has processes synchronised through monitors, waits and signals, structured exception handlers with three classes of exceptions, and direct hardware access mechanisms. Real-Time Euclid allows separate compilation of modules and subroutines.

Since Real-Time Euclid is just an experimental research language, we incorporated its predictability enhancing features into the standardised and widely used industrial language PEARL. We showed that this extended version of PEARL can be implemented on our architecture. The extended PEARL includes elements that directly support such real time functions as time-constrained process operation, event monitoring, and real time performance analysis and verification. Yet, the new language does not deviate from the excellent basic structure present in the conventional PEARL, the structure that made the language come on top in our survey of industrial real time languages. Thus, we have constructively demonstrated that a problem oriented and schedulability analysable real time language, that greatly facilitates the writing of real time software with predictable behaviour, is feasible.

Having defined a schedulability analysable language, we then derived a set of language-independent schedulability analysis techniques. Schedulability analysis of real time programs takes place in two stages. The schedulability analyser consequently consists of two parts: a front end and a back end. The front end is incorporated into the coder, and its task is to extract timing information and calling information from each compilation unit. The front end of the analyser does not estimate interprocess contention. However, it does compute the amount of time individual statements and routine and process bodies take to execute in the absence of calls and contention. These times, serving as lower bounds on response times, are reported back to the programmer.

The back end of the schedulability analyser is a separate program. Its task is to correlate all information gathered by the front end, and predict guaranteed response times and other schedulability statistics for the entire real time application. To achieve this task, this part of the analyser maps the Real-Time Euclid program onto an instance of a real time model, and then solves this instance. The model is represented as a set of constrained sums of time values. The values in each sum are worst-case bounds of various types of execution times and contention. Each overall sum represents a guaranteed response time of a process.

The statistics generated by the schedulability analyser tell the programmer if the timing constraints expressed in the program are guaranteed to be met. If so, the programmer is finished with the timing constraint verification process. Otherwise, the statistics help the programmer to determine how to alter the program to ensure that the timing constraints are guaranteed.

Today, conventional computers are employed to run real time applications. With a minimum of features, viz. process peripherals, user accessible interrupt lines, and general multitasking operating systems, they are adapted to work as embedded systems. We have shown that this approach is to primitive and leads to a number of problems. Specifically, almost all hardware and software features of conventional computers, while improving traditional, averaged performance, do little for or even worsen the prospects for predictable real time performance. These features include common and conventional hierarchical storage management, DMA cycle stealing, pipelining and many other architectural elements. These elements introduce unpredictable delays, unbounded contention and other plagues of predictable program execution and must, therefore, be considered harmful. The state of affairs in using conventional von Neumann architectures in real time computing is thus unacceptable.

We have defined a hardware and software architecture which enables natural support of real time applications. The architecture has no elements that take unpredictably long to operate. This was achieved by designing appropriate alternatives for a number of the above mentioned conventional features causing unpredictability. Moreover, by separating application execution from immediate event recognition and recording, and from complex and time-consuming operating system services, the architecture enables serving a real time request as a natural sequence of predictable and deterministic steps.

Contemporary real time systems do not really deserve to be called real time, since they do not use the notion of real time. Rather, they are slightly modified multitasking systems that allocate tasks on the basis of (often fixed) priorities, and handle real time exceptions in a sudden, unpredictable manner. The architecture we have developed here supports the more appropriate, problem oriented concept of time throughout. The scheduler makes sure that task deadlines are met under all circumstances. By utilising special-purpose hardware, event recognition times can be guaranteed and the time behaviour of input/output operations can be planned precisely.

Our architecture is a parallel one. In contrast to other parallel computing systems, the parallelism does not lead to an increase in software complexity, because the architecture mirrors the parallelism inherent to the external real time environment itself. By allocating intrinsically independent functions to different hardware devices working in parallel, the architecture not only yields increased speed, but also and much more importantly, enhances predictability and dependability. Furthermore, the architecture enables the consequent development of a simple and dependable real time operating system kernel. The semantic gap between hardware and application software is narrowed by incorporating the kernel as firmware into the architecture.

One purpose of our research has been to design a schedulability analysable real time language and a set of schedulability analysis techniques for it. A good way to evaluate our research is to actually use the language and its schedulability analyser in a realistic environment, and see how they perform. For this purpose a prototype Real-Time Euclid compiler, run-time kernel and a schedulability analyser were designed and developed. This implementation was targeted at a realistic multiple-microprocessor system. Using our prototype implementation, two practical real time application programs were developed. The programs were analysed for guaranteed schedulability in the context of four different workloads. The programs were also run on our multiple-microprocessor system, under the same four workloads. The worst-case time bounds predicted by the analyser were compared with the maximum observed times, and found to differ only marginally. When applied to the same two programs, a polynomial-time method resulted in considerably more pessimistic predictions. We thus conclude that our work has been a success.

8.2   Directions for Future Research

The contribution of our work is fourfold: a real time language design contribution, a schedulability analysis contribution, a hardware contribution, and a system architecture and kernel contribution. Thus, it is appropriate for us to give indication in this Section where future research should take place in the four areas.

We believe that applying schedulability analysis to Real-Time Euclid programs has been a success. However, the bulk of the world's existing real time software is written in FORTRAN or assembly languages, only a small fraction is written in PEARL, and even more is to be written in Ada. Thus, a very important question is whether and how we can apply schedulability analysis to these languages. At first, the problem seems unsolvable. Indeed our own survey demonstrated that hardly any existing languages make provisions for schedulability analysis. Does this mean that we are out of luck and should abandon all hope? We feel that the answer is "no". While Ada and FORTRAN may not be real time, the external environments we are concerned about are. As we saw in the first Chapter of this book, real time environments impose critical timing constraints on their embedded software. Thus the programmer is forced to write this software in a schedulability analysable way, regardless of the programming language used. Hence, real time software, if written correctly, is schedulability analysable.

Our original question now reduces to two simpler ones:

1. How do we recognise schedulability analysability of software written in a non-analysable (i.e. general) language?

2. How do we actually do the analysis?

There are no easy answers, though some work has already taken place, as we have stated in Chapter 2.

Even if we address the challenge of making existing languages schedulability analysable in their implementations, this state of affairs is still inadequate, for we must make the languages so in their definitions as well. What is then the next step, following the exercise with Real-Time Euclid and extended PEARL? Since, in industrial real time computing, market considerations play a more important rôle than scientific ones do, other new or extended real time languages are certain to appear. The guiding principle for the development of this next generation of high level real time programming languages should be the support of predictable system behaviour and of inherent software safety without impairing understandability. Language constructs for the formulation of absolute and relative time dependencies and for the control of the operating system's resources must be provided. New, problem oriented synchronisation methods must be devised and provided, which will employ time as an easily conceivable and natural control mechanism. The next generation languages should try to combine the concepts introduced by Real-Time Euclid and extended PEARL, and should also incorporate as many ideas of the inherently safe language NewSpeak [45], as is feasible for real life applications.

While frame superimposition seems to generate good bounds on mailbox communication delays, it is not clear whether the same would be true in the case of a more sophisticated inter-processor communication mechanism. A related question has to do with the amount of time schedulability analysis would take in the case of large, complex communicating systems. Will the analysis still increase the overall compilation time by a small factor, or will the exponential complexity of the analysis make it infeasible? Research is thus quite open in the area of real time systems with complex communication mechanisms.

Most real time software is written in a redundant, fault tolerant way. An important question is: How do we determine guaranteed schedulability in the presence of exceptions? On the one hand, it is overly pessimistic to assume that every exception happens every time. On the other hand, what if all possible exceptions will in fact occur at least once at the same time? One possible solution to this problem is to make the programmer write software in a way that is data flow balanced in time. This means that the amount of time it takes to execute normal code free of exception handling is not substantially different from the amount of time it takes to execute the exception handling code that replaces the normal code. It is not clear whether or not all real time software can be written this way. The question of real time exception handling in the context of schedulability analysis is thus quite open as well.

While we have failed to find, in the existing body of scientific literature, an accurate polynomial-time schedulability analysis algorithm, it is conceivable that one could be developed. We are beginning an investigation into semantics preserving real time program transformations and incremental polynomial-time analysis heuristics that may offer some hope [171].

To achieve temporal predictability and full determinism of system behaviour is a major effort. In the course of this effort many features of existing programming languages, compilers, operating systems, and hardware architectures must be questioned — just as we have first done in this book. To this end, real time systems must be designed to be in all aspects as simple as possible, for simplicity fosters understandability and enhances dependability and operational safety. Even at the cost of losses in (average) speed, all features impairing system behaviour predictability, such as DMA, caches, and virtual memory, must be changed or renounced. To prevent synchronisation problems, parallelism should be implemented physically.

By providing higher and higher levels of integration, innovations in VLSI technology will continue to have the major impact on the entire field of computer design. Within less than ten years, with the advent of gigascale integration, some 100 million to 1 billion transistors should fit on a single die. Then, it will be possible to accommodate up to four processors on one chip. It is one of the theses of this book that these processors do not have to be homogeneous in architecture or use. Some will be general-purpose task processors, others dedicated to fast interrupt recognition and response, yet others used to run the operating system kernel, and for I/O handling. Such an architecture would reflect the parallelism inherent to real time operation and would balance real time performance. A thorough analysis of the application domain will reveal whether this approach is feasible, or whether it would be more advantageous to put the processors on separate chips and to utilise the enormous transistor count for integrated memories and I/O devices to prevent communication bottle-necks instead.

Future hardware functions will be even more readily available than they are today, working at higher speeds, and costing less. Hence, following our new thinking criteria, problem oriented architectures for real time systems that will achieve both predictability and simplicity must be designed. Measures for performance enhancements are only of use, if their effects can be a priori analysed and quantified, and if they behave fully deterministically. As advantageous use of inexpensive hardware we envisage the separation of functions, their encapsulation into standardised and safety licensed modules, and the provision of physical parallelism reflecting the parallelism inherent to the embedding processes. In this book we have worked out first steps in this direction. Thus, real time kernels can be implemented in firmware or hardware and interrupt processing can be delegated to a separate unit, in order to solve a serious problem described by Dijkstra [51] as "... the real time interrupt ... its effect was the introduction of non-determinism and endless headaches ...". Furthermore, entirely new functions can be implemented as well.

As an example, we suggested to provide radio sets in every processing node for the reception of time signals from an official, global time reference, thus replacing contemporary inaccurate and hard to synchronise computer clocks.

To evaluate the feasibility of our co-processor architecture for the real time operating system kernel more thoroughly, we are building a first, coarse prototype. The hardware features as mentioned in Section 5.1 are implemented on the basis of programmable gate arrays. Since speed is not the objective of a prototype, but rather its ease of implementation and high modifiability, the primary and secondary event reaction layers are each modeled by a dedicated personal computer. The first personal computer communicates via a digital interface with a local bus, to which the PGA-board is connected. The first-in-first-out data transfer between the two reaction layers is realised in the form of a standard serial communication link. We are implementing the architecture's operating system kernel (as presented in Chapter 5) using an existing PEARL compiler.

After an empirical evaluation of the first prototype, a second, more realistic one will be built and its performance measured. At each layer, the prototype will be a dual-redundant fault tolerant system, employing VIPER 1A[98] chips as processing elements. The VIPER microprocessor's unique characteristic is that the correctness of its design has been formally proven. Since it is appropriate to prove the correctness of the software as well, we have commenced the process of verifying the correctness of our real time kernel with mathematical rigour. We hope that, once formally verified, the licensing authorities will find our architecture acceptable as platform for safety relevant control systems. This would mean a great step forward since, until now, these authorities do not approve the use of programmable electronic systems for the exclusive control of safety critical technical systems.

Bibliography

[1] *The Programming Language Ada Reference Manual ANSI/MIL-STD-1815A*. LNCS 155. Springer-Verlag, Berlin-Heidelberg-New York-Tokyo, 1983.

[2] Proc. 2nd International Workshop on Real-Time Ada Issues. ACM Ada Letters VIII, 7, 1988.

[3] Proc. 3rd International Workshop on Real-Time Ada Issues. ACM Ada Letters X, 4, 1990.

[4] S. Ahuja and A. Asthana. A multi-microprocessor architecture with hardware support for communication and scheduling. *ACM SIGPLAN Notices*, 17(4):205–209, April 1982.

[5] J. Allchin. Modula and a question of time. *IEEE Transactions on Software Engineering*, SE-6(4):390–391, July 1980.

[6] A. Alvarez, editor. *Ada: The Design Choice. Proc. Ada-Europe International Conference, Madrid*, Cambridge, June 1989. Cambridge University Press.

[7] U. Ammann. Vergleich einiger Konzepte moderner Echtzeitsprachen. In *6. Fachtagung der GI über Programmiersprachen und Programmentwicklung*, pages 1–18, Berlin-Heidelberg-New York, 1980. Informatik-Fachberichte 25, Springer-Verlag.

[8] ANSI/IEEE Standard 716-1985: C/ATLAS Test Language. The Institute of Electrical and Electronics Engineers, Inc., Washington, D.C., 1985.

[9] FORTRAN ANSI X3.9-1978. American National Standards Institute, Inc., New York, 1978.

287

[10] R. Arnold, R. Berg, and J. Thomas. A modular approach to real-time supersystems. *IEEE Transactions on Computers*, C-31(5):385–398, May 1982.

[11] T. Atkinson et al. Modern central processor architecture. *Proc. of the IEEE*, 63(6):863–870, June 1975.

[12] B. Aucoin and R. Heller. Overcurrent and high impedance fault relaying using a microcomputer. In *Proc. 7th Texas Conference on Computing Systems*, pages 2.5 – 2.9, November 1978.

[13] T. Baker. A corset for Ada. Technical Report TR 86-09-05, Computer Science Department, University of Washington, 1986.

[14] T. Baker. A lace for Ada's corset. Technical Report TR 86-09-06, Computer Science Department, University of Washington, 1986.

[15] T. Baker. Implementing timing guarantees in Ada. In *Proc. 4th IEEE Workshop on Real-Time Operating Systems*, pages 129 – 133, July 1987.

[16] T. Baker. Improving timing predictability of software. Working paper, Department of Computer Science, Florida State University, August 1987.

[17] T. Baker and K. Jeffay. Corset and lace: Adapting Ada runtime support to real-time systems. In *Proc. IEEE Real-Time Systems Symposium*, pages 158–167, December 1987.

[18] J. Barnes. Real-time languages for process control. *Computer Journal*, 15(1), January 1972.

[19] J. Barnes. *RTL/2 Design and Philosophy*. Heyden, London, 1976.

[20] R. Barnes. A working definition of the proposed extensions for PL/1 real-time applications. *ACM SIGPLAN Notices*, 14(10):77–99, October 1979.

[21] R. Baumann et al. *Funktionelle Beschreibung von Prozessrechner-Betriebssystemen*. VDI-Richtlinie VDI/VDE 3554. Beuth-Verlag, Berlin-Cologne, 1982.

[22] G. Becker. Die Sekunde. *PTB-Mitteilungen*, 85:14 – 28, January 1975.

[23] A. Berenbaum, M. Condry, and P. Lu. The operating system and language support features of the BELLMAC-32 microprocessor. *ACM SIGPLAN Notices*, 17(4):30–38, April 1982.

[24] G. Berry. Real time programming: Special purpose or general purpose languages. In *Proc. 11th IFIP World Computer Congress*, 1989.

[25] G. Berry, P. Couronné, and G. Gonthier. Synchronous programming of reactive systems: An introduction to Esterel. In K. Fuchi and M. Nivat, editors, *Programming of Future Generation Computers*, pages 35 – 55, Amsterdam, 1988. Elsevier Science Publishers.

[26] G. Berry, S. Moisan, and J.-P. Rigault. Esterel: Towards a synchronous and semantically sound high level language for real-time applications. In *Proc. IEEE Real-Time Systems Symposium*, December 1983.

[27] S. Biyabani, J. Stankovic, and K. Ramanritham. The integration of deadline and criticalness requirements in hard real-time systems. In *Proc. 5th IEEE/USENIX Workshop on Real-Time Software and Operating Systems*, pages 12 – 17, May 1988.

[28] P. Brinch Hansen. The programming language concurrent Pascal. *IEEE Transactions on Software Engineering*, 1(2):199 – 207, June 1975.

[29] L. Brodie. *Starting FORTH*. Prentice-Hall, 1981.

[30] L. Brodie. *Thinking FORTH*. Prentice-Hall, 1984.

[31] G. Bull and A. Lewis. Real-time BASIC. *SOFTWARE — Practice and Experience*, 13(11):1075 – 1092, 1983.

[32] A. Burns and A. Wellings. *Real-Time Systems and Their Programming Languages*. Addison-Wesley, 1989.

[33] G. Carlow. Architecture of the space shuttle primary avionics software system. *Communications of the ACM*, 27(9):926 – 936, September 1984.

[34] P. Caspi, N. Halbwachs, D. Pilaud, and J. Plaice. Lustre — a declarative language for programming synchronous systems. In

Proc. 14th Annual ACM Symposium on Principles of Programming Languages, 1987.

[35] V. Castor. Letter initiating the Ada revision process. *ACM Ada Letters*, IX(1):12, 1989.

[36] CCITT High Level Language (CHILL) Recommendation Z.200. CCITT, Geneva, 1980.

[37] Advances in power station construction. Pergamon Press, 1986. Generating Development and Construction Division, Central Electricity Generating Board, Barnwood, U.K.

[38] G. Chroust. Orthogonal extensions in microprogrammed multiprocessor systems — a chance for increased firmware usage. *EUROMICRO Journal*, 6(2):104–110, 1980.

[39] J. Chung, J. Liu, and K. Lin. Scheduling periodic jobs using imprecise results. Technical Report UIUCDCS-R-87-1307, Department of Computer Science, University of Illinois, Urbana, IL, November 1987.

[40] R. Clapp, L. Duchesneau, R. Volz, T. Mudge, and T. Schultze. Toward real-time performance benchmarks for Ada. *Communications of the ACM*, 29(8), August 1986.

[41] Compagnie d'informatique militaire, spatiale et aeronautique, Velizy. *LTR Reference Manual*, October 1979.

[42] J. Cordy and R. Holt. Specification of concurrent Euclid. Technical Report CSRG-133, Computer Systems Research Group, University of Toronto, August 1981.

[43] J. Cordy, R. Holt, and D. Wortman. S/SL syntax/semantic language introduction and specification. Technical Report CSRG-118, Computer Systems Research Group, University of Toronto, 1980.

[44] B. Corman, P. Wetherall, and P. Woodward. *IECCA Official Definition of CORAL 66*. Her Majesty's Stationary Office, London, 1970.

[45] I. Currie. NewSpeak: a reliable programming language. In C. Sennett, editor, *High-Integrity Software*, pages 122–158. Pitman, London, 1989.

[46] B. Dasarathy. Timing constraints of real-time systems: Constructs for expressing them, methods of validating them. *IEEE Transaction on Software Engineering*, 11(1):80 – 86, January 1985.

[47] DATAPAC standard network access protocol specifications. Computer Communications Group, Ottawa, 1976.

[48] N. Davis et al. Practical experiences of Ada and object oriented design in real time distributed systems. In A. Alvarez, editor, *Ada: The Design Choice. Proc. Ada-Europe International Conference, Madrid*, pages 59 – 79, Cambridge, June 1989. Cambridge University Press.

[49] E. Davison and K. Baker. Private communication. 1986.

[50] E. Dijkstra. Cooperating sequential processes. Technical Report EWD-123, Technological University, Eindhoven, 1965.

[51] E. Dijkstra. The next forty years. Personal note EWD 1051, 1989.

[52] DIN 44300: Informationsverarbeitung. Berlin-Cologne: Beuth-Verlag, 1985.

[53] DIN 66253: Programmiersprache PEARL, Teil 1 Basic PEARL, July 1981; Teil 2 Full PEARL, October 1982; Teil 3 Mehrrechner-PEARL, January 1989. Berlin-Cologne: Beuth-Verlag.

[54] M. Donner and D. Jameson. Language and operating systems features for real-time programming. *Computing Systems*, 1988.

[55] W. Ehrenberger. Softwarezuverlässigkeit und Programmiersprache. *Regelungstechnische Praxis*, 25(1):24 – 29, 1983.

[56] A. El-Sakkary and N. Gough. 25th IEEE CDC Conference, 1986.

[57] T. Elrad. Comprehensive race control: A versatile scheduling mechanism for real-time applications. In A. Alvarez, editor, *Ada: The Design Choice. Proc. Ada-Europe International Conference, Madrid*, pages 129–136, Cambridge, June 1989. Cambridge University Press.

[58] P. Elzer. Ein Mechanismus zur Erstellung strukturierter Prozessautomatisierungsprogramme. In *Proc. GMR-GI-GfK Fachtagung Prozessrechner 1977*, pages 137 – 148, Berlin-Heidelberg-New York, 1977. Informatik-Fachberichte 7, Springer-Verlag.

[59] P. Elzer. *Strukturierte Beschreibung von Prozess-Systemen.* PhD thesis, Institute for Mathematical Machines and Data Processing, University of Erlangen-Nuremberg, February 1979.

[60] P. Elzer. Resource allocation by means of access rights, an alternative view on realtime programming. In *Proc. IFAC/IFIP-Workshop on Real Time Programming*, page 73ff, Oxford, 1980. Pergamon Press.

[61] Fairchild Camera and Instrument Corporation, Mountain View, CA. *F8 Microcomputer System Data Book*, 1975.

[62] E. Fathi and N. Fines. Real-time data acquisition, processing and distribution for radar applications. In *Proc. IEEE Real-Time Systems Symposium*, pages 95 – 101, December 1984.

[63] S. Faulk and D. Parnas. On the uses of synchronization in hard-real-time systems. In *Proc. IEEE Real-Time Systems Symposium*, December 1983.

[64] A. Fleischmann, P. Holleczek, G. Kebes, and R. Kummer. Synchronisation und Kommunikation verteilter Automatisierungsprogramme. *Angewandte Informatik*, 7:290 – 297, 1983.

[65] Specifications for the IBM mathematical FORmula TRANslating system FORTRAN. IBM Corporation, New York, November 1954.

[66] C. Gannon. JAVS: A JOVIAL automated verification system. In *Proc. IEEE COMPSAC Conference*, pages 539–544, 1978.

[67] M. Garey and D. Johnson. Complexity results for multiprocessor scheduling under resource constraints. *SIAM Journal on Computing*, 4(4):397 – 411, December 1975.

[68] A. Ghassemi. *Untersuchung der Eignung der Prozessprogrammiersprache PEARL zur Automatisierung von Folgeprozessen.* PhD thesis, Universität Stuttgart, 1978.

[69] R. Glass. Real-time: The "lost world" of software debugging and testing. *Communications of the ACM*, 23(5):264 – 271, May 1980.

[70] V. Gligor and G. Luckenbaugh. An assessment of the real-time requirements for programming environments and languages. In *Proc. IEEE Real-Time Systems Symposium*, December 1983.

[71] A. Grimshaw, A. Silberman, and J. Liu. Real-Time Mentat programming language and architecture. In *Proc. GLOBECOM 89*, pages 1–7, 1989 1989.

[72] W. Halang. A proposal for extensions of PEARL to facilitate the formulation of hard real-time applications. In *4. GI/GMR/KfK-Fachtagung Prozessrechner 1984*, pages 573 – 582, Berlin-Heidelberg-New York-Tokyo, September 1984. Informatik-Fachberichte 86, Springer-Verlag.

[73] W. Halang. Implications on suitable multiprocessor structures and virtual storage management when applying a feasible scheduling algorithm in hard real-time environments. *SOFTWARE — Practice and Experience*, 16(8):761 – 769, 1986.

[74] W. Halang. On methods for direct memory access without cycle stealing. *Microprocessing and Microprogramming*, 17(5):277–283, May 1986.

[75] H. Hecht. Fault-tolerant software for real-time applications. *ACM Computing Surveys*, 17(10), October 1976.

[76] G. Heider. Let operating systems aid in component designs. *Computer Design*, 21(9):151–160, September 1982.

[77] R. Henn. *Deterministische Modelle für die Prozessorzuteilung in einer harten Realzeit-Umgebung*. PhD thesis, Technical University Munich, 1975.

[78] R. Henn. Zeitgerechte Prozessorzuteilung in einer harten Realzeit-Umgebung. In *GI — 6. Jahrestagung*, pages 343–359, Berlin-Heidelberg, 1976. Informatik-Fachberichte 5, Springer-Verlag.

[79] R. Henn. Antwortzeitgesteuerte Prozessorzuteilung unter strengen Zeitbedingungen. *Computing*, 19:209–220, 1978.

[80] R. Henn. Feasible processor allocation in a hard-real-time environment. *Real-Time Systems*, 1(1):77 – 93, 1989.

[81] R. Herrtwich. Echtzeit. *Informatik-Spektrum*, 12:93 – 96, 1989.

[82] C. Hoare. Monitors: An operating system structuring concept. *Communications of the ACM*, 17(10):549 – 557, October 1974.

[83] R. Holt and J. Cordy. The Turing Language Report. Technical Report CSRG-153, Computer Systems Research Group, University of Toronto, December 1983.

[84] R. Holt and J. Cordy. The Turing Plus Report. Technical report, Computer Systems Research Institute, University of Toronto, February 1985.

[85] R. Holt et al. Euclid: A language for producing quality software. In *Proc. National Computer Conference*, May 1981.

[86] J. Ichbiah et al. Preliminary Ada reference manual and rationale for the design of the Ada programming language. *ACM SIGPLAN Notices*, 14(6), June 1979.

[87] Working draft "Standards for Programmable Controllers", part 3: "Programming Languages". International Electrotechnical Commission, Technical Committee 65: Industrial Process Measurement and Control, Subcommittee 65A: System Considerations, Working Group 6: Discontinuous Process Control, IEC 65A(Secretariat)90-I, December 1988.

[88] INMOS Ltd. *The Occam Programming Manual*. Prentice-Hall, Englewood Cliffs, 1984.

[89] INMOS Ltd. *Occam2 Programming Manual*. Prentice-Hall, Englewood Cliffs, 1988.

[90] Y. Ishikawa, H. Tokuda, and C. Mercer. Object-oriented real-time language design: Constructs for timing constraints. Technical Report CMU-CS-90-111, Department of Computer Science, Carnegie Mellon University, March 1990.

[91] F. Jahanian and A. Mok. Modechart: A specification language for real-time systems. *IEEE Transactions on Software Engineering*, 1990.

[92] H. Johnson and M. Maddison. Deadline scheduling for a real-time multiprocessor. In *Eurocomp. Conf. Proceedings*, pages 139–153, 1974.

[93] R. Johnson and J. Wick. An overview of the Mesa processor architecture. *ACM SIGPLAN Notices*, 17(4):20–29, April 1982.

[94] G. Kaplan. The X-29: Is it coming or going? *IEEE Spectrum*, pages 54 – 60, June 1985.

[95] A. Kappatsch. Full PEARL language description. Technical Report KFK-PDV 130, Kernforschungszentrum Karlsruhe, 1977.

[96] J. Keedy. On structuring operating systems with monitors. *ACM SIGOPS*, 13(1), January 1979.

[97] P. Kelton. Distributed computing for astronomical data acquisition at Mcdonald observatory. In *Proc. IEEE Real-Time Systems Symposium*, pages 83 – 88, December 1984.

[98] J. Kershaw. The VIPER microprocessor. Technical Report 87014, Royal Signals and Radar Establishment, Malvern, Worcs., November 1987.

[99] R. Kieburtz and J. Hennessy. TOMAL — a high-level programming language for microprocessor process control applications. *ACM SIGPLAN Notices*, 11(4):127–134, April 1976.

[100] E. Kligerman. Programming environment for real-time systems. Master's thesis, Department of Computer Science, University of Toronto, 1987.

[101] E. Kligerman and A. Stoyenko. Real-Time Euclid: A language for reliable real-time system. *IEEE Transactions on Software Engineering*, 12(9):941 – 949, September 1986.

[102] Draft Standard on Industrial Real-Time FORTRAN of the International Purdue Workshop on Industrial Computer Systems. *ACM SIGPLAN Notices*, 16(7):45–60, 1981.

[103] H. Kopetz and W. Ochsenreiter. Clock synchronization in distributed real-time systems. *IEEE Transaction on Computers*, C-36(8), August 1987.

[104] F. Krull. Experience with ILIAD: A high-level process control language. *Communications of the ACM*, 24(2), February 1981.

[105] J. Labetoulle. *Ordonnancement des Processus Temps Reel sur une ressource pre-emptive*. PhD thesis, Université Paris VI, 1974.

[106] J. Labetoulle. Real time scheduling in a multiprocessor environment. Technical report, IRIA Laboria, Rocquencourt, 1976.

[107] R. Lauber. Prozessautomatisierung und Informatik. In *GI — 8. Jahrestagung*, pages 381–394, Berlin-Heidelberg-New York, 1978. Informatik-Fachberichte 16, Springer-Verlag.

[108] R. Lauber. *Prozessautomatisierung I.* Springer-Verlag, Berlin-Heidelberg-New York-London-Paris-Tokyo, second edition, 1989.

[109] H. Ledgard. *Ada — An Introduction and Ada Reference Manual (July 1980).* Springer-Verlag, New York-Heidelberg-Berlin, 1981.

[110] I. Lee. A programming system for distributed real-time applications. In *Proc. IEEE Real-Time Systems Symposium*, pages 18–27, December 1984.

[111] I. Lee and V. Gehlot. Language constructs for distributed real-time programming. In *Proc. IEEE Real-Time Systems Symposium*, pages 57–66, 1985 1985.

[112] P. Lee, S. Schaaf, T. Tsai, and N. Srinivasan. Design and development of a real-time system — a case study. In *Proc. IEEE Real-Time Systems Symposium*, December 1982.

[113] D. Leinbaugh. Guaranteed response times in a hard-real-time environment. *IEEE Transactions on Software Engineering*, SE-6(1):85 – 91, January 1980.

[114] D. Leinbaugh and M.-R. Yamini. Guaranteed response times in a distributed hard-real-time environment. In *Proc. IEEE Real-Time Systems Symposium*, pages 157 – 169, December 1982.

[115] D. Leinbaugh and M.-R. Yamini. Guaranteed response times in a distributed hard-real-time environment. *IEEE Transactions on Software Engineering*, SE-12(12):1139 – 1144, December 1986.

[116] J.-T. Leung and M. Merrill. A note on preemptive scheduling of periodic, real-time tasks. *Information Processing Letters*, 11(3):115 – 118, December 1980.

[117] J.-T. Leung and J. Whitehead. On the complexity of fixed-priority scheduling of periodic, real-time tasks. *Performance Evaluation*, 2:237 – 250, December 1982.

[118] K. Lin, S. Natarajan, and J. Liu. Imprecise results: Utilizing partial computations in real-time systems. In *Proc. IEEE Real-Time Systems Symposium*, December 1987.

[119] K. Lin, S. Natarajan, J. Liu, and T. Krauskopf. Concord: a system of imprecise computations. In *Proc. IEEE COMPSAC Conference*, October 1987.

[120] K.-J. Lin and S. Natarjan. Expressing and maintaining timing constraints in FLEX. In *Proc. IEEE Real-Time Systems Symposium*, December 1988.

[121] C. Liu and J. Layland. Scheduling algorithms for multiprogramming in a hard-real-time environment. *Journal of the ACM*, 20:46–61, 1973.

[122] J. Liu, K. Lin, and S. Natarajan. Scheduling real-time, periodic jobs using imprecise results. In *Proc. IEEE Real-Time Systems Symposium*, December 1987.

[123] L. MacLaren. Evolving toward Ada in real time systems. *ACM SIGPLAN Notices*, 15(11):146–155, November 1980.

[124] A. D. Maio et al. DRAGOON: An Ada-based object-oriented language for concurrent, real-time, distributed systems. In A. Alvarez, editor, *Ada: The Design Choice. Proc. Ada-Europe International Conference, Madrid*, pages 39 – 48, Cambridge, June 1989. Cambridge University Press.

[125] J. Marshall. *Control of Time Delay Systems*. Peter Peregrinus Ltd., Stevenage-New York, 1979.

[126] J. Martin. *Design of Real-Time Computer Systems*. Series in Automatic Computation. Prentice-Hall, 1967.

[127] T. Martin. Realtime programming language PEARL — concept and characteristics. In *Proc. IEEE Computer Software and Applications Conference*, November 1978.

[128] D. Moffat. Some concerns about Modula-2. *ACM SIGPLAN Notices*, 19(12):41–47, December 1984.

[129] A. Mok. The design of real-time programming systems based on process models. In *Proc. IEEE Real-Time Systems Symposium*, pages 5 – 17, December 1984.

[130] A. Mok and M. Dertouzos. Multiprocessor scheduling in a hard-real-time environment. In *Proc. 7th Texas Conference on Computing Systems*, pages 5.1 – 5.12, November 1978.

[131] A.-L. Mok. *Fundamental Design Problems of Distributed Systems for the Hard-Real-Time Environment.* PhD thesis, Massachusetts Institute of Technology, 1983.

[132] G. Myers. *Advances in Computer Architecture.* John Wiley & Sons, New York, second edition, 1982.

[133] H. Nägeli and A. Gorrengourt. Programming in PORTAL: An introduction. LGZ Landis and Gyr Zug Corporation, 1979.

[134] National Semiconductor Corporation, Santa Clara, CA. *Series 3200 Instruction Set Reference Manual,* June 1984.

[135] V. Nelson and H. Fellows. A microcomputer-based controller for an amusement park ride. *IEEE Micro,* pages 13 – 22, August 1981.

[136] P. Newbold et al. HAL/S language specification. Technical Report IR-61-5, Intermetrics Inc., November 1974.

[137] C. Ngan. Implementing the Real-Time Euclid compiler. B.Sc. project report, Department of Computer Science, University of Toronto, August 1986.

[138] G. Parnis. Simulation of packet level handshaking in X.25 using the Real-Time Euclid programming language. Student Project Report, Department of Computer Science, University of Toronto, April 1987.

[139] KE-Handbuch. Periphere Computer Systeme GmbH, Munich, 1981.

[140] M. Pickett. ILIAD reference manual. Technical Report GMR-2015B, Computer Science Department, General Motors Research Laboratories, Warren, MI, April 1979.

[141] R. Rajkumar and J. Lehoczky. Task synchronization in real-time operating systems. In *Proc. 5th IEEE/USENIX Workshop on Real-Time Software and Operating Systems,* pages 18 – 22, May 1988.

[142] K. Ramamritham and J. Stankovic. Dynamic task scheduling in distributed hard real-time systems. In *Proc. 4th IEEE International Conference on Distributed Computing Systems,* pages 96 – 107, May 1984.

[143] K. Ramamritham, J. Stankovic, and S. Cheng. Evaluation of a flexible task scheduling algorithm for distributed hard real-time systems. *IEEE Transactions on Computers*, C-34(12):1130–1143, December 1985.

[144] H. Reghbati and V. Hamacher. A note on the suitability of Modula for process control applications. *SOFTWARE — Practice and Experience*, 8:233–234, 1978.

[145] Z. Rekasius. Digital control with computer interruptions. In *Proc. American Control Conference*, pages 1618 – 1621, 1985.

[146] M. Ritout, P. Bonnard, and P. Hugot. PROCOL: Process control language. In *Proc. IFAC Congress*, June 1972.

[147] E. Roberts, A. Evans, and C. Morgan. Task management in Ada — a critical evaluation for real-time multiprocessors. *SOFTWARE — Practice and Experience*, 11(10):1019–1051, 1981.

[148] R. Roessler. *Betriebssystemstrategien zur Bewältigung von Zeitproblemen in der Prozessautomatisierung*. PhD thesis, Universität Stuttgart, 1979.

[149] R. Roessler and K. Schenk. A comparison of the properties of the programming languages ALGOL 68, CAMAC-IML, CORAL 66, PAS 1, PEARL, PL/1, PROCOL, RTL/2 in relation to real-time programming. Technical report, International Purdue Workshop on Industrial Computer Systems and Physics Institute of the University of Erlangen-Nuremberg, 1975.

[150] J. Roos. Real-time support processor for Ada tasking. In *Proc. 3rd ACM ASPLOS Conference*, pages 162–171, 1989.

[151] A. M. Rybezynski and D. F. Weir. DATAPAC X.25 service characteristics. Computer Communications Group, Ottawa, 1977.

[152] J. Schabernack and A. Schütte. Occam2 und Ada. Eine Gegenüberstellung. *Informatik-Spektrum*, 12:3 – 18, 1989.

[153] G. Schrott. *Ein Zuteilungsmodell für Multiprozessor-Echtzeitsysteme*. PhD thesis, Technical University Munich, 1986.

[154] A. Schwald and R. Baumann. PEARL im Vergleich mit anderen Echtzeitsprachen. In *Proc. Aussprachetag PEARL, KFK-PDV 110*. Kernforschungszentrum Karlsruhe, March 1977.

[155] J. Schwartz. Preliminary report on JOVIAL. Technical Report SDC Report FN-L0-34, System Development Corporation, 1959.

[156] L. Sha and J. Goodenough. Real-time scheduling theory and Ada. Technical Report CMU/SEI-89-TR-14, ESD-TR-89-22, Carnegie-Mellon University, Software Engineering Institute, April 1989.

[157] L. Sha, R. Rajkumar, and J. Lehoczky. Priority inheritance protocols: An approach to real-time synchronization. Technical Report CMU-CS-87-181, Carnegie-Mellon University, November 1987.

[158] L. Sha, R. Rajkumar, S. Son, and C.-H. Chang. A real-time locking protocol. *IEEE Transactions on Computers*, 1991.

[159] D. Siewiorek, C. Bell, and A. Newell. *Computer Structures: Principles and Examples*. McGraw-Hill, New York, 1982.

[160] C. Smith. Independent general principles for constructing responsive software systems. *ACM Transactions on Computer Systems*, 4(1), February 1986.

[161] P. Sorenson. *A Methodology for Real-Time System Development*. PhD thesis, University of Toronto, Department of Computer Science, 1974.

[162] P. Sorenson and V. Hamacher. A real-time system design methodology. *INFOR*, 13(1):1 – 18, February 1975.

[163] G. Spur, F.-L. Krause, and L. Sidarous. Development of APT and EXAPT. In U. Rembold and R. Dillmann, editors, *Methods and Tools for Computer-Integrated Manufacturing*, LNCS 168, pages 60 – 67. Springer-Verlag, Berlin-Heidelberg-New York-Tokyo, 1984.

[164] J. Stankovic. Misconceptions about real-time computing: A serious problem for next generation systems. *IEEE Computer*, 21(10):10 – 19, 1988.

[165] J. Stankovic and K. Ramamritham. Editorial: What is predictability for real-time systems? *Real-Time Systems*, 2(4):247 – 254, November 1990.

[166] A. Stoyenko. Real-time systems: Scheduling and structure. Master's thesis, Department of Computer Science, University of Toronto, 1984.

[167] A. Stoyenko. Turing goes real-time... Internal Programming Languages Report, Department of Computer Science University of Toronto, May 1984.

[168] A. Stoyenko. A case for schedulability analyzable real-time languages. In *Proc. IEEE Workshop on Real-Time Operating Systems*, April 1987.

[169] A. Stoyenko. *A Real-Time-Language With A Schedulability Analyzer.* PhD thesis, Department of Computer Science, University of Toronto, 1987. Also available as Computer Systems Research Institute, CSRI-206.

[170] A. Stoyenko. A schedulability analyzer for Real-Time Euclid. In *Proc. IEEE Real-Time Systems Symposium*, pages 218 – 227, December 1987.

[171] A. Stoyenko and T. Marlowe. Analysis of real-time programs using hierarchical clustering. Joint IEEE and IFIP Workshop on Real-Time Operating Systtems, May 1991.

[172] E. Swartzlander and B. Gilbert. Supersystems: Technology and architecture. *IEEE Transactions on Computers*, C-31(5):399–409, May 1982.

[173] T. Teixeira. Static priority interrupt scheduling. In *Proc. 7th Texas Conference on Computing Systems*, pages 5.13 – 5.18, November 1978.

[174] T. Tempelmeier. A supplementary processor for operating system functions. In *IFAC/IFIP Workshop on Real Time Programming*, 1979.

[175] T. Tempelmeier. *Antwortzeitverhalten eines Echtzeit-Rechensystems bei Auslagerung des Betriebssystemkerns auf einen eigenen Prozessor.* PhD thesis, Technical University Munich, 1980.

[176] T. Tempelmeier. Auslagerung eines Echtzeitbetriebsssytems auf einen eigenen Prozessor. In *Proc. Fachtagung Prozessrechner*, pages 196–205, 1981.

[177] T. Tempelmeier. Antwortzeitverhalten eines Echtzeitrechensystems bei Auslagerung des Betriebssystemkerns auf einen eigenen

Prozessor, Teil 2: Messergebnisse. Technical Report TUM-I8201, Technical University Munich, 1982.

[178] T. Tempelmeier. Operating system processors in real-time systems — performance analysis and measurement. *Computer Performance*, 5(2):121–127, June 1984.

[179] S. Thurlow. Simulation of a real time control system using the Real-Time Euclid programming language. Student Project Report, Department of Computer Science, University of Toronto, April 1987.

[180] J. Ullman. Polynomial complete scheduling problems. In *Proc. 4th Symposium on OS Principles*, pages 96 – 101, 1973.

[181] J. van Katwijk and H. Toetnel. Language extensions to allow rapid mode shifting in the Ada programming language. In A. Alvarez, editor, *Ada: The Design Choice. Proc. Ada-Europe International Conference, Madrid*, pages 26 – 36, Cambridge, June 1989. Cambridge University Press.

[182] A. van Tilborg. Preface to the ONR kickoff workshop on foundations of real-time computing research initiative. *Real-Time Systems Newsletter*, 5(1):6 – 7, 1989.

[183] S. Ward. An approach to real time computation. In *Proc. Texas Conf. on Computing Systems*, November 1978.

[184] N. Wilkinson, M. Atkins, and J. Rogers. A real-time parallel processing data acquisition system. In *Proc. IEEE Real-Time Systems Symposium*, December 1988.

[185] C. Williams. The data acquisition, data reduction and control system (DARCS) for the NRCC 2x3m windtunnel. In *Proc. IEEE Real-Time Systems Symposium*, pages 89 – 94, December 1984.

[186] N. Wirth. The programming language Pascal. *Acta Informatica*, 1:35 – 63, 1971.

[187] N. Wirth. Design and implementation of Modula. *SOFTWARE — Practice and Experience*, 7:67 – 84, 1977.

[188] N. Wirth. Modula: A language for modular multiprogramming. *SOFTWARE — Practice and Experience*, 7:3–35, 1977.

[189] N. Wirth. *Programming in Modula-2*. Springer-Verlag, Berlin-Heidelberg-New York, third edition, 1985.

[190] H.-W. Wyes. *Die Omega/CReStA-Maschine — Eine RISC-Architektur für die Echtzeit-Datenverarbeitung*. Hüthig, Heidelberg, 1988.

[191] Zilog Inc., Campbell, CA. *Z80 Data Book*, 1982.

[192] K. Zuse. *The Plankalkül*. GMD-Berichte Nr. 175. R. Oldenbourg Verlag, Munich-Vienna, 1989.

Index